THE HEALING FOUNTAIN

POETRY THERAPY FOR LIFE'S JOURNEY

T0159604

THE HEALING FOUNTAIN

ℰↄ·ℭℜ

Poetry Therapy for Life's Journey

Edited by

Geri Giebel Chavis and Lila Lizabeth Weisberger

NORTH STAR PRESS OF ST. CLOUD, INC.

Cover photo: Ken Stewart, "Bridal Falls."

ISBN: 978-0-87839-189-9

Printed in the United States of America

Published by
North Star Press of St. Cloud, Inc.
Saint Cloud, Minnesota

Dedication

To my husband, Ken, and daughter, Jackie,
special loving companions on my life's journey,
and to all the visionary pioneers and tireless devotees of Poetry Therapy.

Geri Giebel Chavis

To my husband, Gene:
we journey together with love and devotion.
To my sons and daughters:
Gary Stein, Marc Stein, Sharon Groth, and Lori Stein
and my grandchildren Elizabeth, Daniel, Jonathan, Rebecca, Abigail,
Matthew, Rachel, and Chase
—my roots and my flowers and the source of my overflowing joy.
To my trainees—past, present and future:
Gibran says "Work is love made visible."
We work together in that spirit as we go to the healing fountain.
Let us continue our journey.

Lila Lizabeth Weisberger

ACKNOWLEDGEMENTS

At the start of this project, the editors invited the members and friends of the National Association for Poetry Therapy to send poems that they had found to be *particularly* therapeutic in their work with others. We are sincerely grateful to all who responded to our request and wish to acknowledge their contribution in the following list. We also express our heartfelt gratitude to Nicholas Mazza and Alma Rolfs, who, as members of the Poem Selection Committee, provided us with valuable assistance in making our final choices, to Nancy Scherlong for her proofreading assistance, and to Jim Newsome for his help on copyright issues.

Kay Adams
George Bell
Ted Bowman
Rosalie Brown
Geri Chavis
Barbara Dorfman
Rod Farmer
Nancy Fitzgerald
Lisa Friedlander
Deborah Grayson
Judy Gelinske
Sharon Groth

Robert Grunst
Beth Haebel
Sr. Arleen Hynes
Lyndall Johnson
Sandie Johnson
Carol Kanter
Mae Koppman
Babara Kreisberg
Deborah Langosch
Art Lerner
Perie Longo
Nicholas Mazza

Brian O'Neill
Sherry Reiter
Steve Rojcewicz
Alma Rolfs
Charles Rossiter
Joy Shieman
Susan Spindler
Eileen Yeager
Lila Weisberger

TABLE OF CONTENTS

IV. FLOWERS ALONG THE ROAD

CELEBRATING SELF-WORTH 149

By Rosalie Brown, Arleen McCarty Hynes, and Deborah Langosch

BEING WITH NATURE 173

By Barbara Kreisberg and Charles Rossiter

V. SHARING THE JOURNEY: TRAVELING TOGETHER IN AND OUT OF STEP

INTRODUCTION

Geri Giebel Chavis and Lila Lizabeth Weisberger

THIS BOOK REPRESENTS A RICH and unique compendium of experience, exper-
tise, and enthusiasm, a labor of love by a variety of compassionate, innova-
tive, and skilled poetry therapists. While it is built on the fundamental belief
that poetry has therapeutic power, it is equally focused on the lives we lead
and the realities we face because we are human—the joys and sorrows, the
setbacks and advances, the struggles and triumphs, the fears and courage we
experience as we look within, interact with others, and react to the world
around us.

Poetry therapy has both ancient and contemporary roots. In ancient
times, Greek libraries were designated as healing places of the soul, and
Greek tragic theater was viewed as cathartic for the entire community. King
David sang psalms to comfort Saul, and the ancient poets were recognized as
shamans and healers within various cultures. In recent times, within the past
forty years, poetry therapy has been defined as a distinct professional field, a
sister profession to the other creative arts therapies: art, dance, drama,
music, and psychodrama. Pioneers such as Jack Leedy and Art Lerner were
sowing the seeds of poetry therapy as a viable and unique treatment modal-
ity in the early 1970s. Today, the National Association for Poetry Therapy
provides the primary networking, educational and accreditation structure for
diverse practitioners in a wide variety of settings engaged in this therapeutic
mode. While some poetry therapists who are trained as clinicians include
poetry as a part of their therapy, other poetry therapists introduce poems for
those seeking to explore life issues and enhance their development. In both
clinical and non-clinical settings, poetry therapists select poems or other lit-
erary materials to suit their clients' particular needs and goals, facilitate fruit-
ful and frank discussion of these works, and provide exercises to stimulate
and encourage their clients' own creative expressions.

1

This anthology is designed to be a valuable resource not only for poetry therapists and trainees in poetry therapy but also for educators, mental health professionals, creative artists, as well as everyday lovers of memorable, moving poetry who are engaged in their own privately led journey. We expect it to increase awareness of the many ways that the energy of poetic expression can be harnessed to foster growth, help alleviate pain, and improve the quality of life. However, it is important for readers to recognize that incorporating literary materials and creative writing activities into a therapeutic context does not make one a poetry therapist. Specialized training and supervision are required before an individual can become certified or registered in this field.

The initial phrase of this book's title, *The Healing Fountain*, is drawn from W.H. Auden's words, "In the deserts of the heart / Let the healing fountain start." Like the crystalline spouting waters of the famous classical fountain of the nine Muses, poetry inspires and renews us time and again. When we read or hear a poem, our senses, hearts, minds, and souls all participate in the act. Because poems elicit responses at so many levels, they often function as vehicles for enlightenment and healing. Many people have a love of poetry and even use certain words or lines as a mantra, especially in times of trial. With their rhythmical arrangement of images, poems arrest our attention and imagination, moving us between the polarities of what we expect and what surprises us. With a whisper, a shout, a musical cadence, or a sob, the poet's voice conjures up experiences that crackle with immediacy. In "Poetry," Nikki Giovanni captures this exciting intimacy when she writes, "a poem is pure energy / horizontally contained / between the mind / of the poet and the ear of the reader." Through vivid lines of verse, we gain the opportunity to perceive the everyday substance of our own lives transformed magically in language that mirrors and confirms who we are. As Emily Dickinson notes, the "Poet" is the one who "Distills amazing sense / From Ordinary Meanings." Poets achieve a vivid compactness unlikely to be found in any other literary genre. A few well-chosen words and condensed metaphors can tap a well of deep feelings, thoughts, and associations. Poet Stanley Kunitz states: "Through the years I have found this gift of poetry to be life-sustaining, life enhancing, and absolutely unpredictable. Does one live, therefore for the sake of poetry? No, the reverse is true: poetry is for the sake of the life."

Along with the title's "healing fountain" image, the metaphor of the journey in the subtitle captures the spirit and design of this anthology. Each of the six major sections focuses on a key feature of life's journey. The opening section, "Mindfulness," sets the reflective tone as a way of introducing readers to the anthology's creative approach. The middle four sections center on themes or universal aspects of our human journey with its inherent blend of light and shade. Section Two's title, "Twists in the Road," metaphorically suggests the complexity of life's crucial transitional points and the challenging choices we are called upon to make. Section Three invites us to encounter life's shadowy side as we recognize and even affirm the existence of anger, fear, grief, and loss, while Section Four, as a counterpart, celebrates the bright side—the ways we honor ourselves and recognize our place in the variegated natural world around us. Taking into account that our human existence is far from a solitary state, Section Five highlights the parent-child and couple relationships that help make us who we are, both easing and complicating our travels through time. The capstone section, "Finding a Map to Travel By" suggests the ongoing nature of our explorations and provides models of the way we each find valuable truths to help guide us along the way.

Each section of this collection discusses poems designed to appeal to a large audience of readers and is arranged in a similar manner. Each begins with an introductory essay on its theme; follows with a detailed analysis of a selected set of poems, along with questions and approaches to facilitate discussion and writing exercises; and concludes with an annotated bibliography of a larger body of poems suggested as therapeutic resources. While chapter authors quote liberally from all the poems, the exorbitant cost of reprint fees has made it impossible to include the text of all the poems described in this collection. However, the poems we were allowed to reprint free of charge have been appended to each chapter, and the bibliographic information supplied for every poem discussed is designed to enable readers to locate these works.

Embarking on the creative, reflective and sensory voyage that this anthology promises, readers may choose to begin at the shore and set sail on a longitudinal course or may find it more congenial to land here and there randomly at the ports and islands provided. However readers choose to enjoy this expedition, we hope all will find treasures, both personal and professional, to call their own.

REFERENCES

Auden, W.H. "In Memory of W.B. Yeats," Part III (1939). *Collected Poems.* Ed. Edward Mendelson. New York: Vintage Books/ Random House, 1991. pp. 248-249.

Dickinson, Emily. "This is a Poet" (#176) (1862). *Complete Poems of Emily Dickinson.* Ed. Thomas H. Johnson. Boston: Little Brown & Co., 1976. pp. 106-107.

Giovanni, Nikki. "Poetry." *The Women and the Men.* New York: William Morrow & Co., Inc.,1975.

Kunitz, Stanley. Book jacket quote. *Collected Poems of Stanley Kunitz.* New York: W.W. Norton & Co., 2000.

Leedy, J.J. *Poetry Therapy: The Use of Poetry in the Treatment of Emotional Disorders.* Philadelphia: J.B. Lippincott, 1969 and *Poetry the Healer.* Philadelphia: J.B. Lippincott, 1973. Republished as *Poetry as Healer: Mending the Troubled Mind.* New York: Vanguard, 1985.

Lerner, Arthur. *Poetry in the Therapeutic Experience.* New York: Pergamon, 1978.

National Association for Poetry Therapy – Phone: 1-866-844-NAPT (Toll Free) or 954-499-4333; FAX: 954-499-4324; E-MAIL: NAPTstarr@aol.com; Website: www.poetrytherapy.org.

I
MINDFULNESS ON THE JOURNEY AHEAD

MINDFULNESS ON THE JOURNEY AHEAD

Kathleen Adams, LPC, RPT, and Stephen Rojcewicz, MD, CPT

THEMATIC OVERVIEW

WE ENTER INTO A MAGIC TERRAIN, poetry therapy participants and facilitators alike. Our commonwealth is the intersection of the humanities with healing, a locale for the integration of empathy and intuition with organized scientific knowledge. We seek an arena for the taming and transformation of raw, primitive emotions through the discipline and structure of psychotherapy. If poetry therapy is such a privileged example of the fertile amalgam of science and art, then the selection of poems to be used is itself one of the most critical points in the practice of poetry therapy. This skill, needed throughout, is most imperative during the beginning of any group or individual session, when the initial selection can set the emotional tone for months of work to come and imprint a profound legacy on the participants.

Hynes and Hynes-Berry delineate in great detail the criteria for choosing bibliotherapeutic materials. The poems or other written materials must address universal themes, to increase the potential for stimulating recognition among diverse group members. The poems should deal with powerful themes (not trivial ones) and comprehensible themes (passages from complex works such as *Finnegans Wake* or Ezra Pound's *Pisan Cantos*, no matter how powerful or universal, are not suitable for the initial sessions of most poetry therapy groups or sessions). The poems chosen should emphasize positive themes, having a basically upbeat message. The classical *isoprinciple*, developed by Leedy, is paramount. The poem's emotional tone should match the clinical situation or the mood of the group or individual client but should not be excessively negative or glorify suicide or anti-social behavior. Stylistic dimensions are important, but the poem is chosen not primarily for its literary merit but for its usefulness as a tool for awareness, self-discovery, and therapeutic change. In addition to the values of rhythm and imagery, selected poems should be succinct as well as linguistically clear in vocabulary and diction.

Mazza points out additional caveats. The use of pre-existing poems may sometimes force, rather than facilitate, group process. This might occur if the group members see the poem as not connected to their issues but as chosen by the group facilitators for their own or for inscrutable purposes. In addition, a particular poem may be distasteful to a specific group member, or it may evoke feelings that an individual member is not ready to encounter. The situation can even worsen if the group leader is insistent on using that particular poem at that time.

The initial selections of poems, for the above reasons, compel the most judicious exercise of empathy, intuition, and literary expertise. In this chapter, we will focus on poems to be used especially at the beginning of poetry therapy groups or individual sessions, poems that emphasize and reinforce the value of mindfulness—the simple yet profound act of nonjudgmental self-observation—on the journey ahead.

We will examine in depth six poems in a therapeutic context and address additional poems more briefly. The poems in this section emphasize attention to mindfulness, introspection, self-awareness, and the beginnings of a psychological journey into self-knowledge. They provide models of how the course of poetry therapy will proceed.

These selections may take the form of the writer's own experience, may directly address the reader, or may use a third person as the central figure. Lawrence Ferlinghetti's "Dog" even uses an animal as that central figure.

The following poems present the writer's own experience or thoughts in such a way that the reader or poetry therapy participant can readily identify with the issues in question: Mari Evans' "The Silver Cell," Elizabeth Keeler's "Light," Elder Olson's "Directions to the Armorer," Linda Pastan's "Helen Bids Farewell to Her Daughter Hermione," Adrienne Rich's "Upper Broadway," Rainer Maria Rilke's "I am too alone in the world, and not alone enough," Carl Sandburg's "Chicago Poet," W.D. Snodgrass's "looking," and Walt Whitman's "Song of the Open Road."

Additional poems include both a personal experience of the poet and a direct address to the reader: Emily Dickinson's "I'm Nobody! Who are you?" Pablo Neruda's "Keeping Quiet," Mary Oliver's "The Summer Day," and William Stafford's "A Ritual to Read to Each Other." Further poems include the writer and the reader implicitly by using "we": Naomi Shihab Nye's "Living with Mistakes," Mary Oliver's "The Swimming Lesson," Linda Pastan's "An Old Song," "What We Want," and Naomi Replansky's

8

"Housing Shortage." The full text of Auden's classic, "In Memory of W.B. Yeats" sets the stage with a third-person account of the death of W.B. Yeats, then directly addresses the reader and even uses the imperative mood ("follow . . . persuade . . . sing . . . teach").

Delight, fear, quiet contemplation, painful memories, issues of self-esteem, courage, the ability to find oneself while reaching out to others—these themes are addressed in such a manner as to prepare the way for the clinical (psychotherapeutic) or developmental (personal growth or self-help) work ahead.

For purposes of general identification, although with the risks inherent in any brief over-simplification, the content of the poems can be classified as follows. These categories are not mutually exclusive and merely serve as a form of short-hand for an overall catalog. Rilke and Rich focus on the struggle for self-identity, in the context of self-differentiation. Ferlinghetti, Neruda, Oliver's "The Summer Day," Pastan's "Helen Bids Farewell to Her Daughter Hermione," Snodgrass, and Stafford all appeal to careful attention, quiet, and openness. Auden, Berry, Keeler, Nye, Oliver's "The Swimming Lesson," Olson, and Pastan's "An Old Song" call attention to negative emotions, "the bottom of the night," the darkness, painful experiences, or personal mistakes that have to be confronted in order to find oneself. Dickinson, Evans, Replansky, and Sandburg's "Chicago Poet" address issues of self-esteem or forces that narrow our outlook, from insignificance in the eyes of others to the painful legacy of slavery and racism. Pastan's "What We Want" and Sandburg's "Solo for Saturday Night Guitar" illustrate the difficulties of love and desires. Whitman emphasizes exuberance and openness to all of the world, to the point where all his human experiences are indelibly incorporated into himself. Whitman's generosity and openness is a model and goal for poetry therapy, as we work together to achieve mindfulness on the journey ahead.

The chapter authors have successfully used these poems in many different clinical and developmental settings and with a variety of populations, including patients with issues of self-concept and identity, psychiatric patients, people living with HIV/AIDS, and personal growth and self-help groups.

IN-DEPTH FOCUS ON POEMS IN A THERAPEUTIC CONTEXT

1. Lines from "In Memory of W.B. Yeats" by W.H. Auden

This poem, written by the English W.H. Auden as an elegy for the Anglo-Irish poet W.B. Yeats after his death in January 1939, is perhaps the greatest English poem about the power of poetry. The concluding quatrains of the third and final section, beginning with "Follow, poet, follow right / To the bottom of the night" are particularly suitable for use during the beginning groups of poetry therapy.

The meter of this section, quite different from the structure of the first two sections of the poem, is simple and quite catching, almost hypnotic. While this trochaic tetrameter rhythm echoes the meter used in several famous poems of Yeats, it is more readily recognizable as the seven-syllable meter of William Blake's "The Tyger": "Tyger! Tyger! Burning bright / In the forests of the night." Group members may already be familiar with Blake's poem, which is often studied in American high schools.

Auden encourages the poet, great poets such as Yeats as well as any poet such as the group members, to look deeply into oneself, to follow, with courage and openness "right / To the bottom of the night." With the freedom and integrity that come from such an "unconstraining voice," the poet can, despite life's hardships, frustrations, and disasters, "Still persuade us to rejoice."

Some lines occasionally spark confusion in group members: "Make a vineyard of the curse" may be misinterpreted. Some members may think that Auden is encouraging the growth of resentment and vendetta. At times, the poetry therapy facilitator may have to call attention to the preceding phrase, "farming of a verse," and suggest that Auden is describing turning a curse into something fruitful through the power of poetry. There appears to be another connection to William Blake here. The first stanza of "A Poison Tree" by Blake (discussed more fully in the first section of Chapter Three) is often used in poetry therapy, especially when dealing with issues of anger and acting out: "I was angry with my friend: / I told my wrath, my wrath did end. / I was angry with my foe: / I told it not, my wrath did grow." Auden is here elaborating more fully on Blake's dichotomy—"I told my wrath" becomes expanded into "I write about my wrath, making something creative, nourishing, and healing."

The lines about "human unsuccess" and "distress" are universal. All group members can identify with failures, disappointment, and pain. The phrase "rapture of distress," however, may possibly be a distraction to members with self-defeating personality attributes, or sado-masochistic features. The imperative "Sing of human unsuccess" places these issues directly in a creative and therapeutic context, finding lyricism and human dignity in any failure or unsuccess, since it is "human" unsuccess.

The next two lines are among the most therapeutic ever written: "In the deserts of the heart / Let the healing fountain start. . . ." Practically every word is important and can provide inspiration or be the focus of more detailed therapeutic exploration. All group members, whether in a therapeutic or a developmental poetry therapy group, have experienced the "deserts of the heart," ranging from apathy to mild sadness to (in some individuals) the dark night of the soul. These deserts are not just in the brain or the hormones, but in the heart, emphasizing human, interpersonal aspects. It is in these dark recesses of the heart that healing can begin. The verb, "Let," underlines the fact that individuals are not passive but play an active role in healing. They must "let" it begin. Auden is stressing the role of mindfulness on the journey ahead, the willingness for self-scrutiny and increased self-awareness, the preparedness for the healing power of poetry. What begins is the "healing fountain"; this is not a one-time all-or-nothing phenomenon, but a process. A water faucet may be limited to one person or one family; a fountain, by contrast, is community-oriented, available for many. It is associated with relief, cleansing, restoration, coolness. Life-giving fountains are found in biblical scripture and are prominent in many mythologies and narratives of saints, as well as in other therapeutic poems such as "The Fountain" by Denise Levertov.

The therapist can ask individuals to respond to Auden's poem by vividly imagining and describing their own healing fountains and by delineating what processes, images, events, or people helped their particular fountains to start the therapeutic work of healing. The facilitator can direct a group to describe a desert of the heart, with each member contributing an image (cactus, rattlesnakes, heat, dryness, etc.). The members can then create a group poem that constitutes a healing fountain, addressing the specific negative images in the desert (rain to ease the heat, a brook or oasis as a respite from the dryness, a clear path as a protection from rattlesnakes, etc.).

Auden's poem, "In Memory of W.B. Yeats," is a masterpiece. Its concluding quatrains are wonderfully appropriate for poetry therapy and can

11

be especially valuable during the beginning phase, providing an atmosphere of openness, freedom, integrity, with emphasis on the therapeutic value of creativity, sincere self-exploration, and self-understanding.

2. "The Summer Day" by Mary Oliver

Mary Oliver abundantly draws both inspiration and metaphor from her intimate relationship with the natural world, and "The Summer Day" begins with rhetorical musings on the nature of creation itself: "Who made the world? / Who made the swan, and the black bear?" For the next seven lines, the poem explores the particularity and genius of one tiny creation, a grasshopper: "the one . . . who is gazing around with her enormous and complicated eyes." Oliver's telescopic focus on the grasshopper then pulls back into commentary on the art of, and need for, present-centeredness in everyday life, leading into an echo of the questioning that opens the poem. The ending question, however, is anything but rhetorical. In a stunning couplet, it challenges the reader to "Tell me, what is it you plan to do / with your one wild and precious life?"

Oliver is one of the most accessible contemporary poets, with clear use of language and themes that hold near-universal appeal. It is said that she tucks pencils into the hollows of trees she passes on her daily wanderings through the coastal New England landscape, and it is easy to imagine her scribbling lines while perched on a moss-covered rock. It is this matter-of-fact intimacy with the world around her that makes this poem, with its theme of finding the uniqueness within the global, an excellent one to offer a newly forming poetry therapy group.

The specificity of her observations of the grasshopper may invite a discussion on "What is unique about me?" with the encouragement to become just as detail-oriented as the poet: "What, specifically, is unique about me?" A brief writing exercise, using the sentence stem "I am the one who . . ." can be read in a round, creating a group poem.

In one poetry therapy group, a group member could not find anything unique about herself to contribute. "I'm not special," she said. "I wasn't smart in school, I work at a boring job, I don't have a husband or children." Gentle questions by the facilitator did not yield results. "I don't think I'm pretty, I've never done anything interesting, I don't have a hobby." The facilitator invited feedback from the group. "We're all special and unique in *some* way," said one member, who struggled with similar issues of self-concept and invisibility. Another asked, "What was the best day of your whole life?" The first woman softened unexpectedly and said, "When I was twelve, I had my first horseback ride. I'll never forget it." She was then able to contribute to the group process, with the statement, "I am the one who rode like the wind and caught laughter in her mouth." Patterning after the group's contributions, she was able to recall two other microcosms of experience that helped her see her own uniqueness.

The provocative question raised at the end of the poem, "Tell me, what is it you plan to do / with your one wild and precious life?" is an invitation to acknowledge the deeply held desire we each have to be seen, heard, and understood. Each of us has only one life, and it is ours to own and claim through our choices and attention. Often, the silence following the end of the spoken poem will be followed with sighs of satisfaction or poignant yearning.

These lines are also an invitation to chart a mindfulness map for the journey ahead—to begin exercising free will and conscious choice in an intentional, purposeful way. The use of the word "plan," with its assumption of choice and self-determination, is inherently empowering. Any tendency on the part of "over-planners" to assume permission to stay stuck in rigid patterns is immediately disarmed by the adjectives "wild and precious" in the final line. By calling us back to our instinctual natures and simultaneously imbuing this wildness with high (precious) value, Oliver invites us to reach for that which is best in ourselves—that which is both the most universal and the most particular.

The question itself, offered with pragmatic curiosity, is a good one. "Tell me," the facilitator poses to the group, "what is it you plan to do with your one wild and precious life?" Dreams and goals tumble out. "I want to go back to school and finish my degree," says one group member who dropped out to have children. "I want to make a difference in people's lives," announces another whose paralyzing sense of unworthiness inhibits her capacity to engage meaningfully with others. "I want to stay clean and sober," says someone who is in the early, shaky stages of recovery from substance abuse.

It is one short step to a *plan*. What is involved in going back to school, and what is one action step that could be taken now? What type of difference in people's lives will the plan involve, and where are the opportunities to explore? What will it take to continue sobriety on a day-to-day basis?

To conclude the discussion, the theme of present-centeredness can be reintroduced. Before the closing questions in the poem, Oliver states, "I do know how to pay attention. . . ." and describes several circumstances in which she has brought full mindfulness to this one particular summer day. The facilitator might offer a directive to choose one aspect of life experience and practice paying attention to it in the upcoming interval. For clients or group members with self-concept issues, the invitation might be to pay attention to individual uniqueness or preciousness. Others may wish to pay attention to opportunities to take action on their plan. Keeping an "attention log" of notes and observations helps anchor and reinforce the work.

3. "I'm Nobody! Who are you?" by Emily Dickinson

This poem, written by Emily Dickinson circa 1861 and first published in 1891, is often a superb example to use near the beginning of a clinical or a developmental poetry therapy group.

Dickinson begins: "I'm Nobody! Who are you? / Are you—Nobody —Too?" The juxtaposition of "I'm Nobody" with "Who are you?" is very moving. There is a reaching out and finding oneself in a human relationship ("Then there's a pair of us?"), but not in a faceless mob or Bog. This reaching out can be comforting and optimistic. After human contact is made and identification established, Dickinson then cautions, "Don't tell! they'd advertise—you know!" The word "advertise" is unexpected, and adds to the experience of this poem as containing unexpected things. The colloquial phrase "You know" adds to the group member's sense of a relationship with the poet—"we are together," the poem seems to be saying.

Telling one's name can evoke more mixed reactions in certain groups. Some group members may wish to be nameless and would certainly want to avoid the dreariness of a public persona. Some other group members may be hams, enjoy speaking in public, and enjoy even more telling their names.

This poem has often been used in both clinical and developmental groups. In our experiences, it has often brought forth an examination of the theme of conventional insignificance. In one dialogue among group members in a psychiatric hospital for the chronically mentally ill, the participants examined the significance of insignificance. "What is Nobody?" was asked. "Maybe she doesn't stand out in a crowd," one member said. "Everybody's somebody," a third member responded, "but as long as we're part of the mass-es, we're nobody, like salmon going upstream." The group facilitator offered, "Maybe the world thinks she is nobody; but she is somebody."

This statement brought general recognition and acceptance, and led into the related question of "why is it dreary to be somebody?" The facilita-tor suggested that maybe it is not really dreary to be somebody, but if the world forces you to be somebody that you are not, then it is dreary. One member had immediate associations to his combat experience in Vietnam, where the world's expectation was that he should be a hero, somebody he was not. A different member commented that he had been in that hospital for six years, and yet some people still asked what his name was. It made him feel insignificant, he concluded. Further group discussion focused on people trying to make the members what they are not, and the value at times of not being noticed. Those people who like to be noticed were "like a frog," mak-ing noise but not saying anything.

In the above group, Dickinson's poem was a vehicle allowing identi-fication with multiple, clinically significant aspects: feeling insignificant, feel-ing shy, the history of experiencing self as not at all worthwhile. The use of this poem led to the members eventually seeing the poet and themselves, not as nobodies, but as somebodies. From this standpoint, Dickinson's "I'm Nobody! Who are you?" is often a perfect choice for the early stages of either a therapeutic or a self-development or personal growth group. The poem identifies the low self-esteem and sense of insignificance that occur in all of us, not just in psychiatric patients, and with humor and elegance invites identification of the group member with the poet, through the words, "Then there's a pair of us." The group member is now predisposed for further intro-spection. He is inculcated with appropriate mindfulness for the journey ahead.

4. "A Ritual to Read to Each Other" by William Stafford

One measure of the therapeutic usefulness of a poem is the way it arcs across time and space to deliver a specific message of wisdom, hope, or empathic understanding, what the poet Edward Hirsch refers to as a "message in a bot-tle." When the brilliant poem "A Ritual to Read to Each Other" is under-stood in the context of William Stafford's life experience and poetic stance, it is indeed as if we have received a message in a bottle, and the title can be interpreted as a simple imperative from the poet: This poem is a ritual (a repetitive act infused with meaning or intention), and we are to read it to each other.

This is a poem about community and the urgent necessity to value inclusiveness and honor diversity "lest the parade of our mutual life get lost in the dark." Stafford himself is a fascinating study in diversity and paradox. A descendant of Crowfoot Indians, he was born in a small farming town in Kansas on the eve of the first World War. As a young adult, he spent four years during World War II in a conscientious objector camp. The image of a favorite son from the American heartland standing by his ethical allegiance in the face of an entire nation's patriotism offers a window into Stafford's commitment.

The theme of community recurs throughout Stafford's prolific published works. In his Introduction to the anthology *The Darkness Around Us Is Deep: Selected Poems of William Stafford*, Robert Bly comments: "Of all the American poets of the last thirty years, I think William Stafford broods most about community—the 'mutual life' we share, as black people and white people, pacifists and militarists, city people and small-town people."

The poem, comprised of five four-line stanzas, opens with a stanza of caution. We must take the time to get to know each other, not just our social personas, but "the kind of person" we are, or we run the risk of losing touch with what really matters, which to Stafford is deep respect and connection. He speaks to us directly, in a voice of "you" and "I," yet includes in the third line "the world," underscoring his enduring message that the family of Man is at once unique and unified.

In the second stanza, Stafford alludes to a possible etiology of this risk of disconnection. He muses that "small betrayals" and "shrugs"—the ways that we ignore and discount each other, not out of cruelty but out of everyday carelessness—erode not only self-confidence and self-worth, but the "fragile sequence" of the most essential self. If this careless inattention is left unchecked, he warns, the accumulation may let the "horrible errors of childhood/ storm out through the broken dike." Unfortunately, we do not need to look very far in our culture to find the truth in Stafford's words. The proliferation of violence by ordinary citizens, and particularly the murder of our youth by our youth in urban wars and school shootings, has become cultural shorthand for the very despair and primitive rage of which Stafford speaks.

In the first two lines of the third stanza, Stafford offers a brilliant double metaphor of elephants in a circus that may get lost on the way to "the park." Elephants in the wild are highly oriented toward community, with a social order that includes families and bonded groups. The town square or the county fairgrounds is small-town America's gathering place, the hearth of the community, presumably where Stafford himself as a child experienced the circus coming to town. Stafford thus reinforces the message of community, of the necessity of coming together, of not getting lost or separated on the way to our center. He continues with a challenge that "the root of all cruelty" may be the everyday mindlessness and inattention that lead to carelessness and separation from each other, and from our own "fragile" selves.

Stafford stands before us, clear-eyed and insistent, in the fourth stanza. "And so I appeal to a voice," he begins and acknowledges that we are adrift in troubled waters. We may not know how to articulate, our movements toward connection and mindfulness may be awkward and unsophisticated, we may fumble in the dark, but we must begin. Stafford implores us to "consider," to be mindful on our mutual journey. His acknowledgment that the terrain is "important" also offers a glimpse into something inviting and adventurous: The darkness may be shadowy and unknown, but it is the fertile soil of potential.

"For it is important that awake people be awake," he tells us in the fifth and final stanza. This echoes another message in a bottle that lands at our feet from thirteenth century Persia, from the mystical poet Rumi as translated by Coleman Barks: "The breeze at dawn has secrets to tell you / Don't go back to sleep." In the penultimate line of the poem, Stafford guides us to be clear in our messages—"yes or no, or maybe"—but leaves ample room for ambiguity. It is less important, he says, to be definitive as it is to be mindful; an awake "maybe" is vastly preferable to a "yes or no" that comes from the deep darkness of inattention.

Much rich discussion and process evolves from "A Ritual to Read to Each Other." One format that works well is to distribute copies of the poem and to ask each group member to read one stanza, in rotation. If there are more than five group members, the poem is begun again, until all members have read the poem to each other.

Silence may fall after the closing stanza is read. This silence is both appropriate and important. It acknowledges the poem's inherent power and wisdom, the cryptic layers of meaning that deepen and reverberate. It also may offer group members an opportunity to return to certain lines or stanzas that carry meaning or create confusion. Silence in poetry therapy groups need not feel awkward, and the wise facilitator invites it as a time of contemplation and reflection.

"What lines or phrases or images in this poem most speak to you?" the facilitator might ask. The group members might then speak phrases and lines into the circle, and discussion can be introduced on the lines chosen. It is important, of course, to bear in mind that there is no single best interpretation of any poem, and one beauty of a poetry therapy session is the way that individuals will shape the content to fit their own life experiences.

The first two lines of the poem extend an invitation for the newly forming group to get to know "the kind of person" each member is. "What kind of person are you?" inspires a rich round of sharing, particularly when the facilitator suggests that group members focus on their inner selves, rather than external personas. The result is nearly always that group members find they have much more in common in the interior landscape than external appearances might suggest.

The facilitator might close the group with a discussion of the last stanza and the poet's directive to be mindful and attentive in our dealings with each other. This can be a time of bonding, when group members begin to sense that they have come together to travel on a journey and that this group is a place where depth and mindfulness can be practiced.

5. "Directions to the Armorer" by Elder Olson

This poem begins with Olson's request to the armorer to "Make me a sword." The author then asks that the sword not be too sharp. He gives further directions to the Armorer, asking that his shield have easy-to-change insignia, because he is often "A littte vague / As to which side" he is on and in what specific battle he is fighting.

Olson's poem uses good humor to deal with issues of prevention, acting out, and impulsivity. These themes, and the underlying message that the author's problems are due to his own inner conflicts and should not be blamed on other people or on outside forces, make this poem suitable for use with clients who have problems with impulsivity and aggression. In one therapeutic group utilizing this poem, a group member with a history of mental illness, substance abuse, and violence asked: "Do I want a sharp sword, or a dull sword, so, if I go after the wrong guy, I don't do any harm?" He identified with the author, who wants the sword to not be sharp, and "of cardboard, preferably," because "Somehow I always / Clobber the wrong guy." This member concluded by phrasing his dilemma as, "Do I let situations eat me up, or do I talk to staff, so they can arrange a sit-down talk between people, so the situation can be settled?"

Other group members noticed that the author's biggest enemy was not an outside opponent with his own sword and shield, but was inside the author himself. Many members agreed that the author was talking about his own internal problems. This awareness stimulated members to write and talk about their own experience that in some way mirrored Olson's. What followed was a fruitful discussion both of inner conflicts and of the various forms our "armor" takes. The group members saw these conflicts and the multiple forms of "armor" as helping to create the inherent confusion in life, which was compared to "a mixed-up ball game." One person's armor may be a gruff exterior; another's, an automatic anti-authoritarian style; a third person's, a false front of excessive helplessness.

Members reviewed their own history of being stuck in armor, especially a style of impulsivity, and the danger inherent in acting out. At moments of confusion or vagueness, if they prejudge a situation and act impulsively on it, someone can get hurt. In these situations, as Olson writes, "I'm not absolutely sure / I want to win." In contrast, the group members saw self-awareness, asking for help, and even a sense of humor as the most appropriate directions to avoid impulsive acting out. Tough armor promotes rigidity and getting stuck in self-defeating patterns, but the coping skills of self-awareness, the ability to ask for and benefit from help, and humor are seen as useful and self-protective, conducive to growth and healing. Since the issues of managing tempers and impulses are universal, this poem and the process work it invites are equally appropriate for developmental groups or clients in clinical settings.

6. "Song of the Open Road" by Walt Whitman

Walt Whitman is among the first generations of Americans, which makes his beloved status as "America's poet" seem appropriate indeed. "Song of the Open Road" is a joyous 224-line canticle that captures all the optimism and hope for the journey ahead. We shall focus our discussion on Section One, an excerpt that can be very effective for the newly forming poetry therapy group. "Afoot and light-hearted I take to the open road / Healthy, free, the world before me, / The long brown path before me leading wherever I choose." Immediately, the tone is set; we are on our way. In some situations,

Whitman's cheerfulness may ring falsely. People struggling with depression, for instance, may not immediately relate to words like "light-hearted. . . . Healthy, free" as they embark on a new process of discovery. The key is in the last phrase of this stanza, "leading wherever I choose." The poem sug-gests that light-heartedness, health, and freedom are not so much a matter of choice, but an outcome of the choices we make.

The facilitator might frame the beginning poetry therapy group or session in the context of this stanza. The question, "What is this long brown path before us, as we begin the journey?" prompts discussion about what the members hold as ideas or expectations about the group. "Where do you choose to go with this group? If you could imagine any outcome for yourself, what might it be?" Members can be encouraged to borrow from Whitman's vast stores of sturdy cheer if they lack their own.

In one group, the facilitator brought in brown grocery bags, crayons, and felt-tip markers. Each member tore or cut open the bag and drew a map of the "long brown path" and the metaphorical journey ahead, using land-marks, milestones, and obstacles from their own lives.

"Henceforth I ask not good-fortune, I myself am good-fortune, / Henceforth I whimper no more, postpone no more, need nothing, / Done with indoor complaints, libraries, querulous criticisms, / Strong and content I travel the open road." The orientation toward creative self-determination and away from a reactive-responsive locus of control is a vital self-develop-ment skill. Here Whitman offers us a formula for shifting to this orientation. Leave behind whimpers, criticisms, complaints, and expectations, whether they are self-imposed or externally based. Turn instead to the "open road"— the strange and thrilling terrain of possibilities. This stanza is a treasure chest of process questions and points. The facilitator can ask, "Which word or phrase most stands out for you?" Members will usually place themselves in the poem where they see themselves most accurately mirrored, and a follow-up process question offers a chance for articulation.

For example, one woman in an inpatient therapy group was outspo-ken in her negativity. She found fault loudly with hospital procedures and staff. She was especially piqued that her restrictions included not being able to walk freely around the hospital grounds. This woman immediately honed in on the phrase "indoor complaints," which she interpreted concretely. "I complain all the time because I have to stay indoors!" she said. She was invit-ed to say more, and soon identified herself with the phrase "querulous criti-cisms" in the same line. Despite her pessimistic world view, one of her identified strengths was an excellent sense of humor and a capacity to laugh at herself. In the aftermath of this group, and with her permission, the staff person in attendance began gently teasing her, saying "Henceforth, I whimper no more!" each time she began her litany of complaints. This opportunity to see herself reflected in the poem in a humorous way was helpful in developing self-regulation skills.

In the third stanza, Whitman assures those who may be troubled by expectations and demands from harsh internal or external critics that we are exactly where we should be on the journey: "The earth, that is sufficient, / I do not want the constellations any nearer, / I know they are very well where they are, / I know they suffice for those who belong to them." Our modern culture is very different from Whitman's mid-nineteenth century America. Yet there seems to be a common mandate to "reach for the stars," and his permission to not overextend ourselves for goals, to allow the further reach to "suffice for those who belong to them," can bring a sigh of relief and gratitude from group members.

Again, the best starting place with any poetic offering is an invitation from the group to articulate their own interpretation. "What does this stanza say to you? What does it mean, do you suppose, to have the earth be sufficient, to not want the constellations any nearer?" One can almost imagine the twinkle in Whitman's eye as he stage-whispers the final stanza in this section. He acknowledges that a simple decision to embark on the journey to be at choice and to turn away from criticism and doubt may not suffice. What to do about the often painful history and difficult habits we each carry with us?

"(Still here I carry my old delicious burdens, / I carry them, men and women, I carry them with me wherever I go, / I swear it is impossible for me to get rid of them, / I am fill'd with them, and I will fill them in return.)" Whitman's intimacy with his "old delicious" burdens suggests that this business of journeying may be a "both/and" instead of an "either/or." It is not only acceptable but even normal to bring emotional baggage on the journey; we couldn't leave it behind even if we tried. This stanza brings to mind the interpretation of the "trouble tree" fable, where each person is invited to hang their problems on a branch, with the understanding that they must take another's troubles in exchange. As the story goes, everyone eventually reclaims their own troubles, preferring their familiarity and wisdom to any other life lesson they might choose.

"Song of the Open Road" continues for fourteen more sections and over two hundred more lines, exploring the outer journey of adventure and the inner journey of discovery. It closes with Whitman's characteristic and touching habit of reaching out to the reader as if he or she were a cherished comrade: "Allons!* the road is before us! / It is safe—I have tried it—my own feet have tried it well—be not detain'd! / . . . Camerado, I give you my hand! / I give you my love more precious than money, / I give you myself before preaching or law; / Will you give me yourself? Will you come travel with me? / Shall we stick by each other as long as we live?"

Annotated Bibliography of Poems on Mindfulness on the Journey Ahead

Auden, W.H. "In Memory of W.B. Yeats." *The English Auden.* Ed. Edward Mendelson. Boston: Faber and Faber, 1977. Also in W.H. Auden. Selected Poems. Ed. Edward Mendelson. New York: Vintage International, 1989.

> Auden wrote this poem to commemorate W.B. Yeats, who had just died. The concluding section of this elegy, specifically the last twelve lines, emphasizes the therapeutic possibilities of poetry. The poet, and by implication the poetry therapy participant, is encouraged to search the deserts of his or her heart, even to "the bottom of the night." Examination of these deepest personal issues leads to the creation of poetry despite the painful subject matter ("Sing of human unsuccess / In a rapture of distress.") Eventually this poetry will allow the healing process to begin ("In the deserts of the heart / Let the healing fountain start.")
>
> Note: See detailed analysis earlier in the chapter.

Berry, Wendell. "To Know the Dark." *The Selected Poems of Wendell Berry.* Washington: Counterpoint, 1998. Also in Wendell Berry: *Farming: A Hand Book.* New York: Harcourt Brace and Company, 1971 and *A Geography of Poets.* Ed. Edward Field. New York, Bantam Books, 1979.

> This four-line poem of rhyming couplets encourages us to face issues deep within us or develop little-explored parts of our personality ("To know the dark, go dark.") The result, especially in a therapeutic setting, is not despair or horror, but the realization "that the dark, too, blooms and sings."

---

*Allons (French) Let us go.

Dickinson, Emily. "I'm Nobody! Who are you?" (Poem #288). *The Complete Poems of Emily Dickinson*, Ed. Thomas H. Johnson. Boston: Little, Brown and Company, 1960. Poem written circa 1861, first published 1891. Also in *Three Centuries of American Poetry 1620-1923*. Eds. Allen Mandelbaum and Robert D. Richardson, Jr. New York: Bantam Books, 1999; *The New Oxford Book of American Verse*. Ed. Richard Ellman. New York: Oxford University Press, and *Collected Poems of Emily Dickinson*. Eds. Mabel Loomis Todd and T.W. Higginson. New York: Avenel Books, 1982.

In this brief eight-line poem, Dickinson states, "I'm Nobody," and then immediately asks, "Who are you?" / Are you—Nobody—Too?" The poet reaches out to the reader and establishes a human relationship. This poem allows exploration of issues of feeling insignificant, low self-esteem, feeling shy, or feeling worthless. Dickinson suggests an identification of anyone feeling this way with the poet herself: ("Then there's a pair of us.") Readers and poetry therapy participants can then see the poet and themselves, not as nobodies, but as somebodies.

Note: See detailed analysis earlier in the chapter.

Note: See copy of this poem at the end of the chapter.

Evans, Mari. "The Silver Cell." *I Am a Black Woman*. New York: William Morrow & Company, 1970.

In this eight-line poem of very short lines, Evans, an African-American poet, celebrates the dignity and worth of the person, despite on-going obstacles and the legacy of slavery. Facing persistent prejudice and unfair treatment, she does not view her self-worth as totally determined by these impositions from others. If she has been hurt, still she has "never been contained" by these injustices. Evans emphasizes that in addition to the external chains of historical treatment, the strongest chains, those most difficult to overcome, are often those that have been internalized or self-induced. She has never been contained or permanently restricted "except I / made / the prison," unless she herself created the chains. The poem speaks vividly to African-Americans and others who suffer from prejudice or who have lost their freedom through prison. It also offers insight and hope for those suffering from chronic mental illness or those finding themselves slaves to addiction: "I am slave / and I am master," both "bound" and "free."

Ferlinghetti, Lawrence. "Dog." *These Are My Rivers: New and Selected Poems 1955-1993*. New York: New Directions, 1993. Also in *Dog Music: Poetry about Dogs*. Eds. Joseph Duemer and Jim Simmerman. New York: St. Martin's Press, 1996.

In this long poem, Ferlinghetti imagines a dog walking on a street, and describes numerous objects and people from the dog's point of view— puddles, babies, cats, meat in a market window ("the things he sees / are his reality"). Ferlinghetti uses the dog to argue that we should not automatically accept the opinions of others; he emphasizes that each of us has his own reality. The poem encourages us to face this reality, to "reflect upon" it, "touching and tasting and testing everything / investigating everything." Through the unusual point of view, Ferlinghetti demonstrates the concept of mindfulness as seeing the true, essential nature of all phenomena.

Keeler, Elizabeth. "Light." *Cameos: 12 small press women poets*. Ed. Felice Newman. Trumansburg, NY: Crossing Press, 1978.

The first-person narrator, in the midst of winter, needs light. She searches for it among mountain roads, woods, rocky lands, and field. "Trapping it became the end of every afternoon." Despite being crafty, swift and silent, she is unable to trap light—"light was not enticed." Instead of light, she finds the earth with its "stony dusty face" and realizes that she has met her shadow in all the places she searched for light. "My darkness looked at me," she concludes.

This poem is useful in facilitating the acceptance of negative emotions and desires, the shadow side of a participant's personality. The search for light is portrayed as obsessive, "trapping it" instead of finding it in harmony. The search is thus one-sided, and many poetry therapy participants may be led to identify with the narrowness of a point of view that does not recognize any darkness within.

Neruda, Pablo. "Keeping Quiet." *Seeking the Heart of Wisdom*. Ed. Joseph Goldstein. Boston: Shambala, 1987.

Neruda invites us to be mindful through keeping quiet, being unhurried, without rush. "For once on the face of the earth, / let's not speak in any language." The goal is not total inactivity, but a respectful preparation for life. If we were not so lost in everyday hectic activities, "perhaps a huge silence / might interrupt this sadness," and we might then have a chance of understanding ourselves.

Neruda's poem is a good introduction to the value of quiet contemplation as preparation for introspection and personal interaction. Neruda's use of "we" and "us" gathers in all the participants and emphasizes the fact that such an attitude can become a part of the group culture, with each member's authentic mindfulness having the effect of encouraging the other members.

Nye, Naomi Shihab. "Living With Mistakes." *Red Suitcase*. Rochester, New York: BOA Editions, Ltd., 1994.

This short poem of ten lines personifies our past mistakes as living things who "march ahead of us / into our rooms, dripping." The lasting effects of our mistakes are seen as unwelcome and sloppy guests, sitting on a chair, making the fabric wet for days, leaving their imprints on our life. The conclusion to the poem balances the effects of mistakes with the fact that our life goes on and we are free to develop. Nye uses the pronoun "we" instead of "I," acknowledging that we all make mistakes, perhaps suggesting that we can more easily face the consequences of our errors with support from others, and indicating that the mistakes do not have to ruin our lives. Not only can we clearly acknowledge our mistakes, we can "Give them a chair," accept them as part of our past, have them available for mindful review when needed. Some clients might view the concluding lines as supporting denial or avoidance: "We have to talk about / everything else / in their presence." The poetry therapist, however, may help the clients see that these lines can provide a balance—our past not only has an effect on our future, but full acceptance of that past leads to the unity of our personality, a chance to integrate the wisdom that comes from experience into our full personality. We then are "living with mistakes," our life goes on, and we are free to develop; we continue "living," not "dying with mistakes" or wallowing in them.

Oliver, Mary. "The Summer Day." *House of Light*. Boston: Beacon Press, 1990. Also in Mary Oliver. *New and Selected Poems*. Boston: Beacon Press, 1992.

Oliver's poem addresses the themes of finding the unique within the global and invites us to chart a plan of action for the journey ahead. It tells the story of a particular summer day in which the poet is "idle and blessed" and brings attention and present-centeredness to her observations of the natural world. She ends the poem with a provocative question to the reader: "Tell me, what is it you plan to do/ with your one wild and precious life?"

Note: See detailed analysis earlier in the chapter.

Oliver, Mary. "The Swimming Lesson." *New and Selected Poems*. Boston: Beacon Press, 1992. Also in Mary Oliver: *No Voyage and Other Poems*. New York: Houghton Mifflin, 1965.

This poem speaks to life lessons that are learned harshly, by the "sink or swim" method. The first-person narrative begins with the swimmer's immersion into crisis and eventual self-rescue. The narrator retains a nonjudgmental stance toward the "somebody" who had tossed her in, even presuming a positive intention ("had wanted me to learn to swim"), but cautions that lessons learned in this way are more often about survival than life skill. This poem is useful with survivors of trauma who often perceive themselves as having had no control over catastrophe or assault. It can also be helpful for those who are experiencing emotional pain and those trying to find the core of their distress.

Olson, Elder. "Directions to the Armorer." *Collected Poems*. Chicago: University of Chicago Press, 1963. Also in *New Yorker Magazine*, 1959.

The first-person narrator requests the armorer to "Make me a sword," as if preparing for battle. The narrator then qualifies and hedges, asking that the sword not be too dangerous, or even be made of cardboard because "Somehow I always / Clobber the wrong guy." He gradually comes to the conclusion that his problems are due to his own inner conflicts and should not be blamed on other people. This is an excellent poem for prevention of acting out and issues of impulsivity.

Note: See detailed analysis earlier in the chapter.

Pastan, Linda. "An Old Song." *Heroes in Disguise*. New York: W.W. Norton & Company, 1991. Also in Linda Pastan: *Carnival Evening: New and Selected Poems: 1968-1998*. New York: W.W. Norton & Company, 1998.

Excellent for use with groups exploring dysfunctional family-of-origin issues, this three-stanza poem is stark in its language and content. Its theme is the way our "old songs" and refrains—our "childhood demons"—are deeply imbedded to the point where we hear them in the background for years and decades after the trauma has ended. The poem is useful as an empathic statement for the client who is in the early stages of articulating childhood trauma and also for those who are ready to move beyond the "old song" and begin work on creating new core messages of resourcefulness and triumph.

Pastan, Linda. "Helen Bids Farewell to Her Daughter Hermione." *PM/AM: New and Selected Poems.* New York: W.W. Norton & Company, 1982.

The characters of this poem are named only in the title, not the text. Helen of Troy is saying goodbye to her daughter, Hermione, as she prepares to leave Sparta for Troy. The goodbye will probably be forever, in her expectation, but "There is time / before I go" to tell her daughter fundamental things. She calls her daughter's attention to a lily, and how when the root is divided, it can multiply into even more lilies. "I'm speaking now / of love," she explains. Despite the passage of life's events and storms (meteorological and emotional), it is important to pay attention to little details such as how "light slants / across a page," and to be aware of the darkness and vulnerability within ourselves.

The emphasis on awareness and mindfulness make this a poem that can be profitably used toward the beginning of a poetry therapy group. Paying attention to concrete details in the midst of turmoil will provide a model of mindfulness that can eventually suffuse the culture of the group. Some members may identify with Helen's tenderness toward Hermione even while she is preparing to flee. Other members, perhaps those who have experienced divorce or unavailability of a parent, may identify with Hermione, and express resentment or anger at Helen for the abandonment. Whatever their specific identifications, and whatever their own inhibitions and difficulties of expression, group members can learn that they too are "speaking now / of love."

Pastan, Linda. "What We Want." *PM/AM: New and Selected Poems.* New York: W.W. Norton & Company, 1982. Also in Linda Pastan. *Carnival Evening: New and Selected Poems: 1968-1998.* New York: W.W. Norton & Company, 1998.

This short poem invites the nonjudgmental attention of mindfulness to the human condition of desire and the way we accumulate material things in an attempt to feed our deep hunger for meaning. Its language is at once accessible and coded ("We don't remember the dream, / but the dream remembers us") and speaks to the presence and reality of our desire for meaning, which we may not be conscious of, but which nevertheless is our invisible companion.

Replansky, Naomi. "Housing Shortage." *Ring Song*. New York: Scribners, 1952. Also in *Cries of the Spirit: A Celebration of Women's Spirituality*. Ed. Marilyn Sewell. Boston: Beacon Press, 1991 and *No More Masks! An Anthology of Twentieth-Century American Women Poets*. Ed. Florence Howe. New York: Harper Perennial, 1993.

This first-person relational poem is an excellent choice for assertiveness and co-dependency groups. It begins in a tone of apology, with the narrator acknowledging the many ways she has tried to "live small." In the second stanza, the narrator begins to acknowledge her right to take up more space, and the poem swells with her newfound entitlement, which the "you" in the poem "stumble(s) over . . . daily." The third stanza deepens fully into the freedom/closeness dilemma as the speaker's "lungs take their fill" and "you gasp for air." The one-line fourth stanza, "You too dreaming the same," acknowledges both impasse and empathic understanding.

Rich, Adrienne. "Upper Broadway." *The Dream of a Common Language: Poems 1974-1977*. New York: W.W. Norton & Company, 1978. Also in *The Harvard Book of Contemporary American Poetry*. Ed. Helen Vendler. Cambridge: Belknap Press, 1985.

This poem is rich with haunting images of the precarious and permeable boundary between hope and despair ("The leafbud struggles forth / toward the frigid light of the airshaft"). The struggle for emotional survival is captured in metaphors of life, death, and rebirth, one of which appears in the poem's closing lines: "I look at my face in the glass and see / a halfborn woman."

Rilke, Rainer Maria. "I am too alone in the world, and not alone enough." *Selected Poems of Rainer Maria Rilke*. Translated by Robert Bly. New York: Harper and Row Publishers, 1981. Translation of "Ich bin auf der Welt zu allein und doch nicht allein genug." Originally written 1899, and first published in *Das Stundenbuch* (1903).

In this early poem, Rilke develops the insight that "I am too alone in the world, and not alone enough / to make every minute holy." He notes contradictions in his character, contradictions that are inherent in every person. He is "too tiny in this world" but "not tiny enough" to be "a thing / shrewd and secretive." He wants to be with others, "or else alone." At the conclusion, he asks for security, finding comfort in the face of his mother, which he compares to a ship "that took me safely / through the wildest storm of all."

Poetry therapy participants can easily identify with the internal contradictions and the wish for security. Discussion of this poem can lead to recognition of the importance of introspection, personal honesty, and mindfulness for the journey ahead. The poetry therapy experience can metaphorically represent what Rilke calls "the face of the mother," offering security for the exploration of emotions and experience, no matter how wild or self-contradictory. For those poetry therapy participants who speak some German, the original is even more powerful than Bly's English translation. For example, the original German for "like a thing / shrewd and secretive" is "wie ein Ding, / dunkel und klug." Although Rilke often expands the concept of "thing" beyond simple objects to include living animals and even natural processes and phenomena, in this poem the harsh, guttural sounds of "Ding," "dunkel," and "klug" emphasize the materiality and lumpy klutziness of being a thing.

Sandburg, Carl. "Chicago Poet." *The Complete Poems of Carl Sandburg.* New York: Harcourt Brace & Company, 1976. Also in *Carl Sandburg: Selected Poems.* Eds. George and Willene Hendrick. New York: Harcourt Brace & Company, 1996.

"I saluted a nobody," begins this brief poem that captures the psychological process of projection in a story about a man looking in a mirror. The poet realizes that "this looking-glass man" is everything he is and accompanies him everywhere. This poem contains both whimsy and irony and is a good choice when the therapeutic task is to develop insight and self-awareness.

Note: See copy of this poem at the end of the chapter.

Sandburg, Carl. "Solo for Saturday Night Guitar." *The Complete Poems of Carl Sandburg.* New York: Harcourt Brace & Company, 1976.

This poem, written in a style reminiscent of smoky Chicago jazz clubs, begins by comparing time (precise) and love (inexact) and then riffs into a mournful solo on love's difficult beauty. It is a good choice for those enduring relationship difficulties, recovering from broken hearts, or moving into the commitment stages of relationships. Its many metaphors for love offer entry points for those who have a hard time articulating commitment, loss, and grief.

Snodgrass, W.D. "Looking." *Selected Poems 1957-1987*. New York: Soho Press, 1987. Also in *After Experience: Poems and Translations*. New York: Harper & Row, 1967.

Snodgrass describes an episode of forgetfulness, taking the reader on his search for an elusive something, "wondering what I was looking for." His vague wandering travels all over the house yet is poetically contained within a subtle rhyme structure. Taken concretely, this poem is useful as a gently humorous process poem for seniors or Alzheimer's patients. Taken metaphorically, it is a good way to introduce articulation for those who yearn for something ineffable, indefinable, or unknown.

Stafford, William. "A Ritual to Read to Each Other." *The Way It Is: New and Selected Poems*. St. Paul, Minnesota: Graywolf Press, 1997. Also in *The Darkness Around Us Is Deep: Selected Poems of William Stafford*. Ed. Robert Bly. New York: HarperPerennial, 1993.

Stafford's twenty-line poem contains a directive in its title: It is a ritual, and we are to read it to each other. This poem, written in an imperative voice, carries the themes of importance of community and mindfulness. It cautions us to make time to know and connect deeply with each other and to stay awake amidst the darkness that surrounds us.

Note: See detailed analysis earlier in the chapter.

Whitman, Walt. "Song of the Open Road" in *Leaves of Grass. Complete Poetry and Collected Prose*. New York: Library of America, 1981. Also in *Walt Whitman: Complete Poetry and Selected Prose*. Ed. James E. Miller, Jr. Boston: Houghton Mifflin, 1959.

This joyous, exuberant 224-line poem captures optimism and hope for the journey ahead. Whitman's cheerfulness is contagious; he starts out on his journey light-hearted, healthy, and free and offers wonderful role-modeling for positive self-talk as difficulties and challenges arise. He ends the poem with an endearing gesture of friendship to the reader: "Will you give me yourself? Will you come travel with me? / Shall we stick by each other as long as we live?"

Note: See detailed analysis of the first section of this poem earlier in the chapter.
Note: See copy of the first section at the end of the chapter.

I'M NOBODY! WHO ARE YOU?

I'm nobody! Who are you?
   Are you nobody, too?
Then there's a pair of us—don't tell!
They'd banish us, you know!

How dreary to be somebody!
How public like a frog
To tell one's name the livelong day
To an admiring bog!

(1891 version)
Emily Dickinson

CHICAGO POET

I saluted a nobody.
I saw him in a looking-glass.
He smiled—so did I.
He crumpled the skin on his forehead,
    frowning—so did I.
Everything I did he did.
I said, "Hello, I know you."
And I was a liar to say so.

Ah, this looking-glass man!
Liar, fool, dreamer, play-actor,
Soldier, dusty drinker of dust—
Ah! He will go with me
Down the dark stairway
When nobody else is looking,
When everybody else is gone.

He locks his elbow in mine,
I lose all—but not him.

Carl Sandburg

SONG OF THE OPEN ROAD, PART 1

Afoot and light-hearted I take to the open road,
Healthy, free, the world before me,
The long brown path before me leading wherever I choose.

Henceforth I ask not good-fortune, I myself am good-fortune,
Henceforth I whimper no more, postpone no more, need nothing,
Done with indoor complaints, libraries, querulous criticisms,
Strong and content I travel the open road.

The earth, that is sufficient,
I do not want the constellations any nearer,
I know they are very well where they are,
I know they suffice for those who belong to them.

(Still here I carry my old delicious burdens,
I carry them, men and women, I carry them with me wherever I go,
I swear it is impossible for me to get rid of them,
I am fill'd with them, and I will fill them in return.)

Walt Whitman

REFERENCES

Bly, Robert. Ed. *The Darkness Around Us Is Deep: Selected Poems of William Stafford.* New York: HarperPerennial, 1994.

Barks, C., et al. Eds. *The Essential Rumi.* San Francisco: Harper, 1997. p. 36.

Blake, William. "The Tyger." 1794. *The Complete Poems.* Baltimore: Penguin Books, 1977. pp. 125-26.

Blake, William. "A Poison Tree." *The Complete Poems.* Baltimore: Penguin Books, 1977. p. 129.

Hirsch, Edward. *How to Read a Poem and Fall in Love With Poetry.* New York: Harcourt, Inc., 1999. pp. 1-2.

Hynes, Arleen and Hynes-Berry, Mary. *Bibliotherapy—The Interactive Process: A Handbook.* Boulder, Colorado: Westview Press, 1986; St. Cloud, Minnesota: North Star Press of St. Cloud, Inc., 1992.

Leedy, Jack J. Ed. *Poetry the Healer.* Philadelphia: Lippincott, 1973.

Lerner, Arthur. Ed. *Poetry in the Therapeutic Experience.* St. Louis: MMB Music, 1994.

Levertov, Denise. "The Fountain." *Denise Levertov Poems 1960-1968.* New York: New Directions, 1983. p. 57.

Mazza, Nicholas. *Poetry Therapy: Interface of the Arts and Psychology.* Boca Raton, Florida: CRC Press, 1999.

II
TWISTS IN THE ROAD

ENCOUNTERING CHANGE AND LIFE'S TRANSITIONS

Perie J. Longo, Ph.D., RPT, MFT.
and Alma Maria Rolfs, MSW, LICSW, RPT

THEMATIC OVERVIEW

THE EXPERIENCE OF ENCOUNTERING CHANGE and life's transitions, whether it is anticipated, as in the growing up of children and the aging of parents, or unanticipated, as in illness, accidents, relocations, divorces, sudden deaths, and other relationship losses, is one of the great challenges in life's journey. This experience, and associated feelings of confusion, anxiety, and self-doubt, is very often a principal cause in a person's decision to seek professional help. As clinicians and students of human nature, behavior, and expression, poetry therapists know that at such times the customary coping mechanisms and defensive adaptations that have sustained adequate functioning in life's many spheres and protected the individual's vulnerabilities may appear to break down.

The resulting emotional strain can be especially difficult when the transition requires a change in identity and self-perception, the devising of a different answer to the question, "Who am I?" This experience of radical identity-transformation is beautifully expressed by Jerri Nelsen in her book *Icebound*: "Already, I am never the same." Such changes, whether they occur gradually or in one searing, life-changing moment, represent shocks to the psychic system with its collection of familiar, well-known self-images. While these images may inspire a range of emotional responses from cherished to despised, they are, nonetheless, claimed as part of oneself. The incongruities between these self-images and a new factual reality may leave the person in transition feeling extremely disconcerted and anxious. The task then becomes, for example, learning how to reconcile a self-perception of "I am a young woman" with "I am the mother of a teenager, herself capable of being a mother." These disturbing juxtapositions must be faced in order to achieve psychic integration, which is the foundation for healthy psychological, interpersonal, and social functioning.

In the case of transitions involving relationship loss, often the sense of personal identity has been submerged into the relational identity, i.e., the newly widowed woman who can't fathom who she is if she is no longer a wife, or the person who, after years of caring for a sick relative, feels his or her life completely empty of purpose or meaning once that relative is gone. At times when the familiar sense of identity is so shaken, the person may even experience a complete lack of identity, as reflected in the opening line of the poem by Phyllis McGinley, "Portrait of a Girl with Comic Book": "Thirteen's no age at all. Thirteen is nothing."

It should also be noted that in this country where there exists such a high degree of immigration and geographical mobility, physical relocations are so commonplace as to almost go unnoticed, yet they are often accompanied by innumerable small losses and a deep cumulative sorrow. The daily lives of transplanted persons may no longer include greetings from others who know their faces, or their names, or maybe even their family members and histories. Even more disconcerting, individuals may find that their regional or cultural heritage, formerly a source of pleasure and pride and comfort, may, in the new environment, bring discomfort and alienation. Such changes can have a massively disorienting impact, as expressed by Rina Ferrarelli in "Emigrant/Immigrant I": "Neither color, nor shape or size, / nor the face you were born with / can you take for granted anymore."

Frequently the losses necessarily accompanying even positive change are not acknowledged, either by the individual or by others, so that the related grief goes unattended or is actively suppressed in response to admonitions to "look on the bright side" or "never look back." As we know, unresolved grief can lead to depression, a descent from sadness to a state that may include feelings of low self-esteem, guilt, anger turned against the self, helplessness, and hopelessness. In that case, the person may feel mired in a dismal, apathetic state just when almost everything seems strange, difficult, and enormously taxing. These new challenges seem to require high levels of energy, commitment, perseverance, and creativity at the very moment when the person is feeling most psychologically and emotionally depleted, trapped in the dilemma of having to do more with less.

The person in transition seeking help at this moment of both risk and potential growth may be especially able to make use of a poetry therapy experience, since the poems themselves offer fresh perspectives, new voices and ideas, and suggest new alternatives. Particularly helpful is the fact that the voice in the poem requires no response, invokes no obligation, in contrast to all the other actual or introjected voices the distressed person may be listening to or bombarded by. Consequently, the typical often transference-based resistances to suggestions and advice ("easy for you to say," "you can't understand unless you've been through it") are not only defused but rendered unnecessary. The poetry therapist, of course, may suggest or encourage a verbal or written response that may provoke client resistance for any number of reasons, but ideally this occurs in a nurturant context in which the client feels safe enough to either meet the challenge or decline. Furthermore, the opportunity to respond to the poems both verbally and in written form in an empathic supportive environment may tap unrecognized inner sources of strength and creativity, thereby reducing feelings of inadequacy and helplessness, increasing self-esteem and helping to generate hope.

The poems in this section depict moments in which the poet or poem's protagonist faces and responds to change and all the uncertainty, disorientation, and shifting sense of self experienced during important life transitions. These poems poignantly and powerfully deal with themes of loss and replacement, memory and anticipation, holding on and letting go, loss of control and mastery, forgiveness and reconciliation.

There are several important qualities that characterize many of these poems and increase their potential effectiveness for use with clients facing important transitions and "twists in the road." One characteristic is the way in which the voice of the poem models self-observation, speaks from a vantage point that includes both outward sight and insight, that brings both the speaker's situation and his or her internal response to that situation, into one coherent picture. When a person in turmoil can begin to do this, to assimilate and accommodate new information and to include thoughts and feelings as part of the new information, a foundation for healthy change is beginning to be laid. Times of significant transition inevitably demand a capacity for Janusian thinking, a reference to the classic depictions of the Roman god Janus, whose two faces gaze in opposite directions, thus the ability to look simultaneously forward and backward, inside and outside, and to tolerate the anxiety when the normal boundaries of time and space begin to shift. We know both that the ability to tolerate ambivalence is a mark of mental health and that the capacity for Janusian thinking is a hallmark of creativity. Poetry therapy, at times of transition, helps the troubled person develop both of these in the service of freeing and strengthening the spirit for the continuing journey.

The person facing a life change of seemingly seismic proportions is often torn between powerfully felt apparently polar opposites: to stay or to go, to cling or to leap, to honor or to reject. At times of despair, both choices seem dire: to suffocate or fling oneself out alone into the storm. In many of these poems the very act of self-awareness seems to soften some of the painful juxtapositions and lessen their power to hurt. In Sharon Olds' poem "35/10" for example, the mother's sense of competition and envy is present, but robbed of its usual destructiveness (as described by Betsy Cohen in her book *The Snow White Syndrome*) by the mother's tenderness toward her child and by the poet's ability to step back and out to a perspective from which mother and daughter both are part of a much vaster story, the planet's own story. For persons facing difficult transitions and struggling with these and other conflicts and dilemmas, the creative, adaptive, integrative examples offered by these poems may be extremely refreshing and releasing, inspiring in them new creative efforts of their own in the struggle to move from a seemingly catastrophic "either-or" dilemma to a gentler "both-and" resolution. The word "bittersweet" comes to mind, that word so dear to persons moving through bereavement, because it condenses into one experience simultaneously felt opposite emotions and even a host of other mixed associations. The beauty of a sunset, for example, is rendered more poignant by the knowledge that the absent person would have also appreciated it; by missing that person; and by feeling both the pain of the loss and the pleasure of evoking, in heartwarming memory, the beloved presence. Poetry, therapy, and poetry therapy all help develop that creative capacity to find or invent a word or state of mind which can contain and hold the painful opposites. This experience, especially when shared, in turn builds self-esteem and confidence, thereby helping to reverse the downward depressive cycle and beginning to build a foundation of hope.

The poems in this section may be grouped into the following four categories: growing up (from both the parent's and child's perspectives), loss of relationship/loss of home, midlife, and decline and death. Many of these poems model flexibility and self-acceptance, important qualities often unavailable to persons who experience intense anxiety, guilt, and self-blame, and who, under that pressure, rely upon more rigid defense mechanisms. At such times the fear of making bad decisions, or the conviction that misfortune has occurred as punishment for misdeeds or inherent badness, may be immobilizing, leading to further depression and negative self-fulfilling cycles. A poem such as Lucille Clifton's "i am running into a new year" can help nudge someone toward a more self-compassionate attitude.

And finally, some of these poems offer moments of sweetness and of fun, experiences the bereaved, conflicted, confused or overwhelmed person has frequently lost sight of. Transitions, especially those burdened by loss and disorientation, are often not fun. They require the most of us when we seem to have the least to give. And yet the presence of humor, whimsy, or irony can be marvelously lightening, even invigorating. It also serves as a connector—a spark between minds, evidence that, despite the current darkness, in the vast human drama we are not alone.

IN-DEPTH FOCUS ON POEMS IN A THERAPEUTIC CONTEXT

1. "Hanging Fire" by Audre Lorde

This poem poignantly addresses, in simple, direct language, the anguish and isolation of a young adolescent girl as she faces the punishing changes of puberty. The opening statement, "I am fourteen / and my skin has betrayed me," suggests, in the persona of the poem, not only that the external betrays one's age, but also that what a teenager painfully feels about herself may begin with the physical: the color of her skin, its condition, her hair, her shape. The poem continues to free-associate all of the questions the girl has about herself, her boyfriend, her fear of dying, her wondering if anyone would care if she did die. There is no one to talk to, depicted in the heart-breaking phrase laced throughout the poem, "And momma's in the bedroom with the door closed." Each time the line repeats, her loneliness becomes more pervasive and more descriptive of what it is like to be fourteen, to not understand what is happening to her and to have no one to explain it to her. The poem, in just a few lines, captures the theme of Mary Pipher's book, *Reviving Ophelia*, which discusses the trouble young girls experience with the stressors of our culture.

In the second stanza, the speaker of the poem asks if she died tomorrow, would they "finally tell the truth about me." Again the persona of the poem really questions the meaning of her life as she laments her failures, the ugliness of her braces, and having nothing to wear. In the final stanza she wonders if she "will live long enough to grow up." Lorde captures the fear of not only the teenager but all women in transition when the world demands things of them they do not feel capable of delivering.

With this in mind, the poem would be highly recommended for teenage girls, especially those with self-esteem issues, and for groups helping teenage girls talk about how difficult it is to be female, as well as for eating disorder groups, by helping clients express unexpressed conflicts and pressures. It would also be appropriate for mother-daughter groups, bringing to light the daughter's anger and/or depression, so that the mother might understand the pressures her daughter experiences and her resulting inability to talk to the mother. The poem might not be appropriate for those with suicidal ideation because of the lines "suppose I die before graduation / they will sing sad melodies / but finally / tell the truth about me." This could be interpreted as suggesting death as a solution for isolation or for the conflicts of growing up.

Suggestions for Discussion and Writing Experiences:

Before the poem is read, the therapist could ask participants (or the individual) if they feel no one understands them. Often it is helpful to get teens interested in the theme of a poem, before reading it. After reading, in order to encourage discussion, the following sample questions might be asked: What lines do you identify with? What do you need help learning? What do you have to get done that you can't get done? When you want to talk with someone in your family, how do they react? What don't your parents understand about you? How can you tell you are being ignored? In school, what do you want to do that you aren't allowed to do? What don't you like about your body? What do you worry about? Do you feel anyone has betrayed you? If so, what was the situation? Why do you think the author titled the poem "Hanging Fire"?

Writing exercises can be encouraged from answers to these questions. The therapist might suggest that participants begin their poem by stating their age and listing the drawbacks of being that age. Certain lines can be repeated that strike the person as facts of her life, such as, "momma's in the closet with the door closed." Other writing could proceed from how people fail them and how people help also. The therapist might encourage writers not to be logical, but rather to follow thoughts as they come up. They might also be invited to ask questions about their life or life itself. Another poem might follow from complaints and/or thinking about what they are looking forward to.

2. "Edith Gets a Divorce" by Patricia Zontelli

This powerful poem vividly depicts the felt immensity of this moment of transition between a known life and an unknown one, a moment of "no small decisions" and of the inevitable sorting: "What to keep and what to lose."

The language of the poem is spare and clear, filled with strongly physical sensory images such as the opening lines "the sumac bleeds / under a low raw sky / growing closer and closer / to tears as the earth spins" and "the memories snoring / next to her for 20 years." These images capture the tension of such a moment, especially the poet's alternating experiences of time and surroundings rushing or standing still. The poem portrays the intense confusion often experienced at those times in life's journey when one must face and somehow survive unexpected, disorienting changes and transitions, especially those which, like divorce, challenge or compromise an essential sense of identity. Such confusion is reflected in often contradictory impulses: "She needs to warm her hands. / Or run." This poem powerfully expresses and evokes those experiences, culminating in the final, compelling image of the coexistence of fragility and internal strength: ". . . her lightweight / body, her thin sagging / breasts. / Her strong bones."

This poem would be extremely useful in any setting where participants, especially women, are experiencing divorce, separation, leaving an abusive partner, or any other major relationship loss or identity-changing life transition involving the need "to begin again / or become more."

Suggestions for Discussion and Writing Experiences:

In either individual work or a group setting, after reading the poem, clients might be asked which of the images touches them most strongly. Explorations of those responses and associations might be followed by any number of questions, such as: What needs are you feeling now? What "no small decisions" are you struggling with? What are you wanting to keep and to lose? How would you like to become more? What do you think (or fear) the wind will bring? And finally, what can you do to feel, and have faith in, your own "strong bones"?

Writing exercises could flow from any of the above discussion questions, or from using any number of phrases from the poem as a stimulus (i.e., list poems entitled "What to Keep" and/or "What to Lose"), or from having each participant write using his or her own name and context in a poem title, (i.e., "Janet Takes Back Her Keys" "Robert Loses His Job"), a technique which in this poem contributes both to the immediacy and intimacy of the poem and to a certain protective distance afforded by the use of the third person. Ultimately the poem demonstrates both the powerful articulation of the confusion and the capacity to go forward as a whole person, in fully conscious possession of both vulnerability and strength.

3. "i am running into a new year" by Lucille Clifton

This short and energetic poem that is all one breath with no stop or punctuation truly gives the reader the exact experience it describes: a forward rushing; yet the poet's (and reader's) attention, like the wind in her hair, is thrown backwards to the past. The future in the poem is completely unseen and unknown except for the knowledge that "it will be hard to let go of what I said to myself about myself" at the different ages she lists. In the midst of purposeful running forward, the poet pauses—barely—to ask forgiveness from her former, beloved, about-to-be-abandoned self: "and i beg what i love and / i leave to forgive me." What is especially interesting and provocative about using this poem in therapeutic or personal growth settings is the exclusive focus on the relationship with the self. Even the metaphorical movement of time is experienced in physical relation to the poet's body: "the old years blow back / like a wind / that I catch in my hair / like strong fingers," and the various emotions suggested such as disappointment, regret, anger, anticipation, and love are all in relation to the self or selves experienced over time.

This poem is very appropriate for persons who find themselves, intentionally or not, in moments of transition, struggling with identity conflicts; feeling loss, guilt, remorse, or failure, and also, of course, coping with the loss of old dreams, aspirations, and hopes. It is very useful for persons in any kind of recovery process and for obvious marker times such as the beginning of new calendar or academic years, graduations, birthdays and other anniversaries, beginnings and endings of treatment programs or other important endeavors. One strength of this poem is that the language is so simple and vigorous that it can speak to a wide range of clients regardless of their levels of literacy, education, or confidence with verbal expression.

Suggestions for Discussion and Writing Experiences:

In eliciting evoked responses to the poem, one might invite exploration of what the old promises were; what one said to oneself at different ages; what would be hardest or easiest to let go of; what it means to ask or receive forgiveness; or what aspects of one's past selves are most loved, liked, disliked, hated, and why. This poem also offers an interesting vehicle for a beginning exploration of the nature of personality—the cohesive self over time. One might, in this context, suggest that clients look back and trace both changes and continuity in their experiences of themselves.

The opening line, "i am running into a new year," suggesting both energy and intentionality, can also promote an interesting discussion about how we experience the passage of time—are we active participants in time, or is it something that happens to us? Can we make things happen in time or do we wait to see what time brings? This line of thinking could prove very helpful to persons who have lost a clear sense of initiative or control in their lives. For the depressed, apathetic, or even immobilized client, this poem can prompt consideration of what old voices or promises contribute to restraining him or her from moving forward. Similarly, clients moving toward termination, especially clients in recovery programs, sometimes demonstrate their ambivalence about giving up the unhealthy behaviors, symptoms, or substances through expression of conflictual feelings toward their former self-defeating or addicted selves, as though to become healthy and sober is to reject and abandon the former self.

In the context of such ambivalence this poem not only models an attitude of self-acceptance in the face of change, but also evokes exploration of that most important therapeutic achievement: developing the capacity for self-compassion and self-forgiveness. The recognition that all change and growth involve loss underlies the impact of this poem, and applying that recognition to one's own life is an important therapeutic step.

Writing exercises beyond those based on any of the above discussion questions might include inviting participants to change key words in the first line (and, thereby, the mood of the poem) to most accurately express their own experience (i.e., "I am crawling into a new day") or to write about their ages when they had especially significant aspirations or intentions or to write dialogues in which they imagine past, present, and future selves conversing and/or forgiving each other. This poem also lends itself to an accompanying ritual around termination, gathering and discarding written lists of what participants wish to leave behind, for example, or giving a client who is leaving a group setting both good wishes to take along into the new year and, of course, "forgiveness" for leaving.

4. "Men at Forty" by Donald Justice

This poem is about the strange, ambiguous, partly submerged feelings that may arise in midlife—uneasy feelings that have something to do with the replacement chain of the generations ("Deep in mirrors / they rediscover /

The face of the boy . . . and the face of that father"), vague feelings that are partly memory, partly presentiment, mysteriously invisible but clearly felt. The opening lines "Men at forty / learn to close softly / The doors to rooms they will not be coming back to" suggest all the countless small almost unnoticed leavings and endings that occur in the middle years. In the poem, as in the lives about which the poet writes, the "it" in the lines "They feel it moving / beneath them now" is never defined. Nonetheless, "something is filling them," something so "immense" it even fills "the woods at the foot of the slope / Behind their mortgaged houses." While the poem will be especially compelling for men in midlife, it also lends itself for use with any persons experiencing the sometimes vague or free-floating anxieties that accompany more gradual transitions, such as those taking place during the ever-expanding number of years now termed middle age. The tone toward the former boy/self and father is tender, and the private, meditative, mysterious atmosphere of the poem invites quiet, unhurried reflection. The final image of "mortgaged houses," therefore, comes as a shock, with its associations to the pragmatic burdens of middle-age responsibilities which one suspects often keep over-busy men and women in midlife from attending to all that is not immediately visible and tangible in their lives.

Suggestions for Discussion and Writing Experiences:

Participants in a poetry therapy session using this poem might be invited to speculate on the nature of "it" or to associate to how they have closed the doors to "rooms they will not be coming back to." Useful questions might include the following: What might you feel or hear if you stopped to rest on a stair landing and paid attention to the quiet? or What have you discovered "deep in mirrors"? or What "still warm" memories or images do you have about your father? Because of the mystery and ambiguity of the poem and the vague sense of dread or alarm that may be experienced, it would be important for the therapist or group facilitator to be alert to depressive, paranoid and/or anxious responses, for example, to the possibility that "it" refers to death or one's own mortality. Depending on the verbal and psychological sophistication of the participants in the poetry therapy experience, clients could either explore their mysterious submerged feelings or write more straightforwardly of their own experiences as fathers and sons, or be given the instruction to write a poem about their particular midlife learning beginning with a title that includes their own name and age (i.e., "Richard at Fifty-two"). Or clients might be invited to name internal experiences, such as memory or faith, which sometimes seem to be invisible presences inhabiting their lives.

Another exercise might involve writing from the points of view of those others in the mirror, the past and present fathers and sons. For some clients, this poem may stir apprehensions or longings about a spiritual life not easily accessible to them in the midst of the responsibilities of daily living. Because the poem introduces an unnamed, unidentified presence, it may elicit very personal or idiosyncratic material, and, therefore, it would be especially important for the therapist to establish and maintain an environment of respectful acceptance of all personal disclosures. In working with this poem, it would be important to help clients work through any anxieties that may be stirred and gain mastery over troubling underground fears through the process of acknowledging, naming and honoring these feelings.

5. "Midlife Crisis" by Mark Vinz

This is not the usual poem of angst about midlife, but rather one that addresses the subject with a slightly tongue-in-cheek attitude. Vinz begins with the lines: "Mine started early, / but then I always was precocious." We know already he is taking his aging somewhat lightly, but also he is aware that aging is a continual process, not one that hits at a particular age, and so we are always in the process of mourning our losses as we move through life's transitions. As the poem progresses, he allows himself to feel his diminishment, including his lack of physical attributes even when younger. His approach is most sensitive. As he notes his losses, even in the first part of the poem, he also demonstrates insight into what is to come: that each loss has its blessing illustrated in the lines ". . . and as my children say, a wrinkle is / a map to tell you where you've been."

He returns to "old neighborhoods" and his "dreams are litanies of what I've given up." A most important line is that he "laughs to keep from crying." Therein, he captures a psychological mechanism that many use, an important catalyst for beginning a discussion in a given group about what participants do to minimize their losses.

In the second stanza, the tone changes. Vinz becomes serious as he notes it is "the first of October," wind "scrapes" his window, and on a bare tree branch a "fat robin sits watching him." He searches for the meaning of this image in the rest of the poem as it applies to his midlife crisis. The image

49

of a fat robin in fall, suggesting both nourishment and the fullness of life in the season of harvest, is a catalyst for Vinz to admit to himself that he is in the latter part of his life. He then moves beyond this wry admission to find the blessing in this metaphor for acceptance and insight, the message of the moment: ". . . when the tree is bare enough / you learn to move, and see."

The language of this wonderful poem is direct and accessible, appropriate for groups dealing with the aging process because of the message of hope, addressing as it does one of the benefits of aging: the beauty of truly appreciating things you could not before. Other populations that could benefit from this poem are those dealing with depression, substance abuse, grief, and serious illnesses.

Suggestions for Discussion and Writing Experiences:

Questions that could be asked include: What physical features/abilities do you miss? Do you resist aging? When did you notice changes occurring that highlighted your midlife crisis? What dreams did you give up? Have you imagined new dreams? What would you like to do or see that you never have? Where would you like to return?

Writing exercises could grow from the following ideas: Discuss what you do to keep from crying. List complaints about specific ailments and then benefits you have enjoyed or could. What has been learned in your time on earth? (Think small.) You might start with an image in nature as in the first line of the second stanza, "Today the first October wind scrapes my window" and then associate this observation with an internal change within yourself, leading to some insight. Write about a place from your past you would like to visit again, in reality or imagination. What is newly there? Write what your children say about you.

6. "Before You Leave" by Mary Ellis Peterson

The subject of this heart-aching poem is the speaker's regret at not having enough time to learn everything she wants to learn from her grandmother before she dies. At first reading it seems the one "leaving" might be the mother, but mid-poem come the lines: "Teach me with your own hands / . . . hands that birthed my mother, my sister, / . . . hands gnarled with stories / I have not heard." The poem is powerful for anyone dealing with the approaching death of a loved one.

The author begs the grandmother to quickly convey the secret of her glowing skin while she lies in bed "waiting." She wants her grandmother's recipes for "home-made facials," for foods, her "living yeast," her stories. The poem addresses how in the face of death, time looms as a main player on many accounts. There is guilt for not being with the person enough to benefit from her wisdom. As the author says, in a line set off by itself, "I have not put in my time." There is unspoken anger at the dying person for not having told her stories and secrets. Suddenly comes the realization there will never be enough time or enough learned, because it is the person we want left behind, not their recipes or stories. The poem ends with the request of "hurry!"

In processing this poem, the concept from eastern philosophy could be interjected here—that we always have all the time we need. A group reacting to that thought could provoke an emotion-releasing discussion. Populations that could benefit from this poem are those dealing with the death of a loved one, care-giver groups, support groups for those with AIDS or other fatal illnesses, and certainly Alzheimer support groups (for relatives of the patient). An issue here would most certainly include that the loved one may have forgotten all there is to tell, or more sadly, who the person is who is addressing them.

Suggestions for Discussion and Writing Experiences:

Questions that could be considered are: Whom do you want to learn from? What do you want to learn from them? What do you want to say to them before they leave? Do you want to forgive yourself, or them, about something? What is a memory you want to remember that captures the essence of this person?

Writing exercises could grow from these questions. Discuss what you want this person to tell you. Write what you need from this person before they die. Write about stories you want to hear again or a memory you want to relive. This poem focuses on the hands of the grandmother. A participant's poem might do the same. What do the hands remind the writer of? Is there a metaphor for the hands? For life? How will you continue after that person is gone? Starting with the word "hurry," write what naturally follows.

51

ANNOTATED BIBLIOGRAPHY

Clifton, Lucille. "i am running into a new year." *good woman: poems and a memoir 1969-1980*. BOA Editions, Ltd. (92 Park Ave., Brockport, New York 14420), Also in *Cries of the Spirit: A Celebration of Women's Spirituality*. Ed: Marilyn Sewell. Boston: Beacon Press, 1991.

In this short, energetic, breathless poem the protagonist pauses briefly in the onrush of time to consider the past, the promises she made to her former selves, and to "beg what i love and i leave to forgive me." It is an excellent poem for use in moments of life review such as graduations, anniversaries, arrivals, departures, and other important transitions, when one must both look back and look forward, acknowledging both change and continuity.

Note: See detailed analysis earlier in the chapter.

Cofer, Judith Ortiz. "Blood." *The Latin Deli*. Athens, Georgia: University of Georgia Press, 1993.

This is a poem about an old man in a hospital bed after a transfusion, "where the stained sheets / are a testament of shame to the anonymous nights / spent with the stranger his body has become." It describes both his fears and his perseverance in the face of a world comprised of hard, reflecting surfaces: "no place / for an old man avoiding his own face like a good friend / he has offended." This poem would be useful not only for elderly clients or any clients experiencing physical losses and disabilities, but certainly also for those involved in the care of elderly or disabled persons or those close to anyone experiencing physical losses or decline and the related psychic blows to self-image and self-concept.

Ferrarelli, Rina. "Emigrant/Immigrant I" and "Emigrant/Immigrant II." *Looking for Home: Women Writing about Exile*. Eds. Deborah Keenan and Roseann Lloyd. Minneapolis, Minnesota. Milkweed Editions, 1990. Originally published in West Branch #23.

The titles of these paired poems, like the poems themselves, poignantly capture the heart of the emigrant/immigrant experience—one is simultaneously both a person who has exited and a person who has entered. The second-person voice of the poem emphasizes the self-conscious sense of observer and observed characteristic of newcomers: "But you're adaptable. / You stand alone in your new country." Not only is everything outside oneself new, but all that has been familiar about one's own identity has become suddenly unreliable: "Neither color, nor shape or size, / nor the face you were born with / can you take for granted anymore." "Emigrant/Immigrant II" ends with the sense that, despite acculturation, the immigrant remains inevitably dual: "A bridge, a border town." This poem would be very useful for any persons experiencing relocation or loss of home, especially when those changes or transitions affect the experience of identity.

Justice, Donald. "Men at Forty." *Divided Light: Father and Son Poems.* Ed. Jason Shinder. New York: Sheep Meadow Press (5247 Independence Ave., Riverdale-on-Hudson, New York 10471), 1984.

This somewhat mysterious, evocative poem suggests the vague, half-submerged anxieties, memories, and presentiments that can come to people in midlife, taking them unawares and causing them to search for, or listen to, something invisible but felt. This experience may foreshadow unexpected turnings in midlife, such as toward spirituality, art, or nurturing activities like cooking or gardening, or, conversely, may lead to impulses toward adventure and escape. The poem does not go so far but keeps us in the moments of inward listening. This poem would be most effectively used with psychologically healthy persons capable of exploring and articulating subconscious experience without undue anxiety.

Note: See detailed analysis earlier in the chapter.

Koertge, Ronald. "My Father." *The Father Poems.* Sumac Press, 1973.

As the author examines how his formerly vigorous father used to be, before his coronary, it is evident that, between the lines, he is also telling himself to slow down. He describes his father as always "on the run," even treating each sound, on his one vacation, as if it were a "customer." Implicit criticism of the father's life style is strong in this poem, yet there is also great sadness that his life could not have been more. The description of the father resting before a nap, with his "eyes full of ceilings" is a powerful image that sets in motion feelings of grief at the imminent death. This is a wonderful poem to use with caregivers of aging parents, as it processes the anger and sadness that those they love could not do more. Yet it is also a poem that reaches for forgiveness and asks readers in a therapeutic setting what changes they want to make for themselves.

Lorde, Audre. "Hanging Fire." *The Black Unicorn: Poems by Audre Lorde.* New York: Norton, 1978. Also in *Life Doesn't Frighten Me at All,* poems compiled by John Agard. New York: Henry Holt and Company, 1989.

Written in the voice of a fourteen-year-old girl, this poem is heart-rending as it tackles the confusion, fears, and anxiety of that age. The poet lists all the things that she has to do, that she can't do, that she should do. She also fears that she may die before morning, and "momma's in the closet with the door closed," a phrase that turns us inside out for what it depicts: the feeling of isolation and the conviction that no one understands her struggles. She questions whether she will live long enough to grow up. The poem, with its depressed tone, would not be appropriate for teens struggling with suicidality but certainly would be for those teenagers who need to have a forum to talk about their issues, for parent-teen groups, and for teachers to read with their students for discussion and writing.

Note: See detailed analysis earlier in the chapter.

McGinley, Phyllis. "Portrait of a Girl with Comic Book." *Times Three.* New York: The Viking Press, 1952. First published in *The New Yorker.*

This humorous but poignant poem begins "Thirteen's no age at all" and goes on to describe the uncomfortable contradictions and confusions of an age that seems definable only by all that it is not—an age of rather miserable "in-between-ness," an anomalous age that "wants nothing, everything." It would appeal to teenagers, their parents and siblings, and all persons interested in knowing more about the early adolescent girl's experience of herself in relation to others.

Olds, Sharon. "35/10." *The Dead and the Living.* New York: Alfred A. Knopf, Inc., 1975, 1997.

The title of the poem becomes clear with the first few lines which describe a mother's daily act of brushing out her "daughter's dark silken hair" as she also notices the "grey gleaming" on her head (she thirty-five, her daughter ten) in the reflection of a mirror. Olds captures in a short eighteen lines a wide range of emotions that this loving act conjures. She compares her own diminishment with her daughter's maturing body. The language and imagery of the poem are sharp and full at once, holding her sadness of losing her ability to produce yet adoring the one she has produced to replace herself. The poem asks the question "why is it / just as we begin to go / they begin to arrive. . . ?" and also, after a series of powerful, contrasting sensory images, answers it in the final lines: "It's an old / story—the oldest we have on our planet— the story of replacement." This is an exceptional poem to use with groups focusing on issues of children growing up, with women who find themselves dealing with the "empty nest" or the complicated highly charged mother-daughter relationship, with bereavement groups, and also with hospice and parenting groups.

Oles, Carole. "The Explanation." *The Loneliness Factor.* Lubbock, Texas: Texas Tech Press, 1979. First published in *13th Moon,* Winter, 1975.

This poem captures the confused feelings caused by first menstruation, the twelve-year old's painful self-consciousness, the lonely sense of secrecy and shame, the inadequacy of the mother's explanation, and especially the contradiction between the mother's words ("Nothing to be ashamed of") and her secretive, furtive behavior. This poem could be used in any setting in which women's issues are explored, especially concerns around sexuality, gender identity, and mother-daughter rela- tionships.

Peterson, Mary Ellis. "Before You Leave." *Mother Poet.* Ed. Peggy O'Mara. Albuquerque, New Mexico: Mothering Publications, Inc., 1983.

The author captures the universal urgency to learn everything she can from her grandmother before she dies, suggesting that she has not spent the time with her she would have wanted ("I have not put in my time"), not realizing this time would come so quickly. There is also regret in the poem that the grandmother has not taught her what she wanted to learn—"measure me the recipes / your mother made you practice / 'til you knew their feel." The poem is excellent for groups that address death and dying, aging, and grief, as it triggers all the feelings of loss: anger, guilt, compassion, awe, regret, love, and abandonment.

Note: See detailed analysis earlier in the chapter.

Scott, Mary. "Bloodmobile." *Split Verse: Poems to Heal Your Heart.* Eds. Meg Campbell and William Duke. New York: Midmarch Arts Press (300 River- side Drive, New York, New York 10025), 2000.

This short poem describes a moment in which the sight of her ringless finger, "a strip of flesh / depressed and colorless as tripe" requires the protagonist to publicly acknowledge for the first time her recent separation. While the poem captures the dull, numb, apathetic state following relationship loss, it also acknowledges the potential for empathic connection, is not ultimately pessimistic, and would be very useful for persons coping with divorce and relationship loss.

Sexton, Anne. "Little Girl, My Stringbean, My Lovely Woman." *The Complete Poems*. Boston, Massachusetts. 1981.
This is at once a love poem from Sexton to her daughter, a testament to her youthful beauty and approaching womanhood, as well as a poem that speaks, almost bitterly, of her own loss of youth. She warns her daughter of men who will win her by conquest, but she wants her to remember, before they do, how she, the mother, formed her and that she is "lovely." She reminds her daughter that whatever happens, she, the mother, is always there in the background, even though she wishes she could have given her so much more. The longing to be a perfect mother is captured in the lines "If I could have watched you grow / as a magical mother might, / If I could have seen through my magical transparent belly, / there would have been such ripening within." The loss she experiences at the same moment she honors the life she created is poignant and sad, as if she cannot see her own goodness. Those suffering depression will certainly relate to this. Sexton was a magical poet but not a magical mother, in her opinion, as reflected in the poem. Her language is delicious and difficult, hard to understand at times, and the poem is long and, therefore, not for every group. But those willing to tackle it will find many rich lines to process therapeutically such as "women are born twice" and "All that is new is telling the truth." Those who would benefit from discussion of this poem are mother-daughter groups, female teenage groups dealing with transition to womanhood, women dealing with "empty-nest" issues, women struggling with depression around parenting difficulties, and even those re-living their own conflicts growing up and recognizing what their own mothers were not able to give them.

Vinz, Mark. "Midlife Crisis." *Great River Review*, Vol. 7, No. 1, 1986. (211 West Seventh Street, Winona, Minnesota. 55987).
Vinz's poem is one everyone might take to heart on the subject of midlife, with the speaker making light fun of himself as one who "started early," noticing balding, increased waist line, and wrinkles. The nostalgia in the

poem is sure to not only enliven memory but cast light on the shadows of time, helping readers to process times in their lives that held sadness as well as joy. He returns to old neighborhoods and dreams, taking his lesson from the "fat robin" in the tree: that, when a person acknowledges what has been spent "you learn to move, and see." The poem is fitting for a wide range of groups that process the transition from youth to aging and also for those that consider loss, grief, and dreams.

Note: See detailed analysis earlier in the chapter.

Wiegner, Kathleen. "Autobiography After Lu Yu." *Country Western Breakdown*. Trumansburg, New York: Crossing Press, 1974.

This short poem begins "The people I love have pierced my life" and goes on to speak of the sense of both burden and treasure brought by these relationships. The final contrast is between years spent fighting "against possession" and the present "ease in the noose of my life." It suggests exploration of the transition to willing acceptance of responsibility and even sacrifice in the parent-child relationship, and as such would be very appropriate for clients approaching or struggling with issues of parenting or taking on other relational responsibilities.

Zontelli, Patricia. "Edith Gets a Divorce." *Edith Jacobson Begins to Fly and Other Poems*. Minneapolis, Minnesota: New Rivers Press, 1992.

This spare, powerful poem describes the tension and pressure of a time of enormous decision-making, a time suspended between past and future, of needing to choose "what to keep and what to lose," a time after "the breaking and breaking," when one must prepare to take "a big breath" and lean "into the wind." This essentially optimistic poem would be especially helpful for persons facing relationship loss in midlife.

Note: See detailed analysis earlier in the chapter.

REFERENCES

Cohen, Betsy. *The Snow White Syndrome*. New York: Macmillan Publishing Co., 1986.

Nelson, Jerri. *Dr. Icebound*. New York: Hyperion Press, 2001.

Pipher, Mary, Ph.D. *Reviving Ophelia: Saving the Selves of Adolescent Girls*. New York: Ballantine Books, 1994.

ENCOUNTERING DILEMMAS AND LIFE'S CHOICES

Nicholas Mazza, Ph.D., RPT

THEMATIC OVERVIEW

THE RESTORATION OR INSTILLATION OF CHOICE is the central element in most forms of psychotherapy. Every choice, however, involves a loss. Deciding what to hold and what to let go often creates a dilemma. Many times, an individual may feel there are no choices, that he or she is compelled to a certain action. For the clinician, depending upon theoretical orientation, this phenomenon could be classified as learned helplessness, a cognitive distortion, a developmental problem, a defense mechanism, or a storied experience. The common elements among theoretical orientations include choice, action, and empowerment. Poetry serves to validate and universalize feelings, promote self-examination and verbalization and instill hope. The differential use of poetry and poetry therapy methods vary with respect to purpose defined in each theoretical model (e.g., reframe a problem in cognitive theory, promote catharsis in ego psychology, re-story an experience in narrative therapy).

The poems discussed in this chapter address dilemmas and life choices in developmental stages from childhood through elderhood. The life transitions provide a wide range of experiences including childhood activities, gender and role identity, and death. Many of the poems are "open-ended," that is, they contain no specific instruction or message about life but rather invite one to experience a life choice or dilemma and encourage each person's unique response. Other poems are more "prescriptive" or "closed" in suggesting a course of action. The poems examined in this section will be discussed in the light of three different modes of poetry therapy, identified in *Poetry Therapy: Interface of the Arts and Psychology*. Most of the poems will be considered within the receptive/prescriptive mode, which involves introducing an existing poem into therapy and inviting reactions. However, links will also be made to the expressive/creative mode, in which the poetry therapist facilitates client writing and other artistic expression, and to the symbolic/ceremonial mode, involving the use of metaphors and rituals.

IN-DEPTH FOCUS ON POEMS IN A THERAPEUTIC CONTEXT

1. "Tree House" by Shel Silverstein

The speaker in this poem delights in the thought of a tree house where he/she has the opportunity to enjoy a special place ("free house") away from social constraints ("wipe your feet house"). This simple "children's poem" speaks to the importance of personal space, choice, and relationships.

    I have used this poem in clinical practice with both children and adults. The poem works well within the receptive/prescriptive, expressive/creative, and symbolic/ceremonial modes of poetry therapy. In working with abused children, "Tree House" has been helpful in promoting self-expression in the early stages of treatment. The introduction of the poem into therapy (receptive/prescriptive mode) serves as a non-threatening device to promote self-disclosure. By ostensibly talking about the poem, the client begins to talk about self. An art exercise and/or writing exercise (expressive/creative mode) is often used in conjunction with the poem as a point of departure for a discussion of home, family, and friends. Ultimately, the tree house becomes a metaphor (symbolic/ceremonial mode) for a safe place. By allowing the child the freedom to interpret the poem on his/her own terms and to create his/her own artwork, the therapist serves to restore some element of control to the child, thereby empowering him or her. In this way, the poem has implications for both assessment and treatment. "Tree House" is of course therapeutic without being in the context of therapy. The choice each of us faces from day to day, the places we go, the people we encounter often involve relating to "following the rules" and following "the old" and perceived safe way or daring to chart the unknown and engage in change. Such universal themes of anxiety, sadness, and loneliness are poetically addressed by the universality of "Tree House."

Suggestions for Discussion and Writing Experiences:

Facilitative questions include: 1) Could you tell me something about the tree house? the street house? 2) Could you tell me a story about the tree house? the street house? 3) What is it like when you are in the tree house? street house? 4) Who would you invite to the tree house? 5) Is there anyone who should be kept out of the tree house? 6) Do you have a favorite line in this poem? 7) Would you like to add something to this poem? 8) Would you like to get rid of any of the lines in this poem?

For adults, the theme of seeking a safe refuge during times of difficult transitions (e.g., divorce, employment problems, caretaking) is very appealing. Again, simple questions such as the following could serve therapeutic purposes: 1) Do you recall a tree house as a child? 2) If so, what was it like? 3) Do you ever wish you could go back? (or Do you ever wish you had one to go to?) 4) If you could build a tree house now, where would it be? What would it look like? Who would be in it? What can you do there that you cannot do in your present house?

"Tree House" could also be used in a family context to promote interactions among all family members. A collaborative (group) poem on "Our House" could be created by having each member contribute one or more lines to the poem. Or a simple acrostic poem could be developed where the words "Tree House" are printed vertically, thus providing the first letter of each line:

> The story of ....
> Reminds me of ....
> Every ....
> Especially ....
>
> Home is ....
> Outside ....
> Under ....
> Special times ....
> Even though ....

"Tree House" can also be used to promote a symbolic and ceremonial activity in poetry therapy. A special picture, poem, or visit to a special place could serve to conclude therapy and/or mark a significant change. The tree house becomes the image that represents coping with a dilemma and making a choice.

"Tree House" is a poem that can be used within most theoretical orientations. For example, the poem could be used in cognitive behavioral theory within the context of visualization (Let's go to the tree house . . .), assessment of self-talk (What is it that you say to yourself when . . . ?), and cognitive restructuring (change "I am a loser" to "I am a builder . . . I can create."). Within ego psychology, the poem might be used within the context of a therapeutic relationship to promote catharsis and a corrective emotional experience. Within narrative therapy, the poem could serve to externalize the problem (e.g., "street house") and re-story an experience ("free house . . . cozy as can be house").

2. "The Road Not Taken" by Robert Frost

This is perhaps the classic poem used in poetry therapy. The theme of decision-making, as noted earlier, is central to all therapy. Traveling in the woods, the speaker is faced with choosing between two equally appealing roads. The speaker does make a decision but notes that sometime in the far off future, he will probably slant the story to the effect that he took "the one less traveled by." In any case, however, the decision "has made all the difference."

This poem represents the archetypal dilemma that we encounter at various levels and at different times throughout life. The paths in the woods, like the Chinese symbol for crisis, stand for both danger and opportunity. The hope in this poem is reflected in the element of free will. This poem is open-ended because it does not instruct us on what road to take but rather is evocative in highlighting the choice. We can each respond to our own unique fork in the road. Inevitably, with many choices, comes second-guessing. There is no correct path but rather just the one taken and the one left behind. The decision is one of many transitional moments in life.

I have used this poem with clients of all ages. Within the receptive/prescriptive mode of poetry therapy, this poem can elicit the ambivalence associated with difficult decision making. The helping professional can demonstrate empathy by introducing such a poem that relates to the client's experience. The client's response to the poem can serve to clarify problems and perhaps focus on a specific target area to work on. The poem can also instill hope through universalization by suggesting others have "been there." The therapeutic aspects of "The Road Not Taken" are evident in the widespread appeal of the poem. At times we are all "in the wood," and are faced with a choice that may profoundly influence our lives. Struggling for the "right decision" can at times immobilize us. Although we can seek the guidance and support of others, ultimately we are alone in the wood choosing a path. This poem can be used with most theoretical orientations. From an ego-psychology perspective, the poem might be used to examine developmental issues and past decisions (or see how current behavior is an attempt to resolve earlier conflicts). From a cognitive perspective, work on irrational thoughts (e.g., "If I make the wrong decision, my life will be ruined . . .") could be pursued. From a narrative therapy perspective, the ambivalence could be externalized as something to deal with rather than a condition of the client. The story of the person's life could be examined through past decisions and re-storied through "the road not taken."

Suggestions for Discussion and Writing Experiences:

Facilitative questions could include the following: 1) Is there a particular line or image that relates to your own experience? 2) What do you think the speaker in the poem is feeling? thinking? 3) Could you tell me something about your "road"? 4) What has "made all the difference" in your life? The facilitative questions should be altered in each case, based on clinical purpose and what the client reveals in the therapeutic process. I have used this poem with clients struggling over career decisions, relationships, academic issues, ethical issues, legal issues, geographic moves, and the like.

"The Road Not Taken" can also be linked to the expressive/creative mode of poetry therapy by assigning writing tasks associated with decision making (e.g., make a list of your options relating to work, or keep a journal as a means of recording your thoughts, feelings, and behaviors related to making a particular decision). The poem could also be linked to the symbolic/ceremonial mode of poetry therapy, first as a symbol for choice, and secondly as a vehicle for closure in therapy regarding the decision(s) a client has made. The poem might also be linked to writing a letter to someone (e.g., former lover, colleague, family member) or something (e.g., addiction) that might be left behind.

3. "Autobiography in Five Short Chapters" by Portia Nelson

A series of life choices and dilemmas is captured in this poem. The speaker walks down a street and falls into a "deep hole." She walks down this same street two more times and falls into the hole each time. On the fourth walk down the street, the speaker walks around the hole. Finally on the fifth trip, she takes a different street. Interestingly, in the first stanza, the speaker feels helpless and not at fault for falling. In the second stanza, denial is at work through her pretending she does not see the hole. She still maintains it "isn't my fault." In the third stanza, the speaker acknowledges she goes down the street out of habit and is aware of the hole. This time she states that the fall is her fault. In the fourth stanza, the speaker's decision to walk around the hole is made without commentary. In the last one line stanza, she decides to take "another street." Again, no commentary is offered. It appears that in the fourth and fifth stanzas, the speaker feels her actions do not require commentary or excuses. The reader can draw his/her own conclusions.

This story of a life is consistent with narrative therapy. I use this poem to introduce narrative therapy to my graduate social work students. The poem is helpful in conveying each person's unique story. In this poem, the speaker's story in the first three stanzas is one of acting out of habit and convention. Ultimately, the speaker chooses to re-story her experience by first walking around the hole and then choosing to walk down a different street. The metaphor of the hole in the street could of course apply to such things as not working on a relationship, staying in a job that is creating constant stress and frustration, not seeking needed medical attention, or living an unhealthy lifestyle. Perhaps the "known" represents security even if it brings pain. Perhaps initially we feel shocked and disappointed, then there's denial, followed by a recognition that we bear some responsibility for the problem, and subsequently a move to get around the problem. Going "around" the problem, however, often brings discontent. Ultimately, a decision to change is made.

This poem is suitable for most forms of psychotherapy. In addition to the above mentioned narrative therapy, this poem could be used in an ego-psychology model. The poem represents a living model of loss involving separation/ individuation issues. As the individual breaks away from the dependency on individuals or social systems ("same street"), an independent self-identity emerges (takes "another street"). From a behavioral perspective, one could examine what maintains the behavior and select targets for change. From a cognitive perspective, the focus could be on the individual's thematic schemas or belief systems and on helping the client identify, evaluate and respond more effectively to irrational/dysfunctional thoughts or beliefs (for example, "I must walk down that street . . .").

Perhaps part of the appeal of this poem is that we can all relate to making the same mistakes over and over again. We can all relate to wanting to make believe the problem will go away. We try the path of least resistance—walking around the problem. Ultimately, we face living with the problem or making a change (walking down another street).

Suggestions for Discussion and Writing Experiences:

As part of the receptive/prescriptive mode of poetry therapy, this poem can be used to validate the feeling of those who see themselves as locked in a life circumstance and can provide the means for the client to relate the chapters in his/her life. Facilitative questions could include the following: 1) Could you tell me about some of the roads that you have traveled? 2) Why do you think the author feels "not at fault" in the first two stanzas and "at fault" during the third stanza? 3) If a miracle happened tonight and suddenly your problem was gone, what would life be like? Where would you be walking? with anyone? 4) What gives you the strength to walk?

This poem can be linked to the expressive creative mode of poetry therapy by engaging the client to write his/her "autobiography." The client could be asked to complete a sentence stem such as the following: "I walk down the street . . ." The poem is consistent with the symbolic/ceremonial mode of poetry therapy in that the street serves as a metaphor for life experience. The ceremonial aspect could be developed by a personal, family, or community activity to recognize the positive change(s) made. For example, an individual (or all the members of the family) could be asked to draw a street or traffic sign that signifies his/her new approach to life. Some possibilities might include: "Bump Ahead," "Yield," "Fork in Road," and "Leaving Old Castle."

4. "Marks" by Linda Pastan

The speaker in this poem uses the image of an academic grading system to examine how her family members evaluate her role as wife and mother (e.g., received top grade from her husband for the meal she cooked). The last two lines offer a sharp contrast and a rebellion/affirmation of self : "Wait til they learn / I'm dropping out."

"Marks" validates the feelings of those being taken for granted and of course is especially appealing in focusing on gender issues. Self-identity could be examined through this poem. The poem is consistent with feminist and empowerment theories. Recognizing the importance of a gender analysis, the therapist can use this poem to validate the client's reality and promote consciousness raising. The poem serves in an empowering capacity with the last lines where the speaker decides to "drop out." Perhaps from family systems theory, one might examine the intergenerational patterns of role identity and the differentiation process. For example, a female client may have learned from her family of origin that her own well-being should be sacrificed in order to attend to all of the needs of her husband and children. The poem offers a means for the client to discuss her family of origin. It can be used to provide support for behaviors the client chooses that promote her own change and growth, yet are contrary to her parents' beliefs.

This poem can be used in the receptive/prescriptive mode, particularly in group and community activities to promote dialogue and raise consciousness regarding role changes, oppression, and institutional sexism. Speaking out also serves as a symbolic/ceremonial activity that promotes well-being and community development.

The power of this poem lies in part with its capacity to evoke both anger and humor. Most of us (males and females) have been accustomed to seeing how we measure up to others in the classroom, at work, with friends, and at home. Most of us have experienced being taken for granted. This poem provides the means to speak up and take action.

Suggestions for Discussion and Writing Experiences:

Facilitative questions could include: 1) What do you think a typical day would be like for the woman in this poem? 2) Do you feel "graded" in your family? If so, in what ways? 3) What do you think the speaker means by "Wait til they learn / I'm dropping out"? The client could be engaged in the expressive/creative mode by being asked to write her own report card of her family, or to write a letter to her family explaining why she is "dropping out."

5. "Hitch Haiku (After weeks of watching)" by Gary Snyder

The poem depicts the all-too-common experience of staying in a painful or troubled situation for a prolonged period of time until finally we take a small action that makes a profound difference. In this poem (one of a series of haiku in "Hitch Haiku"), solving the problem of a leaky roof was as simple as moving a board.

Fear of the unknown or lack of confidence often keeps individuals in troubled situations. In working with couples, the therapist recognizes that many major marital problems stem from unattended small "leaks" (e.g., feeling ignored, not taking time for each other, resentment over not being involved in certain decisions, misunderstandings that are not discussed). Good therapy occurs in small and timely steps; it is usually not a dramatic insight or intervention that makes the difference.

From a behavioral framework this poem might simply be used to promote action. The poem is consistent with empowerment theory in restoring the element of control to the individual (moving one board). The poem can serve to activate the client by moving him/her from an observer (watch the leaking roof) to a participant in the problem-solving process.

If we wait too long to address problems, they may increase and intensify. The simplicity of this poem in both form and content offers hope to those who dare to take a small step toward change.

Suggestions for Discussion and Writing Experiences:

Facilitative questions could include: 1) In what ways can you relate to a "roof leak"? 2) Can you think of an experience when a small action on your part produced a big change? 3) Why do you think the speaker watched the roof leak for weeks?

This poem can be linked to the expressive/creative mode of poetry therapy by asking the client to write about living in a house with a leaky roof. The metaphor of life as a "roof leak" fits well with the symbolic mode of poetry therapy. The ceremonial aspect could be connected to a "house-warming" exercise wherein a couple has a special dinner to celebrate the restoration of a loving relationship.

6. "When Death Comes" by Mary Oliver

This poem is an affirmation of the speaker's life. Life as a poetic journey and encounter is captured in the lines: "When it's over, I want to say: all my life / I was bride to amazement / I was the bridegroom, taking the world into my arms." Death is portrayed as the unknown part of life. The speaker is curious about what death will be like; however, whatever unfolds in the future, he/she takes responsibility for living in the present with arms wide open.

Similar to previous poems in this chapter, this poem invites the reader (client) to be a participant (take action) in the therapeutic process rather than a recipient (see what happens). A spiritual element is captured in the simple things in life (e.g., "life is a flower"). This poem is consistent with the humanistic theories of psychotherapy particularly as it relates to both contemplation and action ("I want to step through the door full of curiosity, wondering: / what is it going to be like . . ."). Life is a process of discovery. Client-centered therapy, Gestalt therapy and psychodrama focus on the "here and now" and emphasize the importance of self-expression. This poem invites us all to examine our life philosophy. It compels us to define how we want to live. Like the previous poems discussed, the element of choice is a central theme.

Suggestions for Discussion and Writing Experiences:

Facilitative questions that could be used with this poem include the following: 1) In what ways are the author's perceptions of life and death similar to your own? In what ways are they different? 2) What do you think of the author's line: "take the world into my arms"? 3) In this poem, life is pictured as a flower, can you think of any part of nature that represents your life? 4) What gives the greatest meaning to your life?

This poem can be linked to the expressive/creative mode of poetry therapy by using it as a springboard for a physical enactment (dance/movement) of what the poem means to the individual. Clients could be asked to draw an image in the poem that they are closest to (assessment and treatment technique). Writing exercises could include writing your own eulogy, writing a letter to life and/or death, keeping a journal, and completing sentence stems such as "When death comes . . ." The use of metaphors such as life as a flower is consistent with the symbolic ceremonial mode of poetry therapy. Particular exercises that could be used in this mode include rituals for those who have died (e.g., planting a flower, saying a prayer, or writing a letter and then burning it) and ceremonies to celebrate life (e.g., lighting a candle, sharing a meal, or partaking in a recreational challenge such as running).

ANNOTATED BIBLIOGRAPHY OF POEMS
ON DILEMMAS AND LIFE'S CHOICES

Dickinson, Emily. "To fill a Gap." *Final Harvest: Emily Dickinson's Poems.* Selections and Introduction by Thomas H. Johnson. Boston: Little, Brown and Company, 1961.

This brief poem addresses the universal experience of emptiness. The poem takes the form of a lesson with a compelling psychological truth: "You cannot solder an Abyss / With air." This poem has application for a person when the empty space in his/her life relates to the loss of a relationship. One cannot put back what is gone, and simply waiting for the gap to be filled in all likelihood will not work. The experience of feeling a "gap" in one's life can be applied to a wider variety of life's dilemmas (e.g., loss of a physical ability, retirement, and loss of faith).

Frost, Robert. "The Armful." *Complete Poems of Robert Frost*. New York: Holt, Rinehart, & Winston, 1964. Also in *The Poetry of Robert Frost: The Collected Poems, Complete and Unabridged*, Ed. Edward Connery Lathem. New York: Henry Holt & Company, 1979.

In this poem the speaker is trying to carry more packages than he can manage, ultimately drops them, and then regroups. The themes of taking on too much and having problems in letting go ("yet nothing I should care to leave behind") characterize many of life's dilemmas and choices. Populations for whom this poem would be particularly useful include caregivers for the elderly and single parents. Familiar problems which this poem could address include family worries, job responsibilities, and generally too many commitments. The last line is intriguing: "And try to stack them in a better load." For the reader: Is the issue reorganizing or releasing?

Frost, Robert. "Mending Wall." *Complete Poems of Robert Frost*. New York: Holt, Rinehart, & Winston, 1964. Also in *The Poetry of Robert Frost: The Collected Poems, Complete and Unabridged*, Ed. Edward Connery Lathem. New York: Henry Holt & Company, 1979.

The speaker in this poem questions the necessity of a wall between his property and his neighbor's property. He does not see any practical reason for the wall. The neighbor replies "Good fences make good neighbors." The speaker questions the purpose of the wall: "He is all pine and I am apple orchard. / My apple tree will never get across . . ." The speaker wonders what exactly his neighbor is trying to keep in or keep out. Interestingly, the image of this poem involves two neighbors meeting annually to rebuild a wall between them. It has become a ritual, and, ironically, each spring, rebuilding the wall (an act of isolation) is one way the two neighbors are brought together, even if briefly. This would be a good poem to use in facilitating the creation of a dyadic, two-line poem, in which two people each contribute one line. A couple could respond to the poem as a whole or the line: "Something there is that doesn't love a wall."

Note: See copy of this poem at the end of the chapter.

Frost, Robert. "The Road Not Taken." *Complete Poems of Robert Frost.* New York: Holt, Rinehart, & Winston, 1964. Also in *The Poetry of Robert Frost: The Collected Poems, Complete and Unabridged,* Ed. Edward Connery Lathem. New York: Henry Holt & Company, 1979.

This poem is perhaps the classic poem for poetry therapy in that it involves the fundamental element of choice. While walking through the wood, the speaker is faced with making a decision about which of two equally appealing roads he/she should take. Facing the fork in the road is something to which most people can relate. The decision "has made all the difference."

Note: See detailed analysis earlier in the chapter.

Note: See copy of this poem at the end of the chapter.

Giovanni, Nikki. "Once a Lady Told Me." *The Women and the Men.* New York: William Morrow & Company, 1975.

The speaker in this poem reveals a self-affirmation and inner strength amidst the losses associated with elderhood. Refusing to live with her children, she states that she has lived with them before and that now she wants "to live with myself." The speaker recognizes that she might not be able to keep the house very clean and neat; however, she takes pride and comfort in the fact that "it's my life." This poem conveys a positive attitude toward elderhood. For the older children there is the dilemma of wanting to care for their mother yet also needing to respect their mother's wishes. This poem also relates to the all too familiar issues of caring vs. controlling.

Jong, Erica. "Woman Enough." *At the Edge of the Body.* New York: Henry Holt & Company, 1979.

The speaker relates that her priority is being a writer rather than a homemaker. The intergenerational aspects of designated roles for her grandmother and mother are conveyed through images relating to baking and cleaning. Although the speaker enjoys "the kneading of bread," she wishes she didn't have to choose between homemaking activities and writing. However, faced with the choice, she chooses writing. The poem ends with reference to her husband, who although not thrilled, accepts responsibility for such things as cleaning. This poem can address gender issues, intergenerational influences, and the problems inherent with juggling multiple roles and facing others' disapproval.

Kenyon, Jane. "Otherwise." *Otherwise: New and Selected Poems.* St. Paul, Minnesota: Graywolf Press, 1996.

The daily activities of getting out of bed and having a nice breakfast, going for a walk with the dog, and recognizing the preciousness of sharing a special dinner with her mate are appreciated in this poem with the refrain: "It might have been otherwise." Endings and loss are also recognized in this poem as the speaker talks of planning another day similar to the one described, knowing that one day "it will be otherwise." Beauty and spirituality in simplicity are conveyed in this poem.

Nelson, Portia. "Autobiography in Five Short Chapters." *There's a Hole in My Sidewalk.* New York: Popular Library, 1977. Also in *Courage to Heal*, Ellen Bass & Laura Davis. New York: Harper & Row, 1988.

This poem captures the troubling patterns we fall into ("deep hole") and are reluctant to change. The speaker walks down the same street with a deep hole four times. The first three times she falls into the hole. She does not accept responsibility for falling in the first two times. The third time she does accept responsibility. On the fourth trip down the street, she walks around the hole. Finally, in her fifth trip, she takes a different street. The process of change can be threatening and anxiety provoking. The "known" experience, even if painful, sometimes becomes the preferred experience. How many holes do we have to fall into before we dare to change or try something new?

Note: See detailed analysis earlier in the chapter.

Oliver, Mary. "When death comes." *New and Selected Poems.* Boston: Beacon Press, 1992.

In this poem death is depicted as an unknown and inevitable part of life. The speaker celebrates life and conveys an energy and enthusiasm for life as a journey and encounter. The poem contains spiritual and particularly existential elements with respect to the poet's portrayal of "life as a flower" and as "singular." The poet takes responsibility for making the most out of life so that when her life "in this world" is over, she won't be filled with regrets about what might have been.

Note: See detailed analysis earlier in the chapter.

Pastan, Linda. "Marks." *Carnival Evening: New and Selected Poems 1968-1998.* New York: W.W. Norton, 1999.

This poem evokes the speaker's feelings of resentment toward family members' (husband and children) expectations of her. An academic grading system is used to show how the speaker feels evaluated on her performance in the role of mother and wife (for example, her husband gave her an "A'" for cooking dinner). The speaker, however, has the last empowering word: "Wait til they learn / I'm dropping out." This poem serves to validate the feelings of those who feel taken for granted and can provide the stimulus for a discussion of gender identity and empowerment issues.

Note: See detailed analysis earlier in the chapter.

Rich, Adrienne. "Prospective Immigrants Please Note." *The Fact of a Doorframe: Poems Selected and New 1950-1984.* New York: W.W. Norton, 1999.

The element of choice and the resultant risk is captured in the decision to "go through this door / or you will not go through." The speaker contemplates the possibilities and notes that there can be no real assurances in life. In the final stanza, the speaker notes that the door is only a passage and "makes no promises." We are left to trust our internal processes. This poem could be especially useful in working with individuals struggling with cultural dislocation or any major life changes.

Silverstein, Shel. "Tree House." *Where the Sidewalk Ends.* New York: Harper & Row, 1974. Also in *Poetry Therapy: Interface of the Arts and Psychology,* Nicholas Mazza. Boca Raton, Florida: CRC Press, 1999.

The universal theme of seeking a safe and special place is effectively captured through the image of a tree house and the diction of the speaker (e.g., rhyme and sound of ". . . a free house, / a secret you and me house . . ."). The tree house represents freedom, space, and security. It is contrasted with "a street house" that represents rules and social conventions. This poem has appeal to children and adults alike.

Note: See detailed analysis earlier in the chapter.

Snyder, Gary. "Hitch Haiku (After weeks of watching)." *The Back Country*. New York: New Directions, 1976.

The speaker in this poem has been looking at his leaky roof for weeks. Finally, he decides to take the simple action of moving a board. No more leak! Inaction is an all-too-common response to many problems in life. In essence, the metaphor of a leaky roof can apply to a variety of problems that we leave unattended (e.g., relationships, health, career). Ultimately, we are faced with the choice of watching or acting. This poem is also helpful in communicating that small actions can make a big difference.

Note: See detailed analysis earlier in the chapter.

Vogdes, Natasha L. "Snowbound." *Social Work: Journal of the National Association of Social Workers*, Vol. 25 No.1 (January 1980). NASW Press, 750 First Street, N.E., Suite 700, Washington, D.C. 20002-4241.

Tired of the pressures of meeting the needs of other people, the speaker validates her own needs, taking time for self. The image of being "snowbound" is a positive one where one can enjoy privacy and engage in self-transformation. The need to get away and "refuel" is a universal one that is captured succinctly in this poem. In our present age of cell phones and beepers, the last lines "where the only number you dial / is your own" is indeed refreshing. This poem can be used with such problems as burnout, secondary traumatic stress, anxiety, depression, passivity, and relational problems. The use of imagery (subways, airplanes, snow) is especially appealing.

Note: See copy of this poem at the end of the chapter.

MENDING WALL

Something there is that doesn't love a wall,
That sends the frozen-ground-swell under it
And spills the upper boulders in the sun,
And makes gaps even two can pass abreast.
The work of hunters is another thing:
I have come after them and made repair
Where they have left not one stone on a stone,
But they would have the rabbit out of hiding,
To please the yelping dogs. The gaps I mean,
No one has seen them made or heard them made,
But at spring mending-time we find them there.
I let my neighbor know beyond the hill;
And on a day we meet to walk the line
And set the wall between us once again.
We keep the wall between us as we go.
To each the boulders that have fallen to each.
And some are loaves and some so nearly balls
We have to use a spell to make them balance:
'Stay where you are until our backs are turned!'
We wear our fingers rough with handling them.
Oh, just another kind of outdoor game,
One on a side. It comes to little more:
There where it is we do not need the wall:
He is all pine and I am apple orchard.
My apple trees will never get across
And eat the cones under his pines, I tell him.
He only says, 'Good fences make good neighbors.'
Spring is the mischief in me, and I wonder
If I could put a notion in his head:
'Why do they make good neighbors? Isn't it
Where there are cows? But here there are no cows.
Before I built a wall I'd ask to know
What I was walling in or walling out,
And to whom I was like to give offense.
Something there is that doesn't love a wall,
That wants it down.' I could say 'Elves' to him,

But it's not elves exactly, and I'd rather
He said it for himself. I see him there
Bringing a stone grasped firmly by the top
In each hand, like an old-stone savage armed.
He moves in darkness as it seems to me,
Not of woods only and the shade of trees.
He will not go behind his father's saying,
And he likes having thought of it so well
He says again, 'Good fences make good neighbors.'

Robert Frost

THE ROAD NOT TAKEN

Two roads diverged in a yellow wood,
And sorry I could not travel both
And be one traveler, long I stood
And looked down one as far as I could
To where it bent in the undergrowth;

Then took the other, as just as fair,
And having perhaps the better claim,
Because it was grassy and wanted wear;
Though as for that the passing there
Had worn them really about the same,

And both that morning equally lay
In leaves no step had trodden black.
Oh, I kept the first for another day!
Yet knowing how way leads on to way,
I doubted if I should ever come back.

I shall be telling this with a sigh
Somewhere ages and ages hence;
Two roads diverged in a wood, and I –
I took the one less traveled by,
And that has made all the difference.

Robert Frost

SNOWBOUND

There is a time to stop traveling . . .
to get off other people's subways
to halt airplanes from landing in your life.

A time to refuel yourself.

A time to be snowbound
within your own private space
where the only number you dial
is your own.

Natasha Lynne Vogdes

REFERENCE

Mazza, Nicholas. *Poetry Therapy: Interface of the Arts and Psychology*. Boca Raton, Florida: CRC Press, 1999.

III
FACING THE SHADOWS
ON THE ROAD

COPING WITH FEAR AND ANGER

Deborah Eve Grayson, LMHC, RPT

THEMATIC OVERVIEW

IT HAS BEEN SAID THAT ONCE WE FACE the shadow side of ourselves, we can begin to see and have an appreciation and understanding of the light within us. This light is often blocked by the dark, the unforeseen or the unknown or what we call fear. Fear also has a "shadow self" called anger, and it often comes without warning, pretense, or invitation. They often work together as a skilled pair of thieves who rob us of balance, security, or logic. Fear and anger can be seen as tenacious monsters that will not loosen their grip until we beg for mercy, or they may keep us anchored in familiarity and false safety, until we are finally zapped of our strength and inner resources. Yet, fear and anger can also be allies and work as our protection; like a blinking yellow light at a busy intersection or a stop sign at the bottom of a long hill. They are also incessant children who beg for our attention with loud and unavoidable cries until we finally take notice or action.

We have all been intimate with fear and can recognize its voice, even though it assumes many disguises. Sometimes it creeps in like a fog or a whisper, and it leaves just a hint of anxiety or uncertainty, and other times it crashes like a train that has been derailed right into the heart of all sensibility or calm. Most of us have learned that the only way past or around a difficult situation is through it, yet we often have difficulty dismantling it from the power it pretends to hold over us. It is helpful to remember that fear is only as tenacious as we allow it to be and can only take up space where we allow it to sit or lay.

On the positive side, fear is an invaluable stepping-stone for safe passage through bumpy roads or winding paths where it is hard to see the obvious or the slightly obliterated signs. Sometimes, it seems to take a battalion of bravery to stand up to the army of fear and succeed, and, other times, an ounce of courage is enough to make miraculous changes. It is important to remember that action, in and of itself, is courageous and cannot be underestimated.

American Buddhist nun Pema Chödrön reminds us in her deeply meaningful book, *When Things Fall Apart*, that "fear is a natural reaction to moving closer to the truth." Most of us tend to turn on our heels and leave skid marks when faced with the inevitability of truth because it seems too overpowering or dangerous. It is a love-hate relationship because we want to know the truth and seek it, yet we are not always pleased when it is finally revealed. We want it candy-coated and wrapped with ribbons of comfort and ease. There are invaluable lessons that fear often grants us when we are patient enough to ride out the storm and see what happens next.

Chödrön states, "In difficult times, it is only *bodhichitta* that heals. (Sanskrit word that means 'noble or awakened heart'). When inspiration has become hidden, when we feel ready to give up, this is the time when healing can be found in the tenderness of pain itself. . . ."

Like fear, the passionate emotion of anger is also relegated to our shadow side. For the most part, society has given anger a bad rap and a negative reputation. We have been raised to believe that anger distances us emotionally and that outward displays of such an emotion only show that we are destructive and primitive. However, when anger is productively directed, it can help us gain movement when or where we might otherwise be stuck. It can help us clear intersections of miscommunication or redirect us with new-found passion and clarity.

Many of us choose to hold onto our anger as a constant companion. It becomes a friend, a confidant, a source of protection from ourselves or others whose nature may not be as predictable or known. Our anger may serve as an anchor to help us when a more difficult emotion is rocking the boat. Sometimes it is easier to feel anger, for example, rather than bear the brunt of abandonment, shame, depression, guilt, or ridicule. Anger is often the replacement emotion for heartbreak, grief, or shock.

We may wonder what would actually happen if we let our anger loose and allowed ourselves the freedom of expressing it, even if it is unattractive, loud or forceful. We often fear the worst: further anger, confrontation, or misunderstanding. For some of us, expression of anger was never an option in our families. We were told not to air our private issues publicly or to be civil no matter what and come to a quiet resolve without ranting or raving. In a way, we were taught how to "stuff" our feelings, ignore them, or deny whatever was presented in order to circumvent anger's course.

Fear and anger share many qualities. They are both emotions that are difficult to experience because they are often painful or misunderstood, difficult to consciously control, and conflict with experiencing joy or ease. They are also both universal emotions that tend to make us feel isolated, yet can motivate us as well.

It takes a lot of practice, research, experience, patience, mistakes, flexibility, and forgiveness to master the many teachings of fear and anger. Perhaps if we look at both as opportunities for growth or healing, we might begin to take a small step toward embracing our demanding teachers. After all, some of our most memorable learning occurs because we successfully weather the storm of fear or anger in order to reach the shore of safety, security, and knowledge. Even though the journey may be a rough one, we are usually better for the experience of it and find that we often learn more than what we initially thought we have lost.

It takes a lot of courage to do and feel the very things we try to avoid. We must be willing to look silly, to behave imperfectly, to fall down, and to get up again. Most of all, we need to have faith that we can overcome the haunting shadows that fear and anger often bring just by shining a small, but piercing, persistent light along the way.

IN-DEPTH FOCUS ON POEMS IN A THERAPEUTIC CONTEXT

1. "Fear" by J. Ruth Gendler

Fear will both surprise and fool us if we let it. J. Ruth Gendler has written an innovative book that gives human qualities to a wide spectrum of emotions. I have used her piece on fear with a variety of populations with great results because of the universality of her words. Her opening line states that, "fear has a large shadow, but he himself is quite small." Immediately, the reader knows that this is a manageable fear. She tells us that the shadow is often large in appearance (our perception), but the actual thing we are fearing is usually tiny in comparison. The poet is letting us know that when we keep our thoughts and perceptions on a realistic plane, the promise of peace and calm can happen. How often have we made ourselves sick from the expectation of the fear rather than the thing itself? How many times have we allowed fear to determine our actions and the way we relate to the world?

When I use this poem with clients, I first ask them to choose the one line or word that speaks most directly to them. I ask about the line that they wish they had written, calls to them, or tells their story. Sometimes a question like, "What is something that fear does not know about you?" leads to very revealing responses. I may ask them to speak about a current fear that has been haunting them, or possibly make a list of a few more to see what they are truly feeling. Once it is on paper, it is easier to deal with fear more honestly. Clients naturally edit as they speak and write, taking out that which they have already dealt with or questioning their fears for themselves and then letting them go if they are ready. They may then choose to write more deeply about a particular fear, pocket it for another day (literally), or permanently release it. I would also ask them to recall the last time they felt fearful and what (if anything) this experience taught them?

Later in the poem, Gendler lets us know how mysterious and elusive fear can be and that, "he warned us not to talk to each other about him, adding that there is nowhere any of us could go where he wouldn't hear us." She implies that the more we speak about our fears openly, the less damage they will do. Also, the less isolated we are, the better off we will be because fear is diminished when shared with a person of support. This is an invitation to seek someone outside ourselves to talk to so we may receive another viewpoint on what is happening and to gain validation for our feelings. Asking for help is one of the first stepping-stones to healing, and allowing ourselves to receive the help is another.

The next paragraph speaks to the reality and the fantasy aspects of fear. These are often difficult for clients to distinguish. They are guided by their experiences of the past, illusions they need in order to buy into ego, reputation, pride, and a host of other things they hold onto as "truth or excuse." It is helpful to ask leading questions like: "How do you know when a fear is real? How have you handled fears successfully in the past? What might happen if you gave in to this fear? What do you need to fight it? The client may realize he does not fully understand what is creating such fear or what kinds of tools he may already have to conquer it. A direct line of questions helps to magnify that which may have been impossible to see before because the all-consuming shadow was in the way.

Toward the end of this piece we are told, "he is the master of disguises and illusions . . ." and we realize that it is important to be like a detective and seek out clues, follow through, and proceed with caution. We are offered a pragmatic approach to figuring out fear and unmasking this irritating pest once and for all so he may no longer hide out where we cannot see him clearly or haunt us from the deep, dark corners that masquerade as shadows. It is easy to be bullied by the perception of fear, especially when it pretends to be a massive and destructive monster. Many times, fear is a masterfully helpful friend, forcing us to be creative, courageous and victorious. Without fear, we do not extend ourselves or stretch to our full capability. Instead, we remain encapsulated in the facade of comfort and homeostasis and pretend we're satisfied with the results.

Sometimes, I will ask: Has fear ever fooled you? What tactics were used? Who won? How do you know when fear is near?" The answers are always intriguing. They range anywhere from bluffing or boisterous to shockingly honest and brutal such as: "fear can't fool me. I can see it coming a mile away, and it never gets close enough to have any real impact" to "fear is my father's hand turning the knob to my bedroom and coming to my bed when its dark." Certain images in this poem may bring up issues that were hidden for a long time. Good poetry will bypass the usual censors, and a skilled poetry therapist will know how far to go and when to ease up and let the client speak through his own images or story. Readiness cannot be rushed or forced.

The last lines of the poem are particularly encouraging. Gendler encourages us to "speak out boldly. . . . Don't give up. Win his respect, and he will never bother you with small matters." The reader is given a practical recipe for "cooking up success" in fear management. However, just because the poem ends on a hopeful or encouraging note, this does not mean that the client will see it as such. Clients may state that they have faced their fears before and they have been bold about it, but it blew up in their faces anyway. They may express that it just got too tiring to fight, so they gave up and continued along their not-so-merry, fearful way. We have to anticipate any number of outcomes and be prepared to gently guide the client accordingly.

Suggested Topics for Discussion and Writing Experiences:

1. Draw a picture of one of your current fears and the shadow that it casts. Place yourself in the picture with a tool of illumination such as a flashlight, the moon, the sun. Write about what you have drawn.
2. Write a letter to a fear that still nags at you. Be sure to tell it all that you have been holding back and leave no stone unturned! Include a postscript. Many times, the postscript can stand on its own because it is what we have wanted to say all along. The letter is the process and shows us what we had to go through in order to get to the core.
3. Write a dialogue between fear and courage. Use your dominant hand for courage and your non-dominant hand for fear. How are fear and courage

alike? How are they different? This is a way to dissolve the perceived power of fear and empower ourselves with courage.

4. Write a poem that uses all of the senses to describe a current fear. Be sure to include: (1) sound: i.e.: fear is a locomotive in the night, a howling wolf, a haunting whisper; (2) sight: i.e.: it is a black hole, invisible mosquito, a town after a tornado; (3) smell: i.e.: a locker room in summer, freshly peeled orange, crisp scent of snow; (4) taste: i.e.: a bitter herb, a pitfall of salt, a lemon rind in dirt; (5) touch: i.e.: jagged, razor-sharp, rough, deceptively smooth.

5. Write a new poem that turns down the volume on all of the senses. Notice that when we acknowledge fear and embrace its teachings, our need to control it fades, and the fear itself diminishes as well.

6. Imagine that fear has come to your house and is knocking at your door. Write about how you feel when you greet, interact with, and say good-bye to fear.

2. "I Give You Back" by Joy Harjo

Joy Harjo's poem, "I Give You Back" speaks boldly and allows the reader to have both a choice and a voice when dealing with fear. This poem is especially recommended to help clients find a way to stand up to fear on their own terms. Harjo lets us know from the title of the poem and the first lines that this fear is not for keeps. Soon, it will be released, and the reader will be the victor. She begins with, "I release you, my beautiful and terrible fear . . . ," and immediately we see both sides of fear's face. We are introduced to the idea that there can be beauty in fear, perhaps for the lessons it teaches us and how it makes us appreciate joy after the pain; and we see the terror and unforgiving qualities of it as well. The opening line almost has a "farewell my love" quality to it and seems to imply a great intimacy is now lost. Some questions to explore with the beginning of this poem might be, "How can a fear be both terrible and beautiful? Which line stands out the most for you? Which line could be cut from the piece and not be missed?"

Fear is indeed intimate and is also often needy, presumptuous and bossy. In Harjo's poem, however, the greatest power is given to the speaker of the poem. One line stands out on its own and is a most provocative statement. It says: "You are not my blood anymore." This one sentence stands like a tall cypress, unbending in a turbulent storm. It is a statement of clarity that acts like a sword cutting through old beliefs so strength and authenticity may take its rightful place. We have heard that "blood is thicker than water" and that ancestral ties and loyalty for family come before everything else. Many of us struggle with the various ways to confront fear because of certain family messages and patterns. We are told to "put on a brave face and not to air our dirty laundry in public." Often, we are told not to feel a certain way or we are shamed because we do feel the way we do. Yet, when Harjo says, "you are not my blood anymore," we can readily see the disengagement of a familial pattern, the final release of fear as a destructive member of the "family of feelings," and a forward movement toward empowerment as a result of letting go of an emotional anchor.

The third stanza is particularly strong and should be used with great caution for it could easily trigger major areas of trauma and possibly bring on serious consequences such as symptoms of post-traumatic stress disorder. There are references to soldiers who burned homes, children being beheaded, and other brutal injustices such as rape, sodomy, and starvation. These are difficult issues to navigate yet their importance should not be minimized. A possible way to reframe this stanza might be to focus on the narrator's ability to stop carrying the full weight of this fear and to return it, in pieces from whence it came. Harjo deflects the fear and puts it in its rightful place. She gives it back to those who created it, which includes the part of her that cannot deny what has happened because she witnessed the horror with her own eyes that "can never close." For many, the worst fears happen in their imagination or in the constant revivifying of a particular event. When this occurs, there is no rest, no sleep, no ability to close the eyes and "not see."

In the fourth stanza, there's a magnificent line that reads, "I release you fear, so you can no longer keep me naked and frozen in the winter, or smothered under blankets in the summer. . . ." What a perfect example of how fear can take our breath and life away through a feeling of being either on fire or icy cold. These are excellent metaphors for exploration. I can ask my clients to talk about their fiery fear or a fear that has left them cold. Then we can discuss ways to either put out the fire, stop fueling the fire, or find avenues of comfort and warmth. The next few lines are almost hypnotic in nature: "I release you, I release you, I release you. . . ." Here, a statement of truth is declared, and then there is the exhalation of release, spoken like an affirmation. Affirmations allow us to see what we are holding on to so we can also accurately gauge what we are releasing and how it serves us. I might ask, "What does fear make you do?" to elicit a dialogue about how his/her fear may act like a schoolyard bully and how he/she might be able to gain ground and come out the victor rather than the victim. The implication is that fear forces us into a corner until we step up to the plate and accept our part in the healing of the hurt.

The poem continues with these affirmations in the form of a mantra:
> I am not afraid to be angry.
> I am not afraid to rejoice. . . .
> I am not afraid to be full.
> I am not afraid to be hated
> I am not afraid to be loved, to be loved, to be loved, fear.

The affirmations act as a grounding technique, something to hold onto as we step into the shadows, so we can find our way back to courage again. There is a dream-like quality to the line: "to be loved, to be loved, to be loved, fear." The repetition allows the readers to wonder about being loved while reinforcing that they are loved. At the same time, it seems that the writer is directly addressing fear as if to say, "Do you hear me? Do you get it? I said I'm not afraid to be loved!"

Harjo demonstrates that it is love itself that takes over where fear used to live and awakens compassion for the fear that now lies powerless as it dies before her eyes. Her powerful last line stands as a testament to reclaiming the self: ". . . I take myself back, fear . . . / you can't live . . . / But come here fear / I am alive and you are so afraid / of dying."

Her poem gives the reader a chance to release fear, while appreciating why it showed up in the first place, and to receive love and compassion in its place. There is a quality of feeling sorry for the pitiful thing called fear that is now shriveling to nothingness as love and acceptance expands. We see the letting go, the holding on, and the final act of healing: acceptance.

Suggested Topics for Discussion and Writing Experiences:

1. Write about a beautiful fear and a terrible fear. Identify the differences and the similarities.
2. Many are familiar with the acronym of F. E. A. R. It means False Evidence Appearing Real. Write an acrostic poem or a list poem that addresses the theme of fear while using its letters. Here is an example: Forget about reality; food bills, frozen dreams, far-away friends and family,

Exude confidence, excite yourself with possibility, extract the negative,
Allow change to happen, affirm and applaud your accomplishments,
Remember who you are, reflect on hope; remind yourself that you are loved.

3. Write a haiku on fear. Follow the 5, 7, 5 syllable form to help give you a
framework or handle on fear. For example:

> Fear is a small dot
> An annoying stain that spreads,
> We CAN control it.

4. If you could take your fears and "return to sender," where would they go,
who would open the package, and what would the package look like?

5. Complete these sentences:

> I release you, fear, because . . .
> I am not afraid to . . .
> I am . . .

Rewrite some of these statements on post-it notes and place them where
they can remind you of your worth, courage, and conviction. Make sure
they are posted where you live as well as where you work.

3. "Caged Bird" by Maya Angelou

Maya Angelou has focused on the freedom from fear in her beautiful poem,
"Caged Bird." Her opening line, "A free bird leaps on the back of the wind . . ."
moves the reader to feel a sense of freedom and flight beyond the fear of possi-
ble consequences for such actions. The last line of the first stanza speaks to the
free bird who "dares to claim the sky." This line provides a perfect opportunity
to invite clients to discuss what they would dare to attempt if they knew they
would not fail. What would they claim? What would it look like and who, if any-
one, would be there with them in their victory?

In the second stanza, Angelou speaks about the caged bird who can
"seldom see through his bars of rage." How often have we been blinded by
our fear and temporarily paralyzed as a result of it? What might happen if the
bars of rage were removed? She further utilizes images of "clipped wings, tied
feet and nightmare scream" to bring into focus the ways that fear can immo-
bilize us until we use our voice or our song to cry out for the freedom we
deserve—the freedom of our passions, our sense of self, community, and reli-
gion, and our freedom from the injustices imposed by others.

There is a paradox regarding the first line and the title, for we can almost see a before-and-after picture of what freedom means and the need to give voice to the unspeakable or unnameable things in order to break out from the confines of our particular prison. As a poetry therapist, I would explore personal freedoms with the client and find out where his "wings were clipped or how his feet were tied." Of course, the standard questions of, "Where are you in this poem?" or, "Which line do you identify with right now?" might also be used. From there, we can also explore when the client feels the most freedom or restraint, with whom do they feel this way, and what have they already tried to access more of what they need.

Often, I will use the story of the poet if it is pertinent to the issue that has been brought to the table. Angelou is highly regarded as a playwright, actress, writer, and public figure, yet she gains even more respect and appreciation when her own story is revealed. Many do not know of her rape at the age of eight and her decision to be mute for two years after this incident, her bearing a child out of wedlock at sixteen, being raised by her grandmother, or other struggles that further define her courage, strength, and message. Clients may benefit from knowing that a highly visible role model such as Maya Angelou is a person first, a human being who is not immune to pain, fear, or discord. She has had struggles and triumphs. She learned to by-pass, confront, and build a life for herself in spite of the blocks in her way. The implied message is that people can break free and fly if they choose it for themselves.

Poetry serves as our saving song when our throats appear to be paralyzed or voiceless in the midst of fear's grip. Angelou further reminds us that when the longing or intent for freedom is predominant, success will follow.

Suggested Topics for Discussion and Writing Experiences:

1. Write about your life from the perspective of a caged bird. What kind of a bird are you? What does your cage look like? Who/what feeds you?
2. Write your own poem from these sentence stems:
   A free bird . . .
   A caged bird . . .
   I am looking forward to . . .
   I am looking back on . . .
3. Write about a time when you felt most liberated or free. How old were you? How has your view of freedom changed or remained the same?

4. "A Small Green Island" by Jelaluddin Rumi

One of the ingredients for combating fear is faith, and it comes in a variety of forms: faith in what cannot be seen, faith that things will get better, faith in ourselves, and faith in something bigger and better than us at that given moment. In Rumi's poem, "A Small Green Island," the story is told of a cow who grazes contentedly during the day on the meadow grass yet panics at night and "grows thin as a single hair." The cow worries about what she will eat tomorrow and fears that nothing will be left in the morning, even though the meadow has always provided her meals and has faithfully been a rich resource of life and sustenance. Her worry convinces her that this far-fetched fear is a reality. What a familiar scenario this is! Most of us have gone through times of such darkness ourselves. Perhaps we worry because it motivates and drives us toward action, or perhaps it is a bad habit we cannot seem to break. Either way, this is a good poem to use for exploration of how to be present with possibility and be opened to its unfolding. Rumi gives us a vehicle to look inward as well as outward in a more global sense.

Rumi says: "The cow is the bodily soul. The island field is this world . . . that grows lean with fear and fat with blessing. . . ." This one line is pivotal to the entire piece. We can choose to worry and grow thin from anxiety or we can fatten ourselves with blessings and gratitude. I might ask my client, "What do you worry about, and when does the worry stop? When did you last express gratitude or give thanks for what you have received? Is your sense of worry equivalent to your sense of appreciation?"

The last line is one of wise counsel. Rumi urges us not to "make yourself miserable with what's to come, or not to come." He is stating that faith and gratitude happen in the present moment and it does little good to be miserable with thoughts of fear. Rumi's poem is also good for clients who tend to ruminate excessively and need a gentle push in a positive direction. The last line is almost a gentle warning or reminder that life is what you create it to be, so choose carefully.

When we lose our faith, it is easy to panic and forget what we know. We flounder in the dark, gasp for air, and become blinded by the unseen. It is helpful to get used to the dark and allow time for our eyes to adjust. When we can get comfortable and still, our knowingness becomes clear, and we are then capable of ushering ourselves through the greater challenges with ease.

Suggested Topics for Discussion and Writing Experiences:

1. Write about a place of faith. This can be a real place or one from your imagination. Note whether this is an internal or external landscape. Is it easy to get there? When was the last time you visited? What happened the last time you were there? What do you take with you when you go? What do you leave behind?
2. Write the word "worry" on a page and free-write everything you know about that topic for five minutes. Now, do the same for the word "concern." What do you notice?
3. Fold a piece of paper in half lengthwise. Write a list of your top ten fears on one side of the page and a list of actions you've utilized in the past to conquer these fears. Now turn the page over (you're about to "turn over a new leaf") and do the same thing generating new techniques that you will now put into action.

5. "Anger" by Linda Pastan

Linda Pastan's poem, "Anger," speaks directly to the rabid, biting nature of anger in comparison to a tamer version that is described as "dull with disuse." The poem begins, "You tell me that it's all right to let it out of its cage. . . ." The "you" in the poem could be the therapist, the friend, the someone other than ourselves who gives permission or encouragement to unleash this emotion, yet the speaker of the poem holds onto the wild nature of anger like a sword. There is a particular amount of pride or protection in the closing line that states, "mine is a rabid thing, sharpening its teeth . . . and I will never let it go." We get a clear picture of a dog pulling on a bone, shaking its head from side to side, teeth bared, a low, guttural growl coming through the clenched jaw. This may not be a pleasing picture to see or experience, but it puts a definitive metaphor into the mind's eye. I might ask my clients any number of questions when using this poem. Some might be as benign as, "What is your general feeling about anger?" or "What happened the last time you showed anger?" I might delve further and then ask, "What does your anger want everyone to know?" or "How does your anger play into your fear?" This way, we can give equal voice to both the speaker and the emotion itself. I might also simply ask "Where are you in this poem?" This is an excellent question for discovering one's placement in the scheme of things. Together we can see if our clients are outsiders to anger or if they are on the front lines. We can have a discussion about how anger was handled in their family of origin as well as how it is handled in their current family and begin to piece together the various roles that anger played or plays in their lives as both an ally and an enemy.

Suggested Topics for Discussion and Writing Experiences:

1. What are some synonyms for the word "anger?"
2. How do you feel when you express anger? Where do you feel it in your body? Mind? Spirit? Is it different when expressed with strangers, family members or friends?
3. What is it like to be the recipient of anger? How is it different or the same as being the one who delivers it?
4. What does your anger look like? What forms does it take? Write a "first thoughts" statement using these sentence stems:
   My anger is . . .
   My anger is not . . .
   An animal that best describes my anger would be . . .
   Some of the things I've learned about anger . . .
   In my family, anger was . . .
   Choose the sentence that has the most meaning for you right now and write a poem about it.
5. Write a character sketch on anger and play with the numerous roles. For example, you may write about anger as a soap opera star, a dentist, a magician, a movie director, a Buddhist monk, a cosmetologist, a two-year old, an archaeologist, a librarian, an astronaut, or a disc jockey.
6. Write a short story in the third person about Anger. Tell about its adventures and the characters Anger meets along the way. Describe Anger's landscape. Where does the journey take the characters? What do they learn?

6. "Harlem" by Lansgton Hughes

Langston Hughes' famous poem, "Harlem," asks about what happens when a dream is put off indefinitely and when the emotions associated with the disappointment are stuffed, ignored or denied. His images are strong in their implications. Words like: dry, fester, stink, rotten, sag, heavy load, and explode are utilized to graphically reveal anger and its consequences.

This poem has garnered great results when used with middle-school and high-school-aged children to help explore individual issues with anger as well as collective or societal anger. In the face of the continued violence and new challenges in our school system, this poem is a great tool for constructive anger management. I enjoy using this poem with groups because it lends itself well to a group process. The first line is a perfect opener for a group discussion: "What happens to a dream deferred?" We can talk about family dreams, individual goals, or dreams in a larger context outside of ourselves. Some of the responses I have received over the years when using this first line are: "I die like the dream itself," "I give up," "I create another dream or another way of obtaining it," and "It depends on the dream." I would invite the group to write a collaborative poem, formed from each group member's response to Hughes' opening line. The new poem might look something like this:

What Happens to a Dream Deferred?
It melts away like chocolate on a hot sidewalk,
leaving a big, sticky, brown stain.
It flies off on the wings of the wind.
It screams for your attention and it won't quit!
It haunts you when you sleep,
creeps into your thoughts when you're not looking,
whispers annoying nothings into your deaf ear.

Young adults love to share their images with their peers and will sometimes try to "outdo" one another. Similar to rap, blues, and hip-hop, the rhythm of a poem will often carry students to new heights. I encourage them to speak from a place of authenticity that will allow them to find their own rhythm and set their poems to music or sing them like rap songs. I have had wonderful results from this exercise ranging anywhere from a personal theme song entitled, "Ya Just Don't Get It Blues" to a musical autobiography. This poem, as well as others for which Hughes is known, have a voice and rhythm that speaks clearly to today's youth. In fact, I often use the autobiography of the poet to bring in a different viewpoint and appreciation for the work. Kids are fascinated with personal stories, and they want the details of one's life to "prove" they're worthy of the poem, song, or story. When I give details of the poet's life, the poet becomes more like a friend rather than another somebody who just does not understand. This background information brings credibility into the classroom and a chance to enliven words and give them a human focus.

For example, Langston Hughes was born in Joplin, Missouri, in 1902 and died in 1967. Great writing exercises and discussions can come from imagining what life must have been like then for a black man in the South. Sometimes students are intrigued to know that this poet also wrote short stories, an autobiography, song lyrics, essays, humor, and plays and that he was also gay. He was the recipient of numerous awards and grants that included the Guggenheim and an American Academy of Arts and Letters Grant. After presenting this background, I might ask the following: "What would you like to ask this great writer if you had the opportunity to speak with him in person? What advice might come from this exchange?"

Suggested Topics for Discussion and Writing Experiences:

1. Write about a dream you have had to defer. Write about a dream that has come true. What is the bridge that allowed you to go from one to the other?
2. Who are the people who support you in your dreams or goals and believe in you? Do you have any role models you look up to regarding accomplishments? Write about a dream or a goal they have accomplished and how it is similar to yours.
3. List some of your greatest accomplishments and assign yourself the appropriate award.

   Example: ACCOMPLISHMENT   AWARD
             Finished my degree   Persistence Pays Award
             Got married   Gotta Kiss A Lot of Toads Award
             Received a scholarship If They Could See Me Now Award

   Have fun with this! You may imagine you've won the Pulitzer Prize as well, and why not? Everything is obtainable and possible when we reach for it and remain persistent in our quest.
4. Number a page from 1 to 31 and fold it length-wise in half. On one side, make a list of all the things you are angry about now. On the other side, write a list of ways you have handled anger in the past. You can repeat if you want to. Once you have done this, read over your list and note the similarities or themes that occur. For example, you may find the things that make you angry are things you cannot control. You may find that the way you mostly handle anger is by ignoring it and hoping it will just go

away. Now, choose the number that corresponds with today's date. For example, if you are doing this exercise on the fifth of the month, look at the number five. Do a seven-minute write on this topic. Review your poem. Note the changes as a result of your writing.

5. Write about a time when you forgave someone or someone forgave you. Give your piece a title. What might it sound like if it were written as a song? or look like if it were a photograph? a piece of artwork in a museum?

6. Write a poem of gratitude, a prayer of anger, a recipe for anger, or an antidote for anger.

7. Complete these sentences:
Words of wisdom regarding anger . . .
Anger has shaped my life by . . .
If I could change one thing about my anger . . .
The next time I feel angry, I might . . .

ANNOTATED BIBLIOGRAPHY OF POEMS ON COPING WITH FEAR AND ANGER

Angelou, Maya. "Caged Bird." *And Still I Rise*. New York: Random House, 1978.

Freedom from fear is the focus of this well-known poem by one of America's most revered writers. Easy to understand and utilize with mixed groups, this poem offers a before-and-after peek at fear by comparing freedom through strength and voice vs. bondage from fear. Angelou's personal triumphs lend to the authenticity of the opening lines, "A free bird leaps on the back of the wind. . . ." An excellent piece to use with both groups or individuals.

Note: See detailed analysis earlier in the chapter.

Anonymous. "This Woman."

The author speaks of coming to grips with a particular aspect of anger that is hard to lasso. She speaks of the shared connection of emotion. There is an exchange of warmth, understanding, and respectfulness. She says, ". . . she has no whip in her talk, no snarling teeth . . . and I let her stand in my field, unharmed." There is an acceptance and a reverence for one who shares a space of pain or difficulty with us. We can relate to the "understanding someone," whether it is a poem that shares

our thoughts and feelings or a person who can accept us uncondition-
ally. We feel safe and whole and can then begin to heal from the
wounds of our anguish. Sometimes, just knowing we are not alone in
what we feel is enough to begin the healing process.

Note: See copy of this poem at the end of the chapter.

Blake, William. "A Poison Tree." *Fine Frenzy*. New York: McGraw-Hill,
1972; *The Complete Poetry and Prose of William Blake*. Ed. David V. Erdman.
New York: Doubleday, 1965.

In William Blake's well known, "A Poison Tree," we are told that when
we express our wrath, it ends, and when we do not, we and our loved
ones suffer the consequences. This is a classic poem with a classic mes-
sage: "speak of your anger honestly and gain a friend in the process."
Most people know the popular lines that open the poem: "I was angry
with my friend / I told my wrath, my wrath did end. / I was angry with
my foe / I told it not, my wrath did grow."

The first stanza gives us a recipe for success in expressing anger. Blake
states that telling your anger to a friend will end the possible destruction
that anger may cause. He lets us know that we need to gain favor with our
enemies. This is a classic poem that works well with older adults because
they will recognize these words by Blake from their school days and may
be able to recite it from memory. Poets such as Blake, Wordsworth, Poe,
Shakespeare, and Millay were mainstays in English studies. Although
words like "foe" and "wrath" are not readily used today, they are great
words for further exploration. The poetry therapist might ask the client,
"Do you know who your friends and foes are and what part they play in
your life?" "What are some of the ways you have worked through troub-
ling issues with either your friends or your enemies?"

We can see by the second stanza, the anger that was initially thought
of as being somewhat benign is now larger than life because it has been
fortified with fear and deceit. It grows the more the speaker tries to
rationalize it, numb it, or ignore it until finally, it bears fruit. The ques-
tion remains open as to who "won" this particular fight and how was it
done. Was the enemy lured into the garden under false pretense of
friendship? I like to ask clients to add another verse to this poem to find
out "what happens next." In this way, we can put our own conclusion
to this particular war.

Note: See copy of this poem at the end of the chapter.

Bowman, Ted. "Safe Places." *Journal of the American Academy of Psychotherapists*. Fall 1991, Vol. 27, No. 3.

The poet speaks of long-ago times when safety included games we constructed and controlled. Back then, there was an innocence and a simplicity of things where a child could wrap himself around a parent's leg and scream, "[Y]ou can't get me, I'm safe here!" It was a time when safe places included: "Bases where we were safe and free; Lines that the monster intruder couldn't cross. . . ." As children, our world was small and somewhat protected. However, even if we didn't have the adult version of concerns such as paying bills or being responsible for a major corporation, our fears of monsters, of big brothers that tattle-tale, and of being left out or throwing up in the car, were just as big and real. We learned early what it was like to be rejected, ridiculed, or punished, and we learned defenses for maintaining dignity, control, and individuality. The poem concludes that as adults our fears seem to know the safe places where we used to hide and it is up to us to fight back with our courage, faith, and will. Like Angelou's and Rumi's poem, the emphasis is placed on utilizing tools to strengthen our conviction in times of need.

The last line, "courage and faith, my only legs to stand on," implies that even though these may be the "only" things left, they may also be the very qualities needed to diminish feelings of "being left." Poetry therapists could ask clients how they maintain safe boundaries for themselves as adults or ask when do they feel the safest? An exploration of what safety means could also be discussed.

Other facilitation questions might be: "Where were your safe places as a child?" "What did you fear then?" "Where are your safe places now?" "With whom do you feel safe?" The goal of the poetry therapist would be to create a safe environment for this type of discussion and to help clients resolve both past and present fears through building trust, maintaining boundaries and utilizing techniques to assist in developing safety in their relationships as well as within themselves.

Note: See copy of this poem at the end of the chapter.

Chandler, Janet C. "I Give You My Anger." *The Colors of a Marriage*. Grass Valley, California: Lenox Press, 1982.

Janet C. Chandler's "I Give You My Anger," is perfect for couples who may need support or encouragement in communicating more effectively. Anger can be used as a passionate connection and as a tool to help couples get back to intimacy. In this poem, we are shown that the burden of one's anger is not easily given, nor is it to be shared with just anyone. We see anger as something sacred and intimate that "we give only / to each other / and to those / we love and care for. . . ."

Note: See copy of this poem at the end of the chapter.

Gendler, Ruth J. "Fear." *The Book of Qualities*. New York: Harper and Row, 1988.

This ingenious and illustrated book gives human qualities to a range of emotions that includes jealousy, whimsy, doubt, inspiration, loyalty, courage, excitement, and worry, to name a few. Each line in the emotion described can be used as a starting point for discussion or writing. For example, "Excitement wears orange socks . . . Fear conducts horror music in the middle of the night . . ." are wonderful sentence stems that can lead to individual awareness and invite exploration. Poetry therapists can assess the client's particular mood, fear, resistance, or pattern and match a quality that might help to illuminate areas the client cannot see. Gendler cleverly switches pronouns every other quality and speaks in third person. This allows for an effective "distancing" so the clients may safely observe from another perspective and not have to "own" anything before they are ready. Many clients are resistant to saying "I feel" or "I am," but when they are offered the option of reading "She skates on thin ice with Doubt" or "Fear almost convinced me he was a puppet-maker and I was a marionette," the spontaneous responses are encouraged. Clients may choose to either be the quality or the "she" or the "he" who shares the space with the quality described. They don't have to personalize a particular quality if they are not ready for that leap. The book is also very hopeful in that it offers solutions on how to minimize overwhelming emotions. It is easily adapted to all populations and works well with groups or individuals. The simple line drawings are helpful additions because they put a human face to elusive or unattractive emotions and make them more approachable or palatable.

Note: See detailed analysis earlier in the chapter.

Harjo, Joy. "I Give You Back." *She Had Some Horses*. New York: Thunder's Mouth Press, 1983/1997.

Joy Harjo's poem is a timeless victory song that gives readers strength in reclaiming their authentic voice and sense of self. The poem beautifully releases the ills of anger, fear, resentment, pain, and bitterness by reaffirm-ing, "I am not afraid to be angry . . . I am not afraid to rejoice . . . to be black . . . to be white . . . to be loved. . . ." These statements also say: "I am loved in spite of all that has happened and all that I am because I choose it. I release all that no longer serves me." Perhaps the strongest line is "I take myself back, fear." This one statement declares a return to courage, faith, responsibility, power, and all of the other characteristics that give an individual roots to build a strong foundation as well as room to grow.

Note: See detailed analysis earlier in the chapter.

Hughes, Langston. "Harlem." 1926. *Selected Poems of Langston Hughes*. New York: Knopf/Vintage, 1954.

This highly anthologized poem asks the reader to answer the question of "What happens to a dream deferred?" Graphic metaphors are utilized to help readers see what might happen if they ignore their dreams or compromise their ideals. The last line "Or does it explode?" could mean an explosive movement in a positive direction or an eventual dissolv-ing or disintegration of a hope or a dream. Either way, the reader is challenged to weigh the alternatives and consider the consequences of not seeing a dream to fruition.

Note: See detailed analysis earlier in the chapter.

Kavanaugh, James. "Anger Leaks Out." *Sunshine Days and Foggy Nights*. New York: EP Dutton & Co. Inc., 1975.

James Kavanaugh begins his poem with a subtle approach to the ways that anger is expressed and then ends with a twist. In "Anger Leaks Out," he says, "Anger leaks out in strange ways. . . ." It is true that we are often caught unaware of the undercurrent of anger. It may ooze out through our attitude or mood, our patience or impatience, or even our health. It may affect our sleep pattern, eating habits, or the way we relate to those closest to us. Kavanaugh closes the short list poem with "You and me making love!" It's a surprise ending because we don't nor-mally view anger as something that is communicated in our lovemak-ing. We are left to examine for ourselves if this is true and if so, then what? Kavanaugh shocks us with the closeness of anger and its ability to be intimate with us in ways we may not always recognize.

Pastan, Linda. "Anger." *A Fraction of Darkness*. New York: Norton, 1985.
This poem speaks directly to the rabid and biting nature of anger. The speaker chooses to hold onto her anger and "never let it go" because it serves her well. Her anger insulates and protects her from the outer world and its inhabitants. She is almost proud of her anger and all that it gives her. She says, "Ah, you think you know so much . . ." as a kind of mockery to others who may feel they know her better than she knows herself. This is a good poem for exploring ways that anger feeds or starves us and for identifying other aspects of anger that we may not see on a conscious level, such as anger as a protector, an ally, or a way of coping with trauma or loss.
Note: See detailed analysis earlier in the chapter.

Piercy, Marge. "How Divine is Forgiving?" *Available Light*. New York: Alfred A. Knopf, 1988. Text of poem is also available on www.google.com/search <http://www.google.com/search> (type title using quote marks).
Marge Piercy asks us whether or not we forgive due to acceptance, rationalization, time, or understanding or because our love is stronger than our anger. "How Divine is Forgiving?" is a poem filled with strong images, and it forces readers to reflect on the role that forgiveness plays in their lives. The poem's title asks, how divine is forgiving? We can interpret this question many ways: as one of sarcasm, realism, or self-reflection. Do we see forgiveness as something only God can do? Is this what the author means by the word "divine?" Piercy then says, "It's a nice concept / but what's under the sculptured draperies?" We get the feeling that there is more to forgiveness than saying we are sorry for whatever wrong we have done or that there is something hidden behind our apology. It takes a long time to understand the true meaning of our personal anger and sometimes even longer to accept the meaning we are given.

Rumi, Jelaluddin. "A Small Green Island." *The Soul Is Here for Its Own Joy: Sacred Poems from Many Cultures*. Ed. Robert Bly. New Jersey: Ecco Press, 1995.
One of the ways we can combat fear is through faith that our situation and whatever it is presenting can and will shift. In "A Small Green Island," Rumi takes a spiritual and symbolic approach to addressing fear of the unknown. This is an effective poem for exploring mindfulness and gratitude in order to reduce anxiety and appreciate the unfolding of the present moment. Rumi cleverly uses a cow to symbolize people,

101

or self, and the small green island to illustrate the world. He allows us to be both introspective and global in our thinking so we can take a step outside of ourselves and see life in a broader spectrum.

Note: See detailed analysis earlier in the chapter.

Sutheim, Susan. "For Witches." *No More Masks! An Anthology of Poems by Women.* Eds. Florence Howe and Ellen Bass. New York: Doubleday/Anchor Press, 1973. Also in *No More Masks! An Anthology of Twentieth-Century American Women Poets.* Ed. Florence Howe. New York: HarperCollins, 1993.

Many unattractive sayings have been used to describe anger such as, "wild with rage, beside himself/herself with anger, having a hissy fit, fit to be tied, spitting mad, a sputtering, spewing maniac, or blind with rage." In Susan Sutheim's poem, "For Witches," we are shown the difference between rage and tempering oneself or finding strength in refusing to accept that which is no longer acceptable. When the speaker says, "you step on my head / for 27 years . . . / and . . . I have been trained to excuse you," we see the struggle of having to rationalize our behavior or acquiesce to someone in order to keep the peace. Many of us are trained not to ruffle feathers, to be good or polite, lady-like or mute. We have been taught that "silence is golden," and that we should not "rock the boat." Often, it is not to our benefit to keep silent when our very world is being rocked by injustice, but we have not been thoroughly trained in the fine art of assertiveness.

In this particular piece, the narrator states that in finding her temper, she finds herself because she has been authentic and true to her individuality and feelings. The poem ends with the statement of finding oneself: "today i began / to find / myself / tomorrow / perhaps / i will begin / to find you." Even though the poet speaks from a small "i" perspective, her statement is at least a beginning for unraveling the grip of anger and finding personal freedom. She clearly understands that self-acceptance and care have to come before acceptance of anyone else. This is also a rich poem for deciphering the good that can come from a strong and sometimes scary emotion.

White, Ann. "A Nameless Anger." *Parents and Other Strangers.* Grayson, Deborah & White, Ann. New York: Ashley Books, 1987.

One of our greatest challenges is learning how to define anger and find ways to communicate it without hurting ourselves in the process. Ann

White writes about this in "A Nameless Anger." Most of us have experienced what the author describes. It is not foreign so much as it is elusive. We may describe it as a knot in our stomach, a headache, a depression, apathy or any combination of these symptoms. Sometimes we call it something else altogether. Anger can be difficult to pinpoint and even more difficult to embrace for any length of time. It is not usually comfortable or even remotely friendly, but it is necessary to define so we may find a way to safely and effectively express it. This is a good poem for helping clients put a name to the unspeakable and to help put a container around that which may have escaped their grasp.

Note: See copy of this poem at the end of the chapter.

THIS WOMAN

This woman
    talks to me
    in a warm language
    between her feelings
    and mine.
    She has no whip
    in her talk,
    no snarling teeth,
    She does not need to
    see the color of my blood
    to know me.
    This woman,
    seeing the gap in my fence,
    walks through it
    knowingly; and I,
    let her stand in my field,
    unharmed.

                    Anonymous

A POISON TREE

I was angry with my friend:
I told my wrath, my wrath did end.
I was angry with my foe:
I told it not, my wrath did grow.

And I water'd it in fears,
Night and morning with my tears;
And I sunned it with smiles,
And with soft deceitful wiles.

And it grew both day and night,
Til it bore an apple bright;
And my foe beheld it shine,
And he knew that it was mine.

And into my garden stole
When the night had veil'd the pole:
In the morning glad to see
My foe outstretch'd beneath the tree.

William Blake

SAFE PLACES

As children
Our games included safe places:
Bases where we were safe and free;
Lines that the monster intruder could not cross;
Areas off limits, out of the games;
Parents around whose legs we wrapped ourselves yelling,
"You can't get me, I'm safe here!"

Now older
I'm still looking for safe places
But, the fears inside
Seem to know the safe places I seek.
They wait there patiently for my arrival,
Courage and faith, my only legs to stand on.

Ted Bowman

I GIVE YOU MY ANGER

I give you my anger
hot clear direct
sharp as lightning jag
then you give me yours
and we resolve
our differences.

If I keep my anger
it smoulders
makes me sick.

Our anger is a gift
we give only
to each other
and to those
we love
and care for.

Anger is not
something
I can give
just anyone.

Janet Carncross Chandler

Reprinted by permission of Dan Chandler

THE NAMELESS ANGER

Observe,
it's like our very hairs turning toward
their follicles
nothing
reached to silence
only
teeth touch
and our bodies
heavy
   and cold as icebergs
  in some aimless ocean
drift.

                      Ann White

Reprinted by permission of Ann White

REFERENCES

Chödrön, Perna. *When Things Fall Apart, Heart Advice for Difficult Times.* Shambala Publications, Inc. Boston. 1997.

COPING WITH GRIEF AND LOSS

Sherry Reiter, Ph.D., CSW, RPT/MS, RDT/BCT
and Lila Lizabeth Weisberger, MS, RPT/MS, CASAC

THEMATIC OVERVIEW:

WHAT SHALL WE DO WITH OUR GRIEF? Shall we sit on it, dialogue with it, be seduced by it, learn to love it, or push it into the shadows? Death, illness, and loss are all uninvited guests that accompany our heartbreak. Sometimes we resign ourselves to this uninvited guest; at other times we are rendered speechless. Often the words we cannot yet form within ourselves are expressed by the poets with directness and clarity. Reading or hearing the words of others may touch our pain and inspire us to write and to communicate our grief in words. By speaking and breathing out words, we send them into the air; by writing we release our laments and desires into the universe and simultaneously contain them in a home of their own that we can visit again and again.

"When despair for the world grows in me/My sadness has no seasons," states James Kavanaugh. Our reasons for sadness are both large and small. Whether we have lost loved ones, physical or mental abilities, jobs, dreams, or self-images that we treasure, grief is a part of our lives that is inevitable. Poet Ha-Jin suggests the power of grief when he writes, "words line up in our throats / for a good whining, / grief seemed like an endless river / the only immortal flow of life." The small losses of everyday life have the power to deaden us or agitate us; they may call us to battle or to retreat. The large losses may stun us, freeze us or galvanize us with feelings of anger, betrayal, and depression.

Regardless of our attachments and our wish to remain as we are, we cannot control the flow of life. We do, however, have the potential to control how we deal with loss. As Judith Viorst explains in *Necessary Losses*, the nature of life is such that there will always be changes and challenges with which we must deal. We may lose a person, thing, or quality which results in a great sense of fear, anxiety, and/or sadness.

As therapists, our task is to elicit emotions and help the client to find words to articulate feelings. A major task is helping the bereaved to have the capacity to tolerate the feelings of grief and move through its dark shadows. In *Macbeth*, Shakespeare writes: "Give sorrow words; the grief that does- not speak / Whispers the o'er-fraught heart and bids it break." Poetry thera- py, when used by a trained facilitator, is a valuable, supportive tool that cushions the blows of grief and provides a path to new understanding and hope. We turn to the poets, the scribes who record their journeys of travail. When we read words that touch our spirits, we know that we are not alone. Grief is universal.

In her brilliant poem "In Blackwater Woods," Mary Oliver wisely reminds us that there are three things that are necessary in this life. The first is to love. Second, she admonishes that this love be guarded zealously. And third, she tells the reader to hold this "mortal love against your bones know- ing / your own life depends on it; / and, when the time comes to let it go, / let it go."

Our success in life rests on our ability to embrace all aspects of life with an open heart: to find a way to forgive, to accept, to hold on and to let go. We hold on for dear life to those we trust and love, and to whom we have given our hearts. When we go on the roller coaster of life, we hold on regard- less of the speed or steepness of the ride. Ironically our success in coping with loss requires the opposite skill—letting go. It is essential to achieve psycho- logical balance in an ever-changing, topsy-turvy world. May Sarton compares this letting go to the natural process of a tree letting go of its leaves in "Sonnet Two of the Autumn Sonnet": "If I can let you go as trees let go / their leaves, so casually, one by one; / If I can come to know what they do know, / That fall is the release, the consummation. . . ."

This incessant rhythm of holding on and letting go is with us from conception. We see it in the suckling infant as his tiny hands contract and expand, and in the very life pulse of the human heart. Rumi's words of wis- dom capture this thought perfectly, as he describes the opening and closing of one's hand, stating that if it were always a fist or always stretched open, the person would be paralyzed. "Your deepest presence is / in every small contracting and expanding, / the two as beautifully / balanced and coordi- nated / as birdwings." When our hands are stretched open, we may receive, but there is also the possibility of loss.

While physicians and therapists have tried to chart a predictable path for bereavement and sorrow, each individual grieves in his/her own way. Perhaps the most famous model is Elizabeth Kübler-Ross' five stages of grief. This paradigm is also widely misunderstood. Dr. Kübler-Ross herself has stated that not all persons go through all stages, and not necessarily in the order outlined; nevertheless there is a mistaken notion that there is a "right" way to grieve. The value of the Kübler-Ross model lies in the fact that it has identified some of the most commonly experienced aspects of grieving: 1) denial, 2) anger, 3) bargaining, 4) depression, and 5) acceptance.

In Linda Pastan's superb poem "The Five Stages of Grief," she moves us through each stage until she finally reaches the place of acceptance with this poignant conclusion, "But something is wrong. / Grief is a circular staircase, / I have lost you." This is a reminder that while the scab protects our wound, a scar becomes part of our very being. The loss is forever; one can accept it and move on, but there is no replacement for what specifically is lost. Nevertheless, there may be amazing opportunities, fulfilling events and relationships if one can grieve and understand and accept that what is, is.

Losses bring about a change in our sense of self and our place in the world. While this may be invisible to the outside world, it is dramatically experienced by the individual who has sustained loss. The perspective of the outside world is sometimes so different that the person grieving may feel the gulf widening between what is real and unreal, as well as a piercing sense of loneliness. Others cannot possibly understand unless they have been there.

Generally those closest to the grieving person want a quick recovery and do not want to be confronted with the harsh images of loss. These images are frightening and remind us that if such tragedy can happen to someone else, perhaps we are not out of harm's way. We have a need to feel in control, and, therefore, we may blame the other person for the illness. Or we may feel guilty about something that we did or did not do as though our actions could have stopped the death or loss. It can be frightening to acknowledge that so much is completely beyond our control.

In the face of grief, friends and loved ones become silent, awkward, uncertain of how to comfort the bereaved. More often than not, the task is bungled. Interestingly enough, Kübler-Ross' framework for grieving may also be used to reflect the reactions of persons who are interacting with the grieving person. Certainly we see denial ("It's not the worst thing in the world; she was ninety-one and had a long life"), rationalization ("It's for the best"), bargaining within the relationship ("If I'm good to this person now, then . . ."), anger ("I'm sick and tired of seeing her mope around; I can't put up with it much longer!").

If we are truly fortunate, loved ones will arrive at acceptance, listening sensitively to hear the needs of the grieving person, while treading softly and compassionately. Bereavement counselors suggest that the concept of "being there," even if it is in silence, may be more important than anything else. The definition of loss is the absence of something or someone important within one's universe. Although the presence of another cannot make up for the specific loss, it may decrease the isolation and sense of loneliness that loss brings.

Our loved ones are not always successful in living up to our expectations. The bereaved person may have difficulty understanding why this is so. We all know someone who says he/she cannot make visits to a friend who is seriously ill in the hospital. When you are the one lying in the hospital bed alone, this is difficult to accept. The friend may have the inability to cope and look illness or loss directly in the face. Some bereaved persons are able to be generous and not judge their friend's inability harshly, even though they may acknowledge their disappointment.

Conversely, the person who is grieving might not be able to accept the hands reached out to him. C.S. Lewis explains in his journal *A Grief Observed*: "There is a sort of invisible blanket between the world and me. I find it hard to take in what anyone says. Or perhaps, hard to want to take it in. It is so uninteresting. Yes, I want the others to be about me. I dread the moments when the house is empty. If only they would talk to one another and not to me. . . . And no one ever told me about the laziness of grief. Except at my job—where the machine seems to run much as usual—I loathe the slightest effort. Not only writing but even reading a letter is too much."

C.S. Lewis writes poignantly about the death of his wife in his journal. He tells us that grief feels so much like fear. He states: "There is one place where her absence comes locally home to me, and it is a place I can't avoid. I mean my own body . . . Now it's like an empty house. But don't let me deceive myself. The body would become important to me again, and pretty quickly, if I thought there was something wrong with it. . . . It doesn't matter whether you grip the arms of the dentist's chair or let your hands lie in your lap. The drill goes on. . . ."

Regardless of the support or lack of support one may receive, mourning is a private journey, painful and at times filled with anguish. In the poem "Surviving" by Gail Tremblay, she tries to forget how much she has lost as she states, "Nothing insulates me from memory." The hungers of the body remain but the body itself, once young and graceful, cannot perform as it once did. "Now there is no speed, / only the struggle of muscle working to cross space, / the deliberate choice to survive pain, / and the will to remember love is inescapable."

This striking last line suggests that while the decline of the body is inevitable, love may hold the key to survival. Although the will to remember love may haunt us and even taunt us, this memory may also have the power to sustain us. Our memories of the body celebrating itself at peak moments can never be forgotten, even when the body is a shell of its former self. Tremblay writes, "I dream of dancing naked under stars, / the dew on grass dampening my ankles, / the moon, sensuous ancestor, calling to my blood. I dream the impossible. . . ." Our memories contribute to the composite self or self-concept, made up of the past, present, and anticipated future. Memory enables us to reach beyond the fleeting moment. This is a strength, a comfort, and often an inspiration.

Our eventual rendezvous with grief cannot be avoided. Sooner or later, grief will make overtures and wind its arms around us in an embrace that may be hard to escape. We form a relationship with grief. This is the concept that is put forth in Denise Levertov's poem "Talking to Grief": "Ah, grief, I should not treat you / like a homeless dog / who comes to the back door / for a crust, for a meatless bone."

How can we have a relationship when our first impressions are that this unwelcome stranger is dominating, strangling, engulfing, and completely out of our control? First we try to banish this dark stranger and send it from our doorsteps in disbelief or anger. But what if the stranger were announced and beckoned into the parlor? What if we dialogue with this peculiar "other"? What if we allow this interaction to naturally evolve? What if we make a place for this uninvited guest in our homes? Sooner or later we must accept the fact that we have a relationship with grief. Dialoguing with grief rather than trying to ignore its presence is a sign of growing acceptance.

There may be a period of time when the only visitor a mourning person wants is grief. The outside world may temporarily hold no interest. Grief may hold the person tightly in its grasp like a vice, or it may embrace the person softly, suspending the bereaved with a hypnotic, lulling lullaby.

Ownership of grief is a critical task in the bereavement process. Once the grief is owned and the relationship is clearly articulated, the loss itself can be honored and memorialized. In time, a person's grief slowly undergoes a transformation. Eventually grief is not the dominating relationship in one's life, and there is a hunger for life and all that we love. Virginia Hamilton Adair pounces upon this hunger as a source of salvation: "Forgive me, Life, the famished ache / To swing across eternity—my line holds fast and do not break / I do this for my hunger's sake."

Eventually we are forced to make a decision. Which shall we love more: our despair or the grace of the world? Wendell Berry tells us about this decision in his marvelous poem, "The Peace of Wild Things." The larger world beckons to us, calls to us to come and see the "day-blind stars." His spirit is nourished by nature, and his despair and fear are temporarily set free.

Such calm and acceptance becomes difficult in the case of ambiguous loss as described by Pauline Boss. People hunger for the certainty of closure, but many experience the everyday slowness of loss inch by inch. When a person watches loved ones lose their capabilities because of Parkinson's Disease, MS, dementia, or Lou Gehrig's disease, the onlooker suffers from ambiguous loss. Ambiguous loss is also experienced by mourners who have loved ones missing in action. In our society we have rituals and rites that give support when there is a clear loss. Loss is complicated when it is ambiguous. The people involved are on a roller coaster, and it is never clear whether one should hold on tight or start to let go. When loss occurs drop by drop, there is no safe harbor or delineation of boundaries. The situation is so fluid that it is hard to be resilient because of the stress factor. When the ambiguous loss continues over a long period of time, we may feel helpless and not know how to move along.

Psychotherapists and doctors have embraced the Kübler-Ross model because its stages offer predictability and a sense of order. In reality, the stages do not always follow one another, and dying follows no set formula. One of Kübler-Ross' most important legacies is her message that each individual should be supported to grieve and die "in character," being true to one's self. We learn to be resilient when the lesson hits home; this is "what is." We have no choice but to find a way to accept reality. How does one find hope and optimism in this struggle?

Emily Dickinson states "Hope is a feather . . . And it asks nothing of me." The hope involves finding a way to accept and manage what is. As Mary Oliver reminds us in her poem "Journey," the only person you can save is yourself. The goal is to let go of what is not within our grasp while we love as long as we can. An essential task is not to be frozen in caring for ourselves and those we love.

Poetry therapists working with clients who are experiencing loss and bereavement must have an openness and have successfully worked on their own issues in this area. They must be able to listen, to hear, and be present with the person on his/her individual journey. The poetry therapist accompanies the client on his/her journey facilitating creative expression by selecting appropriate poetry and introducing writing experiences.

There is an abundance of poetry about grief and loss, and the following poems discussed in this section are only some of the many available to poetry therapists. We have chosen those poems that have been most effective in our work. In *Poetry Therapy*, Dr. Jack J. Leedy suggests the isoprinciple (choosing a poem to match the emotional tempo of the client) as a method that some facilitators may find helpful. Generally, some congruence is necessary for identification to take place.

It is also important for the facilitator to avoid the use of confusing, hopeless, and depressing material that offers no resolution or insight into coping with negative feelings. The poetry therapist chooses poems in which the metaphoric content builds upon and integrates images clearly and consistently. This clarity leads to clear thinking and a deeper emotional impact.

When we choose exercises and poetry, we must take into consideration the cohesiveness of the group and the readiness of the group for certain material. The appropriateness of each selection will depend on the emotional status of group members and the aspects of grieving previously mentioned.

IN-DEPTH FOCUS ON POEMS IN A THERAPEUTIC CONTEXT

1. "One Art" by Elizabeth Bishop

Perhaps what is most striking about Elizabeth Bishop's poem "One Art" is the use of a tightly controlled poetic structure to contain the expression of uncontrollable grief. This structure is the villanelle, a poetic form of five tercets, two rhymes, and two refrains: "The art of losing isn't hard to master" with variations on "It wasn't a disaster." Bishop provides us with a poem that serves as a tongue-in-cheek, little instruction book on loss. Her tone is flip as she compares grieving to an art that one may get better at with time and experience. Bishop herself started losing at an early age, with the death of her father as an infant and the breakdown of her mother at age five. She was raised by her grandparents, and her biography chronicles the staggering losses which she sustained during her life.

The poem's narration of these collective losses reminds us of the unique cumulative character of grief itself. While some of us may aspire to live up to the Buddhist ideal of non-attachment, most of us fail miserably in the endeavor. We are attached to our favorite things, be it a favorite necklace, a beloved easy chair, or a cherished book. We are attached to the people whom we love. Sometimes we feel they are extensions of ourselves. Often the relationships that we have with others are the most vibrant source of energy and joy in our lives. The fact is that we humans sustain multiple losses. What is not thoroughly grieved at the time will settle like sediment on the floor of our emotional oceans to be kicked up again in future storms.

Bishop's treatment of loss is doused with wry humor. She uses understatement and irony: "Lose something every day. . . . Then practice losing farther, losing faster." The poem progresses from small losses to larger ones. Bishop starts with keys, then the loss progresses to her mother's watch, and moves on to two cities, two rivers, a continent, and finally in the last quatrain, "Even losing you." Her diatribe is couched in intellectual resistance with some measure of denial, which may be considered part and parcel of the grieving process. However, by the end of the poem, there is some recognition of the catastrophe of losing her love, a slow dawning, which suggests a coming to terms with loss. Her command "Write it!" is a way of coping with loss, and one which all poetry therapists espouse.

Suggestions for Discussion and Writing Experiences:

1. Using Bishop's first line "The art of losing isn't hard to master" as a refrain, write your own poem chronicling your losses. Start with the small losses and begin with a distanced, flip tone. See where it goes.
2. Using magic markers and paper, draw a "Grief Time Line." Represent all your losses, both great and small. When your time line is complete, write one word or one paragraph about each loss. Share with the group.
3. Draw a line down the middle of a page. Make a list of small losses on one side and large losses on the other. Choose one of the small losses, or allow an item on your list to choose you and expand upon this in prose or poetry. Another option would be to work in twos, sharing your small losses and lists with your partner. In the beginning phases of a group, focusing on smaller losses, rather than larger ones, is an appropriate starting point. Once the group is cohesive, this exercise can be open-ended, and participants can choose to focus on large or small losses. The list may serve as a map surveying the grief, giving an over-all picture of what losses have been sustained.
4. Draw a line down the middle of the page. On one side list what you have lost. On the other side list what you are afraid of losing. Dialogue with the lost or anticipated lost person or object.

5. The above three exercises may be done with a list of gains and accomplishments.

2. "Talking to Grief" by Denise Levertov

In this striking poem, Levertov likens grief to a dog who "comes to the back door / for a crust / for a meatless bone." This metaphor allows the individual to identify and explore the relationship that one has with grief. Grief, in the embodiment of the dog, is a separate object from the person. While they may be keeping each other company, it is important for the bereaved person to acknowledge that he/she is a separate being. Grief may be so overwhelming at times, that the boundary lines between the person and the emotion may become blurred. The person may feel like he/she is the embodiment of grief itself. This state reinforces a "stuck" position in which the person experiences a loss of self, because the only emotion that is felt is grief.

This poem performs an essential therapeutic task by separating the emotion from the person, providing us with an externalized observing point. The dog metaphor becomes an effective container facilitating an exploration of what often feels like an unmanageable and uncontrollable emotion. By utilizing the dog metaphor, Levertov has also given us a subliminal message. After all, aren't we the masters of the dog? Surely the dog is not our master.

This dog is clearly not a threat. "You long for your real place to be readied. . . . You need your name, / your collar and tag." It appears to be in need of a home. "You think I don't know you've been living / under my porch." If the grieving person were aware of the dog living there, until now she has denied that it existed. In this poem, there is finally an ownership of grief. "You need / the right to warn off intruders, / to consider / my house your own / and me your person / and yourself / my own dog." Levertov is suggesting that grief has some rights and should be treated with some dignity rather than skulking around like a homeless dog. If we liken grief to an uninvited guest, it makes sense that the more one tries to ignore the presence of this "other," the more unsuccessful one will be. Someone is using your guest bedroom, and grief is not a tidy guest leaving your house exactly as it once was.

"You need / the right to warn off intruders." If the uninvited guest is taking up time and space in your home, you will not be able to devote as much time to the outside world. There may be people that are disrespectful or insensitive to the needs of the grieving person. Boundary lines may need to be clearly defined for relatives and friends who mean well but who may mistakenly deny the presence of the invisible guest. The grieving person may need to set limits. He/she needs to balance the time spent with the new house guest and the time spent with the outside world. Because loss itself is intrusive and may be experienced as a fragmentation of self, it is the therapist's task to help the individual to create a safe healing and "holding" space. Denial ultimately brings greater fragmentation. Acceptance works toward the unity of disparate parts.

Suggestions for Discussion and Writing Experiences:

1. In the Levertov poem, grief is embodied by a dog. If you were to choose an animal or object to represent your grief, what would it be? Write a dialogue between you and your grief, using first person (I) and second person (you), as modeled by the poem.
2. How do you usually contain your grief? If you were to represent grief as baggage or a bundle on your back, what would this look like? Using art materials, can you create, sculpt or draw a new container that can hold grief and get it off your back?
3. Draw a representation of your home. Show how much of your home is being occupied by grief. In a second drawing, show how much space you would like to allot to this uninvited guest. Write about it.
4. What are the things in your life that are uninvited? What are your houseguest rules for the uninvited guest? How can you employ limit setting and take control of this situation?

3. "Five Stages of Grief" by Linda Pastan

Pastan's poem recreates the labyrinth of grief, and using Elizabeth Kübler-Ross' five-phase model, shares one person's journey through each phase. She utilizes her voice in the first person and addresses us intimately and directly. There is an ironic juxtaposition of confusing and overwhelming emotion as Pastan takes us through the highly structured five-phased journey that is, in reality, anything but neat and simple. By the end of the poem, Pastan writes: "Grief is a circular staircase / I have lost you." We can only conclude that there is no formula for the resolution of grief. What is ultimately understood and is beyond our attempts at denial, bargaining, and anger, is the stark and painful truth of accepting the fact that something dear and precious has been lost.

Suggestions for Discussion and Writing Experiences:

1. Can you give examples of denial that you see in others? In yourself?
2. Can you create a metaphor for each phase of grieving? For example, "Denial is an aardvark," "Acceptance is an elderly man bearing fruit." After you have personified or symbolized each aspect of grief, choose one to write more about.
3. Have you attempted to make any "deals" or bargains with G-d or yourself? Have you ever said to yourself, "If I do such and such, then the consequences will be—"? As suggested by the common lines, "Step on a crack, break your mother's back," many of us are superstitious. Write about your own specific practice of "magic." If it is helpful, use the form, "if   , then" to explore some of your wishes.
4. Draw a ladder of healing, with various rungs. What phase are you in now? Place yourself in the picture depicting your current position. What is your goal? Label your goal as the top rung of the ladder. Label each rung drawing upon your unique personal journey. Then choose one aspect of your journey to write about.
5. Utilizing personification, choose one of the five phases to be the villain or hero. Write a fairy tale, writing in the voice of the third person. Another option is to become one of the characters and tell your story in the first person from the point of view of a character called by the name of one of the five phases: Denial, Anger, Bargaining, Depression, or Acceptance.

4. "The Peace of Wild Things" by Wendell Berry

This beautiful poem begins with despondency and fear: "When despair for the world grows in me / and I wake in the night at the least sound / in fear of what my life and my children's lives may be. . . ." Berry speaks to us directly and poignantly in first person. He is quick to take action and does not allow these heavy emotions to paralyze him: "I go and lie down where the wood drake / rests in his beauty on the water, and the great heron feeds. . . ."

Berry's poem offers us a way of coping. "I come into the presence of still water." This line reminds us of one of most popular and calming psalms ever written, Psalm 23: "The Lord is my shepherd / I shall not want . . . He leadeth me beside the still water." This particular image of "still water" is a very powerful metaphor. The ocean and sea are universal symbols of birth, rebirth, transformation, and change. However, the symbol of still water has a very different quality. There is no turbulence, only consistent quiet, depth, and serenity. There is no movement here. We always know what to expect. In a world that is constantly changing, this symbol provides us with a sense of security and calm. Nature provides us with constancy and predictable seasons: "And I feel above me the day-blind stars / waiting with their light."

Berry states, "I come into the peace of wild things." By leaving the fear and despair and entering a different place, he retrieves a part of himself that was left. Psalm 23 states, "He restoreth my soul." This restoration is the ultimate goal. Faith will be a boon to those who have religious values; others may be helped by finding a belief system or world view that provides some security and respite from turmoil. Nature provides us with order, beauty, and reassurance. When we return to the wildness in nature and ourselves, the appreciation for life and beauty kindles our instinct to survive. While some losses can be replaced, others are irretrievable. We can never replace a person we love. Nevertheless, it has been said that in life, one loves many things. This being true, eventually we make the choice to be in touch or not be in touch with what is still beautiful in our lives.

Suggestions for Discussion and Writing Experiences:

1. What gives you a sense of peace? Make three columns and list places, persons, and activities that help you to feel calm and peaceful.
2. Berry comments about the anticipation of loss: "I come into the peace of wild things / who do not tax their lives with forethought / of grief." Do you find yourself anticipating future losses? Is this helpful or productive in any way?
3. What is "the grace of the world" for you? How can you enter into "the peace of wild things"? Write about a time in your life when you have experienced this. Take us there, so we can feel what you have experienced.
4. What is beautiful in this world? Write a list of 100 things that are beautiful to your sight, hearing, touch, taste, and sense of smell.

5. "Sonnet 2 from the Autumn Sonnet" by May Sarton

In this poem, Sarton utilizes the seasonal imagery of trees letting go of their leaves as paradigms for the bereavement process. She addresses her lost beloved directly using an irregular rhyme scheme and a calming rhythm that is close to the human heartbeat. Sarton wishes that she could let go of her beloved with the same natural "release" and "consummation" she sees in nature. Letting go is part of the natural life cycle: "If I can take the dark, with open eyes / And call it seasonal, not harsh or strange. . . ." Sarton's wish is to be like a tree: "Stand unmoved before the change, / lose what I lose to keep what I can keep, / the strong root still alive under the snow, / Love will endure—if I can let you go."

The poem is eloquent and hopeful; at the same time it is practical and prods our instinct for survival. Sarton's imagery and poetic devices (alliteration, rhythm, and rhyme) are powerful and persuasive. The image of the tree losing its leaves is a universal and powerful symbol, strongly reminiscent of the Tree of Life. However, this tree is not in full bloom. It has weathered wind and storm and sustained loss. Life—and love—will endure if we can "let go" of what is not ours to keep.

Suggestions for Discussion and Writing Experiences:

1. Are there other images in nature that are inspiring and hopeful to you? Draw an image that speaks to you. Write a poem in which you capture the image. Help us to see and understand this image by describing it in detail.
2. What do you lose and what do you keep in bereavement? Draw a line down a page and list "What I Lose" on one side of the sheet, and "What I Keep" on the other side.
3. How will love endure if we "let go" when it is necessary to let go? How do we know when to hold on and when to let go? When is "letting go" a sign of weakness and when is it a strength? Discuss.
4. Draw one closed door. What door are you shutting? Write about what is behind that door. Draw an open door and write about what doors you may open in the future.

6. "Musée des Beaux Arts" by W.H. Auden

This is a complex poem since it refers to a painting with which the reader may be unfamiliar. This powerful poem describes a scene depicted in a painting by Brueghel. In this painting a terrible tragedy is happening to Icarus and his son, while a ploughman leisurely and peacefully continues with his work. Auden describes the tragedy and the turning away, "how everything turns away / Quite leisurely from the disaster."

Arleen Hynes refers to this poem in her book, *Bibliotherapy—The Interactive Process: A Handbook*, describing it as a difficult work yet one with a theme so universal that she highly recommends using it in poetry therapy work. Hynes explains that it has been used successfully with both clinical and developmental groups. Through discussion, group participants are helped in exploring what suffering means to them personally and how they have dealt with the isolation that suffering may involve. Auden's poem reminds us that we are all separate beings, and we may suffer alone while others are involved in their own preoccupations. Auden says ". . . it takes place / While someone else is eating or opening a window or just walking dully along. . . ."

This powerful poem is multidimensional and touches on many life issues. In addition to suffering and isolation, there are issues of boundaries, self-protection, and awareness of the pain of others. The poem raises questions about the scope of what is in one's line of vision, and the limits of one's tolerance. To be effective there is a need for empathy, and yet the need to walk away for one's own renewal must also be respected. How does this feel to the suffering person? To the caregiver? When do we keep on leisurely and peacefully ploughing our field and when do we help? Caregivers, as well as those persons working in mental health, medicine, and education have their own fine balance to maintain. Auden writes about a universal dilemma. We strive to maintain our emotional equilibrium at all costs, while not turning away from those in need.

Suggestions for Discussion and Writing Experiences:

1. Discuss suffering and the many forms it comes in. How have participants helped themselves through times of pain and crisis?
2. What does the grieving person choose to turn away from or need to ignore? Is choice involved or is a self-protecting mechanism operating automatically?

3. Draw a picture in which you delineate boundaries to protect yourself from other people and things. Using a second colored marker, show the boundaries that you feel others have delineated. Using a third colored marker, identify which boundaries you wish did not separate you from other people and things.

4. Do we block ourselves off from tragedy or do we open doors and windows to view the disaster and participate in it? This discussion may segue to exploring some well-known poems on doors and walls.

5. There have been several different paintings depicting the tragedy of Icarus. Copies of these paintings may inspire writing. Group members may also create their own scenes or collages.

6. Select the line of the poem that you connect with the most and use that as the title of your own poem.

ANNOTATED BIBLIOGRAPHY OF POEMS ON GRIEF

Aldington, Richard. "New Love." *The Complete Poems of Richard Aldington.* London: Allan Wingate, 1948.

> Epigrams in the three-line stanza poem, "New Love," speak of rebirth and recovery. It is a poem of hope and acceptance. The little almond tree is a metaphor of the necessary and routine changes in life. It pointedly speaks of the hurt and reality of loss, but the poet gives the message that there is a cycle of change and recovery after hurt. "She has new leaves / After her dead flowers. . . ."

W.H. Auden. "Musée Des Beaux Arts." *W.H. Auden: Collected Poems.* Ed. Edward Mendelsohn. New York: Random House, 1968.

> The suffering person experiences a separateness from the rest of the world. A tragedy may happen to one person while someone else is experiencing joy. In our culture, we may be reading news articles about fires and wars or watching tragedies unfold on television while we are eating our dinners and in the safety of our homes. How much do we take in about the tragedies around us and how much do we shut ourselves off for self-protection and self-preservation?
>
> Auden brings this concept to us through his reference to a famous painting, Brueghel's "Icarus," which depicts everyone turning away, or oblivious to a disaster happening. Auden states, "About suffering they

were never wrong. / The Old Masters; how well they understood / Its human position; how it takes place / While someone else is eating or opening a window or just walking dully along. . . ."

Note: See detailed analysis earlier in the chapter.

Author Unknown. "Do Not Stand at My Grave and Weep."

Absorbing the full impact of loss may take months or years. Sometimes we continue to search for traces of our loved one in the universe. Where has the person gone? This poem attempts to address this issue and speaks from the point of view of the person who has died. Written in rhyme with a steady, calming beat, the poem uses cyclical nature images (the autumn rain, the stars that shine, the birds in flight) to reassure us of the continuity of life. Our beloved has become one with the universe. "Do not stand at my grave and weep / I am not there, / I do not sleep." This anonymous poem has been passed from person to person and survived because it addresses the universal issue of mortality at a very basic level. Death is a mysterious phenomenon. This poem may be used as a catalyst to discuss group members' personal philosophies, as well as how the deceased person is kept alive and reflected in the personal environment and universe of the mourner.

Note: See copy of this poem at the end of the chapter.

Berry, Wendell. "The Peace of Wild Things." *Openings: Poems by Wendell Berry*. San Diego, California: Harvest Books, 1980.

While Berry's poem begins with despondency and fear, it offers us a way of coping. Berry reminds us that nature provides us with order, beauty, and reassurance. When we return to the wildness in nature and ourselves, the appreciation for life and beauty kindles our instinct to survive.

Note: See detailed analysis earlier in the chapter.

Bishop, Elizabeth. "One Art." *The Complete Poems 1927-1979*. New York: Farrar, Straus & Giroux, 1983.

Bishop's treatment of loss is doused with wry humor, using understatement and irony. The poem progresses from small losses to larger ones. Bishop starts with keys, then the loss progresses to her mother's watch, and moves on two cities, two rivers, a continent and finally in the last quatrain, "Even losing you." Her diatribe is couched in intellectual resistance with some measure of denial, which may be considered part and parcel of the grieving process. Her command "Write it!" is a way of coping with loss, and this poem is a superb catalyst for exploring small and large losses.

Note: See detailed analysis earlier in the chapter.

Dickinson, Emily. "After Great Pain, A Formal Feeling Comes." *The Poems of Emily Dickinson*. Ed. Thomas H. Johnson. Cambridge, Massachusetts: Harvard University Press, 1983.

The poem begins, "After great pain, a formal feeling / comes—." In Dickinson's narrative the grieving person becomes hardened like a stone and experiences a host of physical mechanical changes. The person overwhelmed by pain may become robotic when "the hour of lead" is experienced; the person goes through the motions of living but is not really there. This poem may be used as a catalyst to explore physical as well as emotional symptoms of grief.

While some may experience this poem as hopeful, others may interpret Dickinson's description of the grief process as overwhelming and brimming with pain. Dickinson's last verse describes the "Hour of Lead" as "Remembered, if outlived, / As freezing persons, recollect the Snow—First—Chill—then Stupor—then the letting go—." Letting go may be interpreted as a healthy end to a painful loss. It is possible to interpret "letting go" as giving up or submission to death. Facilitators should be aware of possible counter-therapeutic interpretations.

Dickinson, Emily. "Hope is the thing with feathers." *The Poems of Emily Dickinson*. Ed. Thomas H. Johnson. Cambridge, Massachusetts: Harvard University Press, 1983.

This is a short poem that inspires hope and tells us to hold on. Dickinson uses the image of a bird: "Hope is the thing with feathers. . . ." The poem serves as an effective catalyst for exploring the role of hope in group members' situations. The facilitator may ask the following questions: "What do you hope for?" "What does hope ask of you?" "Are its demands exorbitant, or does it ask nothing of you?"

Note: See copy of this poem at the end of the chapter.

Gardner, Lewis. "When I Was Fourteen." *Search the Silence: Poems of Self-Discovery*. Ed. Betsy Ryan. Scholastic Magazines, Inc., 1974.

In this poem composed of four quatrains, Lewis Gardner captures the tremendous feeling of insecurity that comes with a fall as a teenager. This fall is accompanied "with fatigue in my bones for being human, / since even Mother Earth / could not be trusted / to stay beneath my feet." Years later, this feeling returns to him, although it is not brought on by a fall. The sensation of falling may serve as a metaphor for loss, change, and vulnerability. When we lose loved ones, the earth beneath our feet shifts and it is difficult to center ourselves and restore balance to our lives. This poem may help readers to explore their own personal metaphors for loss. The facilitator may ask: "What is your grief like?" "How does your body experience grief?" "What can you do to restore balance in your life?"

Henley, William H. "Invictus." *A Concise Treasury of Great Poems*. Ed. Louis Untermeyer. New York: Pocket Books, 1968 (Also 1953, 1964, 1967).

This famous classic poem uses strong rhyme and rhythm and should be read aloud more than once for appreciation of its poetic elements. Henley prides himself on his "unconquerable soul" and the fact that he has not cried aloud: "Under the bludgeonings of chance / My head is bloody, but unbowed." While some readers will be inspired by this heroic stance, others may reject it as pompous braggadocio. This poem is an excellent catalyst for a discussion on participants' responses to suffering. Do we hide our pain from the world or exhibit it proudly? Do we take a heroic stance? If so, what words are used? Do participants agree with Henley's statement "I am the captain of my soul." If the individual is not captain, who is? Participants may explore their personal metaphors to describe their own relationship with destiny. The oral interpretation of this poem is highly therapeutic and is recommended.

Note: See copy of this poem at the end of the chapter.

Hughes, Langston. "Island." *Selected Poems of Langston Hughes*. New York: Vintage Books, 1987.

This poem acknowledges the power and depth of sorrow as well as the strong instinct for survival, which is in each of us. Langston Hughes' opening lines are "Wave of sorrow / Do not drown me now." The journey of sorrow is treacherous, but an island or oasis lies ahead. The metaphor of the ocean as emotion and the island as a safe haven captures the opposing forces, which are often a part of sorrow's journey. Even if we feel ourselves drowning, it is important to tread water and have faith in the existence of a safe haven that may be just out of reach. This poem speaks with simplicity and power reminding us not to lose sight of hope.

Hughes, Langston. "Still Here." *Selected Poems of Langston Hughes*. New York: Vintage Books, 1987.

> This is a powerful poem that sings out about survival. One can sing this poem, yell it out, recite it. It speaks of an endurance of physical and emotional scars, and the ability to survive despite shattered hopes. This poem can be seen as a statement of strength and empowerment, yet some may experience it as denial. The poem ends with the lines, "But I don't care! / I'm still here."

Kavanaugh, James. "My Sadness Has No Seasons." *Will You Be My Friend?* New York: E.P. Dutton, Inc. (1971, 1984). Also in: *The Seashell Anthology of Great Poetry*. Ed. Christopher Burns, New York: Park Lane Press, 1996.

> Poet James Kavanaugh insists that his sadness has no seasons, nor can he account for the reasons behind his grief. "There are no reasons for my sadness / Except living, and maybe dying." Sadness is part of the human condition. The poem suggests that while we may not always understand it, we must sustain it throughout our lives and survive its comings and goings.
>
> Kavanaugh writes, "I wish I were a planet so my sadness would have seasons." The facilitator may raise the question of whether or not sadness has a season. Is grief confined to specific losses? Or are there daily occurrences that make us sad? If we were to compare our grief to a season, what season would it be? Is it possible to experience joy when a person is in mourning? Participants may be asked whether joy has a special season and to identify what brings them joy.

Levertov, Denise. "Talking to Grief." *Life in the Forest*. New York: New Directions Books, 1978.

> In this striking poem, Levertov likens grief to a dog who "comes to the back door / for a crust / for a meatless bone." This metaphor allows the reader to identify and explore the relationship that one has with sorrow. This poem performs an essential therapeutic task by separating the emotion from the person, providing us with an externalized observing point.
>
> Note: See detailed analysis earlier in the chapter.

Longo, Perie. "Sometimes A Life." *Journal of Poetry Therapy*, Vol. 12. Number 2. New York: Human Sciences Press, Winter 1998.

This poem captures the enormous impact of the death of a loved one, which cannot be reduced or contained fully, even by the greatest of poets. The poem acknowledges our own feelings of inadequacy in coping with grief: "Sometimes a life is too much to fit on a page . . . Sometimes a love is too grand to fit on a page." How can we express feelings so large? The ending of the poem calms us and reassures us that we can manage these emotions, even though our world has temporarily become a darker place. "Let us be dark for awhile. After all, the moon is full / and the world once too large to fit on this page / has become small." This poem is an excellent catalyst for discussion about issues of emotional containment, expressiveness, and practical strategies for grief management.

Note: See copy of this poem at the end of the chapter.

Merlin-Molstad, Karl. c 1994. "One Leaf."

This poem quivers with hope even as the narrator speaks of his own dying. He speaks about feeling alienated from the rest of the universe, yet wanting to leave his mark on the world. This poem may be used as a catalyst for a discussion to explore what legacies the deceased has left behind that are immortal. Participants may also explore what they hope to leave behind someday. The concept of living legacies is a way of memorializing the one who has died, as well as giving hope and sustenance to survivors.

Note: See copy of this poem at the end of the chapter.

Millay, Edna St. Vincent. "Lament." *Collected Poems*. New York: Harper-Collins, 1923 (also 1931, 1951, 1958).

Millay uses the narrative voice of a mother speaking to her children informing them of their father's death and instructing them on how life will proceed in his absence. There is a deep irony in this classic poem, as the mother tries to compensate for the death by telling the children about all that will be theirs. In fact, the mother is helping the children to incorporate pieces and parts of their missing father to make the loss more bearable. "I'll make you little jackets; / I'll make you little trousers / From his old pants." His son will have pennies to save, and his daughter will have his keys.

This poem serves as a catalyst for exploring the ways that we may incorporate the lost person in our everyday life. Is there a favorite article of clothing or possession that has become important? Or has the person in mourning found it necessary to remove objects and posses-sions? The ending of this poem is morose, but may ring true for some readers. "Life must go on; / I forget just why." Why, indeed? The facil-itator needs to be prepared to tackle this fundamental question. Perhaps the answer lies in the ability to incorporate and remember the lost loved one.

Note: See copy of this poem at the end of the chapter.

Millay, Edna St. Vincent. "The Wood Road." *Collected Poems*. New York: HarperCollins, 1923 (also 1931, 1951, 1958).

This poem suggests that we need a greater perspective than that offered through the eyes of grief. We need to be able to mark the maple spray coming into leaf as well as the burrs beneath a tree. In this Millay poem, the reader understands that life and death co-exist. In the life cycle we do not have one without the other, yet death's visitation in our lives leaves us surprised and dumbstruck, as if we are shocked that death exists at all. This poem uses images to bring this point home: the vitality of life itself is captured in the image of "a rock maple showing red." Yet in the next line, Millay's attention is drawn to the process of decay or entropy: "Burrs may rot upon the ground." What will the grieving person's field of vision encompass? And how can we expand the field of vision?

Pastan, Linda. "The Five Stages of Grief." *The Five Stages of Grief: Poems*. New York: W.W. Norton & Co., 1978.

Pastan's poem recreates the labyrinth of grief, and using Elizabeth Kübler-Ross' five-phase model, shares one person's journey through each phase. She utilizes her voice in the first person and addresses us intimately and directly. There is an ironic juxtaposition of confusing and overwhelming emotion as Pastan takes us through the highly struc-tured five-phased journey. By the end of the poem Pastan writes: "Grief is a circular staircase / I have lost you."

Note: See detailed analysis earlier in the chapter.

Pastan, Linda. "Go Gentle." *Claiming the Spirit Within: A Sourcebook of Women's Poetry*. Ed. Marilyn Sewell. Boston, Massachusetts: Beacon Press, 1996.

This is a short poem about letting go. The narrator is a grown child entreating the parent to let go; this is in direct contrast to the plea to rage against the dying of the light in Dylan Thomas' poem "Do Not Go

Gentle into That Good Night." The person who does not rage may go with the natural order of things. While some may rage, it is instinctive for others to let go, to accept rather than submit. Elizabeth Kübler-Ross reminds us that there is not a right or wrong way to die. She says that each person dies "in character," and this will differ for each individual. This poem, in conjunction with Thomas' poem, provides two alternatives and may lead to a discussion exploring possible ways to say goodbye.

Pastan, Linda. "I Am Learning to Abandon the World." *PM/AM: New and Selected Poems*. New York: W.W. Norton & Co., 1982.

This poem may be experienced from the point of view of the dying person or a person who is in mourning. The grieving individual may feel abandoned and also may experience a need to abandon the world. To love is to be invested in something, and loss is a price we pay. "Already I have given up the moon / and snow, closing my shades / against the claims of white." "Closing the shades" suggests disillusionment and depression, but also a delineation of boundaries in the service of self-preservation. "And the world has taken / my father, my friends." This poem records a litany of losses and things that have been given up.

"But morning comes with small / reprieves of coffee and birdsong." The last verse suggests hope and acceptance. This poem may be used to discuss the negative and positive aspects experienced by participants in mourning. What have been participants' experiences of abandonment? Do they want to abandon the world before the world abandons them again? Are amends or reprieves possible?

Pastan, Linda. "Old Woman." *The Five Stages of Grief: Poems*. New York: W.W. Norton & Co., 1978.

In this poem Pastan uses the metaphor of mourning doves flying high in the sky to embody the distance that we try to put between ourselves and grief. Unfortunately these mourning doves "come back / wearing disguises." No matter how we try to escape the clutches of grief, we cannot. Thankfully, most grieving persons do experience moments of what Pastan terms "amnesia of sun." This poem may be used as a catalyst to explore the phenomenon of momentary amnesia of grief; such moments may be important to our survival. This poem concludes on a note of hope: "When my griefs sing to me / from the bright throats of thrushes / I sing back." The grieving process may incorporate a dance that vacillates between crying and singing, between forgetting and acceptance.

Rilke, Rainer Maria. "Again, Again!" *Selected Poems by Rainer Maria Rilke.* Translated by Robert Bly. New York: Harper & Row Publishers, Inc., 1981. This is a poem of hope and acceptance that describes the person who persistently stays with life and keeps trying despite bad odds and experiences. This person does not abandon what he has or give up on what might be. The narrator tells us that even though we have experienced pain and loss, we walk out and face the sky. "Again, again, even if we know the countryside of love, / . . . we walk out together anyway / . . . again, among the flowers, and face the sky."

Sandburg, Carl. "Different Kinds of Good-By." *The Complete Poems of Carl Sandburg.* New York: Harcourt, Brace and Jovanovich, 1970.
What is "good-bye"? How many different kinds of "good-by" are there? Using a tone of wry humor, Sandburg lists definitions, ending with "the big grand good-by." The poet plays with the concept of good-bye and encourages us to do the same. Participants may be inspired to write a list of what they have had to say good-bye to, and contrast this with a list of what they would like to say hello to. Participants may choose to emulate Sandburg's wry humor or experiment with exaggeration, sarcasm, or even telling lies about what is easy to give up.

Sarton, May. "Sonnet 2 from the Autumn Sonnet." *Cries of the Spirit; In Celebration of Women's Spirituality.* Ed. Marilyn Sewell. Boston, Massachusetts: Beacon Press, 1991.
In this poem, Sarton utilizes the seasonal imagery of trees letting go their leaves as a paradigm for the bereavement process. Sarton wishes that she could let go of her beloved with the same natural "release" and "consummation" she sees in nature. The poem is eloquent and hopeful; at the same time it is practical and prods our instinct for survival.
Note: See detailed analysis earlier in the chapter.

Skeen, Anita. "The Woman Whose Body Is Not Her Own." *I Am Becoming the Woman I Always Wanted.* Ed. Sandra Haldeman Martz. Watsonville, California: Papier-Mache Press, 1994.

This poem powerfully captures a woman who is in deep mourning after a mastectomy. Skeen bluntly states, "She is not herself anymore." The amputation of a body part alters one's self-image irrevocably. Simultaneously, she is receiving messages from friends and relatives that are in discord with her felt experience. While her friends may rationalize that she is lucky to be alive and lucky to lose "something she doesn't need," their message does not lessen the mourning. In fact, the perspective of the outside world is sometimes so different that the person grieving may feel a piercing sense of loneliness.

Spady, Susan. "Two." *Claiming the Spirit Within: A Sourcebook of Women's Poetry*. Boston, Massachusetts: Beacon Press, 1991.

This poem, written in third person, depicts a woman who has lost not only a breast, but a sense of self and her own lovability. As she traces her tender scar, she asks "Could a man stroke this? / And find her?" The poem poses many questions such as: "Does a man / with no legs have a spirit / sliced off like bread? / And does it grow back?" Questions about the body are juxtaposed with questions about the spirit. Readers may be encouraged to write a list of their own questions that their specific loss has raised for them. Using this poem as a model for creating a narrative, participants may write their own personal experiences, using third person ("she" or "he") to achieve distance and attain a different perspective.

Spigel, Naomi Halperin. "A Living Will." *I Am Becoming the Woman I've Wanted*. Ed. Sandra Haldeman. Watsonville, California: Papier-Mache, 1994.

This poem is narrated in first person, and the voice reflects a person who has lost her ability to speak and cannot make her feelings known. "When they say I'm past / all caring, brush my hair / and braid in ribbons." While the narrator evokes compassion in us, the last stanza may arouse feelings of guilt or regret in persons who have been caregivers: "When they tell you / to go home, stay with me / . . . inside I will be / weeping." She is pleading with the caregiver to stay, but can the caregiver provide what she wishes? When does one's own self protection enter this picture? The poetry therapist may ask the following questions of the caregiver: What are your limitations in your own care-giving situation? Can you balance someone else's needs with your own? Can you voice what you need? How do we show love through touch rather than words?

Tennyson, Alfred Lord. "Break, Break, Break." Originally published in 1842. *A Treasury of Great Poems.* New York: Simon and Schuster, 1956.

This is a mournful poem that uses poetic device to set the mood through rhythm and rhyme. It should be read aloud for its full impact. The form of this poem plays a key role in communicating the tension between the restraint and release of the emotions of grief. Each quatrain has two lines that rhyme and a rhythm that captures the ongoing movement of the world. The rhythm of the waves is unrelenting, as are the waves of grief to the person in mourning. "Break, break, break, / On thy cold gray stones, O Sea! / And I would that my tongue could utter / The thoughts that arise in me." As Tennyson watches the waves break against the cold stones, there may be a vicarious release of emotion for the reader. It is, however, a mournful poem but some hope and reassurance is provided in the ongoing activities of the world: "O, well for the fisherman's boy, / That he shouts with his sister at play! / O, well for the sailor lad, / That he sings in his boat on the bay!" This poem may act as an effective catalyst for a discussion about how participants find ways to safely release and express their grief.

Note: See copy of this poem at the end of the chapter.

Thomas, Dylan. "Do Not Go Gentle into That Good Night." *The Top 500 Poems.* Ed. William Harmon. New York: Columbia University Press, 1992.

This classic poem reflects the feeling of a son watching his father die. It is in the form of a villanelle, a hypnotic iambic chant consisting of six stanzas with a rhyme in the first and third line. The repetitive refrain, "Rage, rage against the dying of the light" is a powerful plea and has the semblance of a ritualistic chant for life. In the poem, the son directly addresses his dying father, urging him not to submit gently to death. He yearns to see a show of strength and fierceness in his father, saying, "Old age should burn and rave at close of day." This poem captures the frustration and pathos of the son in a situation over which he has no control. Thomas' poem may serve as a catalyst to explore the following questions: What were your emotions as you watched your loved one growing weaker? What was your one plea or repetitive thought in your grieving process before, during, and after your loss? Is there a "right" or "wrong" way to die?

Note: Please see Pastan's "Go Gentle" for a contrasting poem.

Tremblay, Gail. "Surviving." *Claiming the Spirit Within: A Sourcebook of Women's Poetry*. Boston, Massachusetts: Beacon Press, 1996.

This free-verse poem poignantly recalls the pleasures of the flesh and powers of youth while dealing with losses incurred by age and illness. Written in first person, the narrator recalls the physical feelings of the past. "Now there is no speed, / only the struggle of muscle working to cross / space, the deliberate choice to survive pain, / and the will to remember love is inescapable." This is a wonderful poem to address the physical changes that are universal to the human condition. It is important to be able to accept the changes and remember the triumphs and joys of the past. This is a hopeful poem. Although loss and decay are inevitable, Tremblay reminds us that love is inescapable.

Updike, John. "Perfection Wasted." *Collected Poems 1953–1993*. New York: Alfred A. Knopf, 1993.

This poem begins, "And another regrettable thing about death / is the ceasing of your own brand of magic." This poem is both mourning and celebrating the loss of the individual personality that occurs through death. It speaks directly and eloquently to the fact that life will never be the same because each individual is irreplaceable. "Who will do it again? That's it: no one: / imitators and descendants aren't the same." This poem can be used to acknowledge the depth of our loss as well as the specific gifts that were ours because of a loved one's presence in our lives.

Von Eichendorff (1788-1857). "On My Child's Death." *In the Midst of Winter*. Ed. Mary Jane Moffat New York: Vintage Books, 1982.

The death of a child is a violation of the natural order in life and is considered to be the most difficult loss to overcome. In this poem, Joseph von Eichendorff effectively juxtaposes the inner world of the mourning person, who may feel tired and lonely, with the peaceful eternal slumber of his child. In the last verse, there is a denigrating tone as the poet writes: "We are poor, poor stupid folk! / It's we, still lost in dread, / Who wander in the dark— / You've long since found your bed." This poem may serve as an excellent catalyst for a discussion about the regrets with which the bereaved often torture themselves. It is important, however, for the facilitator to provide some hope and resolution to offset the deep melancholy in this poem.

Williams, William Carlos. "The Bare Tree." *Selected Poems*. New York: New Directions, 1985.

This poem provides a metaphor for loss and change by utilizing the image of a tree in its various stages. Williams writes: "The bare cherry tree / . . . last year produced / abundant fruit. But how / speak of fruit confronted / by that skeleton?" When he ends the poem, suggesting that we cut down the tree "and use the wood / against this biting cold," he advises us to observe the changes that exist and make constructive use of what remains.

Wordsworth, William. "Sonnet—Surprised by Joy—." *The Oxford Authors William Wordsworth*. Boston, Massachusetts: Oxford University Press, 1984.

This poem may require several readings because of the classical language. Reading it aloud may also be helpful and will capture the beautiful sounds of rhythm and rhyme that grace this poem. Wordsworth reminds us that loss is irrevocable. In this poem, the narrator turns to share a joyous feeling with a loved one, but the loved one is long gone and will never return. The narrator expresses surprise that he/she has had even a moment of not being conscious of loss. "But how could I forget thee? Through what power, / Even for the least division of an hour." Yet there are moments when a grieving person may be blind to his/her loss. "Have I been so beguiled as to be blind / To my most grievous loss!—That thought's return / Was the worst pang that sorrow ever bore." This poem may be used as an effective catalyst to explore what is most painful to each person as they move through the grieving process. It may also provide a valuable opening to a discussion on the role of guilt.

Note: See copy of this poem at the end of the chapter.

DO NOT STAND AT MY GRAVE AND WEEP

Do not stand at my grave and weep.
I am not there.
I do not sleep.
I am a thousand winds that blow.
I am the diamond glint on snow.
I am the sunlight on ripened grain.
I am the autumn rain.
When you awake in the morning brush,
I am the swift uplifting rush
Of birds circling in flight.
I am the stars that shine at night.
Do not stand at my grave and weep.
I am not there.
I do not sleep.

Author Unknown

"HOPE" IS THE THING WITH FEATHERS

"Hope" is the thing with feathers
That perches in the soul,
And sings the tune without the words,
And never stops at all,

And sweetest in the gale is heard;
And sore must be the storm
That could abash the little bird
That kept so many warm.

I've heard it in the chillest land,
And on the strangest sea;
Yet never, in extremity,
It asked a crumb of me.

Emily Dickinson

INVICTUS

Out of the night that covers me,
   Black as the pit from pole to pole,
I thank whatever gods may be
   For my unconquerable soul.

In the fell clutch of circumstance
   I have not winced nor cried aloud.
Under the bludgeonings of chance
   My head is bloody, but unbowed.

Beyond this place of wrath and tears
   Looms but the horror of the shade,
And yet the menace of the years
   Finds and shall find me unafraid.

It matters not how strait the gate,
   How charged with punishments the scroll,
I am master of my fate;
   I am captain of my soul.

William E. Henley

SOMETIMES A LIFE

Sometimes the world is too large to fit on a page,
the woods eventually closing us out. I must stop
giving myself these impossible tasks.

Sometimes a life is too much to fit on a page.
I tried today, tried to describe their coming
and going, our laughing and weeping.

Sometimes a day is too complicated to fit on a page,
how it suddenly changes from bursts of red trees
to gray. Best I not talk about love.

Sometimes a love is too grand to fit on a page.
It needs a city to contain its edges and alleys,
not an open woods filled with wolves and tall spires.

Sometimes you need a whole night to weep
too much containment. Now that she is gone
let us be dark for awhile. After all, the moon is full
and the world once too large to fit on this page
                    has become small.

                                        Perie Longo

ONE LEAF

Riding over in Jessica's car,
Hot, stuffy breezes blowing in,
I watch the runners and rollerbladers
Circle the lakes in a narcissistic daze.
Poor human beings: we loll and stretch
In the sun like cold sponges,
Hungering not just for heat,
But warmth.
I look at these people
Like an alien from the planet of dying.
I hid the prospect of running
Like a talisman in my pocket
To take out on my fiftieth birthday;
But in a few weeks
I was stripped of my strength.
Now if I ran, I might fall
Or spend the rest of the day unconscious.
I am still attached to the tree of life,
Feel the tug of each breath of wind,
Frail as a leaf,
My connection slight and rough.
So many more flowers I hoped to bear
So many stories and poems
Burgeoning in my brain.
Will they be the harvest
Not grown, not gathered?
I grieve what I wanted to accomplish,
But never may.
And yet I write,
Even now pressing the patterns
Of my mind into the paper—
Clear, tough, and intricate.
Perhaps those who come later
Will find these words,
Like a leaf left in a big Bible,
And dream of summers past—

The splendor and the light
Splashing through elms and maples
On the boulevard as if I were
Entering heaven again and again,
Moment after moment.

Karl Merlin-Molstad c. 1994

LAMENT

Listen children:
Your father is dead.
From his old coats
I'll make you little jackets;
I'll make you little trousers
From his old pants.
There'll be in his pockets
Things he used to put there,
Keys and pennies
Covered with tobacco;
Dan shall have the pennies
To save in his bank;
Anne shall have the keys
To make a pretty noise with.
Life must go on,
And the dead be forgotten;
Life must go on,
Though good men die;
Anne, eat your breakfast;
Dan, take your medicine;
Life must go on;
I forgot just why.

Edna St. Vincent Millay

BREAK, BREAK, BREAK

Break, break, break,
  On thy cold gray stones, O Sea!
And I would that my tongue could utter
  The thoughts that arise in me.

O, well for the fisherman's boy,
  That he shouts with his sister at play!
O, well for the sailor lad,
  That he sings in his boat on the bay!

And the stately ships go on
  To their haven under the hill;
But O for the touch of a vanished hand,
  And the sound of a voice that is still!

Break, break, break,
  At the foot of thy crags, O Sea!
But the tender grace of a day that is dead
  Will never come back to me.

Alfred Lord Tennyson

SONNET

Surprised by joy—impatient as the Wind
I turned to share the transport—Oh! with whom
But Thee, deep buried in the silent tomb,
That spot which no vicissitude can find?
Love, faithful love, recalled thee to my mind—
But how could I forget thee? Through what power,
Even for the least division of an hour,
Have I been so beguiled as to be blind
To my most grievous loss!—That thought's return
Was the worst pang that sorrow ever bore,
Save one, one only, when I stood forlorn,
Knowing my heart's best treasure was no more;
That neither present time, nor years unborn
Could to my sight that heavenly face restore.

William Wordsworth

REFERENCES

Adair, Virginia Hamilton. "Dark Lines," *Ants on the Melon*. New York: Random House, 1996.

Boss, Pauline. *Ambiguous Loss: Learning to Live with Unresolved Grief*. Cambridge, Massachusetts: Harvard University Press, 1999.

Ha-Jin. "Ways of Talking." *Poetry Journal*. Chicago: Modern Poetry Association, July, 1994.

Hynes, Arleen and Mary Berry-Hynes. *Bibliotherapy—The Interactive Process: A Handbook*. Boulder, Colorado: Westview Press, 1986; St. Cloud, Minnesota: North Star Press of St. Cloud, Inc., 1992.

Kübler-Ross, Elizabeth. *Death: The Final Stage of Growth*. Englewood Cliffs, New Jersey: Prentice-Hall, 1975.

Leedy, Jack J., Ed. *Poetry Therapy*. Philadelphia, Pennsylvania: 1969.

Lewis, C.S. *A Grief Observed*. New York: Bantam Books, 1976.

Oliver, Mary. "The Journey." *New and Selected Poems*. Boston: Beacon Press, 1986.

Oliver, Mary. "Blackwater Woods." *American Primitive*. Boston: Little, Brown & Co., 1983.

Rumi, J.: *The Essential Rumi*. Translated by Coleman Barks. San Francisco: Harper, 1995.

Shakespeare, William. *Macbeth*. Act IV, Scene 3, lines 210-211. New York: Clarendon Press, 1990.

Viorst, Judith. *Necessary Losses*. New York: Simon & Schuster, 1986.

IV
FLOWERS ALONG THE ROAD

CELEBRATING SELF-WORTH

Rosalie Brown, BA, RPT; Arleen McCarthy Hynes, O.S.B., RPT;
and Deborah Langosch, ACSW, CPT

THEMATIC OVERVIEW

THIS SECTION ON CELEBRATING SELF-WORTH focuses on transformation. It helps us to appreciate the journey from sometimes dark and despairing places to the discovery of strength, survivorship, and awakening of the "good self." This process of change often involves discovering small and beautiful aspects of ourselves or helping our clients to identify those qualities that sustain and stabilize them, despite all that they have endured.

Our sense of self is established from both internal and external sources. It originates from early identifications with parents or caregivers and later from experiences with the outside world. Healthy self-esteem, as authors Moore and Fine tell us, is understood as "pride and pleasure in one's body and mind, in one's achievements and in family, nation, and possessions."

Often our clients have traveled a tumultuous road towards establishing positive self-worth, as they have encountered trauma, crises, and what Hartmann calls a less than "average expectable environment." They describe how devalued they feel, much like in Ronald Wallace's poem, "Hot Property": "I'm a near miss, a close second / an understudy, a runner-up. / I'm the one who was just / edged, shaded, bested, nosed out." Emily Dickinson's poem, "I'm Nobody / Who are you?" is another significant example. In this poem, she asks, "Are you nobody too?" and then suggests whimsically that as a pair, it does not have to be so grim. Our clients' paths to healing can be arduous and painful, yet with adequate therapeutic support and sufficient ego strength, there is opportunity for growth and healing from early damaging experiences.

Validating self-worth also has a critical place in work with our healthier clients. Here we can focus on helping clients discover their own strengths and healthy aspects of the self, almost in a preventive mental health model. Helen DeRosis describes the importance of this shift away from pathology to this more innovative model and notes that in a therapeu-

149

tic session: "Undoubtedly pathology will be talked about, but it would seem that equal or greater emphasis might be placed upon talking about and/or experiencing the healthy features of the patient's character structure, environment and development. To discover, identify and describe these features may take greater skill than to deal with pathology."

Poetry lends itself to validating self-worth through its use of metaphor, imagery, condensation, identification, and generalizing. Our clients can share the experiences of the poets in their quest to feel less isolated, more whole and confident. They can be helped to internalize their positive strengths and celebrate their self-worth.

The poems in this chapter can be categorized into four themes, and these are:

1. Survivor Poems
2. Transformation and Journey
3. Facing old conflicts, letting go, moving to newness
4. Awakening

IN-DEPTH FOCUS ON POEMS IN A THERAPEUTIC CONTEXT

1. "Saint Francis and the Sow" by Galway Kinnell

This poem is a rare gift for it leads us directly to a sense of our own worth. The successful facilitator of this poem is likely to be firmly convinced of the worth of each individual in the group and throughout the world, and of each sow or puppy dog that exists.

"The bud / stands for all things" are the first two lines of the poem, and we are launched into what seems to be a circuitous journey from the bud to "everything" that "flowers, from within, of self-blessing," to the last half of the poem describing the sow. As the facilitator reads the poem aloud to the group, some may find it a light reflection on a very lowly animal—the sow, especially if the session has begun with a newspaper photo of the winning sow at the State Fair. Perhaps a tentative chuckle spreads through the group, and incredulity grows because the participants say to themselves, "No one writes a page-long poem about a sow." Even the "earthen snout" is mentioned, "through the fodder and slops to the spiritual curl of the tail" (louder chuckles at that one), and "the hard spininess spiked out from the spine," down "through the great broken heart" to the "sheer blue milken dreaminess spurting and shuddering" into the mouths of the fourteen piglets, and culminating in the last line—"the long, perfect loveliness of sow."

In many ways each of us vitally needs to celebrate, with all the confidence and delight the word means, our unique self-worth. Not just the noteworthy qualities, but the small, trivial but essential and integral aspects of each of us that set us apart from anyone else. In short, "the long, perfect loveliness" of each of us and, in this poem, of the sow. Just because the insignificant details of sowishness are so strange to us, the poem helps us accept our own minute qualities more readily. In fact, is it not exactly when we are relaxed and accepting of ourselves just as we are, that we can unassumingly accept our "long, perfect loveliness"?

Children and youth need to learn the message about loving oneself from "within, from self-blessing" in the formative years so that the basic self-confidence arising from the core of one's being will be lasting. If there is a group of young parents interested in developing parental skills, this poem would be an excellent choice. Older persons may need to re-learn to love themselves as they grow in the use of common sense and practical wisdom but are losing their memories about incidental matters and are feeling devalued in our society. Almost every group needs to hear Kinnell's message as he formulates it in those early lines.

Suggestions for Discussion and Writing Experiences:

As the dialogue begins about this complex poem, it might be helpful to look at the photo of a prize-winning sow found in a newspaper and re-read the poem aloud—together. Poet Robert Bly says something about reading a poem aloud twice. The first time, listening with the ear of the mind, the second time, with the ear of the heart. Reading aloud together carries the message deeper than merely listening to a poem.

Together we form the words, and breathing in and out, we are conscious of articulation. The sense of hearing and sound, is added to that of reading and sight. The nuances of the lines are heightened when one pays attention to the community of the poetry therapy group reading in unison. One has to pay attention to the pace the others are using, the pauses, and the emphases. Thereby, the meanings of the lines may be enriched. If the first reading is uneven and rough, we consider that a "practice session" and go through it again, more smoothly, this time, enjoying the experience.

After this oral reading, the group is likely to perceive more depth in the poem than previously and is ready to answer a question like, "What does it mean to say that 'the bud / stands for all things, / even for those things that don't flower?'" It is useful to explore the varying interpretations several members give. Or the facilitator might not need to ask this question if a member brings up an opinion of the meaning of the twice repeated sentence, "for everything flowers, from within, of self-blessing." How significant do members think the phrase "self-blessing" is? And what various meanings can these words have?

Have any of the members an example of how someone might "re-teach a thing its loveliness?" Has someone helped you? Or have you been the one to "re-teach" yourself or others? The facilitator would not want to rush through this teaching dialogue and can invite each member to think of an example of teaching through "words and in touch." Invite the sharing response, but never pressure anyone to join in the discussion.

Group members might also be asked if they themselves remember "re-telling" another, or an animal, that "it is lovely"? A full session could be devoted to the discussion, closing with a go-around of members telling each other which line or lines they will take away in their hearts as the key message of the poem. Or the dialogue might be suspended before everyone is talked out. Then there will be some things left unsaid to write about. Use one of the following topics:

1. Write a reaction to the phrase, "The bud / stands for all things."
2. Work around the idea of: "and the sow / began remembering all down her thick length / . . . the long perfect loveliness of sow."
3. Clarify the terms, "self-esteem" and "self-blessing." What are the differences and/or the similarities?
4. Describe in your own words what you saw in the photo of the sow. Did reading the poem change your perception or insight?

On occasion, when it is important for a particular group to get the message of flowering "again from within, of self-blessing," the first eleven lines of Kinnell's poem—down to the semi-colon—can be presented as one poem with the title, "The Bud Stands for All Things." It should be indicated at the bottom of the page that this is an excerpt from "St. Francis and the Sow." The message of these eleven lines is so powerful that it can well take the full session to explore the meanings for each person. Since it is customary to provide each group member with a copy of the material being used, it is a good idea to type (or stamp) at the bottom of each copy of a poem to be handed out to group members, words such as: "This material is for educational or therapeutic use only" in accordance with the copyright laws.

After a good discussion of the general meaning of what "a bud" means to each person in the group, and then why or how it can stand for "all things," including themselves, the discussion can move on disclosing how each member responds to the fourth line, "for everything flowers, from within, of self-blessing." Each phrase needs to be examined. Each person in the group needs to personally examine for him or herself what this sentence means. Words not used in the poem, like "being yourself," "personal honesty," or "self-esteem," may also be examined. Each person in the group will find the second half of the poem easier to grasp if he or she has experienced how "everything flowers, from within, of self-blessing."

The next session becomes a follow-through meeting with the second part, also retyped, using Kinnell's title, "St. Francis and the Sow." It begins (line twelve), with Saint Francis putting "his hand on the creased forehead / of the sow," and bestowing upon her "the blessing of earth." In response, the sow begins to remember her unique beauties (her forehead, snout, curl of the tale, spine, heart, milk, and the fourteen teats), right down to "the long, perfect loveliness of sow."

You may want to concentrate on what it is the sow remembers that seems so lovely to her, and then ask group members to acknowledge the details of their own "lovable" selves that they recognize. Maybe some will have specific memories of a grandmother or a teacher or favorite uncle telling them something about themselves that surprised them, or the group leader may try to draw out the features each person regards as significant about themselves—that which "flowers from within, of self-blessing."

2. "Variation on a Theme by Rilke: The Book of Hours, Book 1, Poem 1, Stanza 1" by Denise Levertov

The poem begins, "A certain day" was "confronting me—a sky, air, light: / a being." The poet treats the day as if it were a person, telling us "it leaned over and struck my shoulder," and thus reminding us of how valiant young men were knighted in the past. And, as in the ancient ceremony, it was "granting me honor and a task." The "day's blow / rang out, metallic—or it was I, a bell awakened." This is only a ten-line poem, but its last line is powerful. How many will hear, "my whole self saying and singing what it knew: *I can*"?

Levertov's poem has the potential for appealing to almost every group: children, adolescents, healthy and mentally ill adults; in short, any group the facilitator thinks would profit by examining the force of self-esteem. It would also lend itself to an exploration of the ordinary behaviors of persons who possess self-confidence. Or, when emphasizing personal strengths, group members can focus on their own attributes and how their strengths influence their lives.

Suggestions for Discussion and Writing Experiences:

Useful questions to ask in relation to this poem are: "Is this a poem about you? Do you wish it were? Are you inspired to make it be so? What were your feelings about the phrase 'or it was I?' What about the punch line, 'I can'?"

A group of teenagers or chronically ill mental patients might react if you asked them to briefly relate this poem to the story of "The Little Engine that Could." Ask for details they remember of the story to contrast or compare with the poem. Does the work "plucky" for the Engine and the word "inspired" for the "bell awakened" come up? Is there a big difference in the word choice in the long run? A good facilitator wants to excite each participant to become aware of his/her own potential, whichever word is used. The question might be asked, "What awakens that 'can do' bell in you? Tell us what happens." If anyone recognizes the experience of suddenly becoming aware of a new potential to take action on in their lives, did this awareness happen in the past or recently? Does anyone feel awakened simply by the zest of the poem? Does anyone think the awakening may now happen about a project he/she is planning? And if this piece leaves anyone indifferent, the facilitator will want to investigate that as well.

Self-worth and self-esteem are comparable and especially significant for dialogue in a poetry therapy group of children or adolescents or the elderly. Both these terms involve ways in which a person values self. To begin the exchange about recognizing self-esteem, you might ask the members to describe the actions of individuals who possesses it. Does their tone of voice sound different if they are talking to someone "important," than if they are talking to ordinary friends? How do they treat and talk to children and the elderly or the poor? Self-confident persons rarely seem to be the ones who argue with others. Have you observed that people who accept themselves have a sense of humor and can laugh at themselves? What does something as basic as the way persons carry themselves, their posture, tell you about self-assurance? Do poised persons seem to need others' approval before they can start a project? Do those with self-esteem need to brag about their achievements?

Another way the group can be led to share their reactions is to ask them to write three or four words or phrases about their own strengths. Your convincing attitude and dynamic tone of voice will assure them that they do indeed have strengths. Give them some time to think about these words, then ask them to write about the ways these strengths influence their lives. As they share their insights, focus on the strengths listed.

You can also inquire about the different meanings the poem has if you read it correctly, "or it was I, a bell awakened," or if the plausible misreading was made, "or was it I?" How do those meanings differ? And how does the change from a stated self-assessment to a question about self, change the impact of the poem?

As they think about it, which members of the group believe their success requires a sharp motivation like, "I can," or which ones deliberately, carefully, and slowly plan all details before they begin a project? Is there only one right way to success? Why is it important to know one's manner of procedure?

Group members can be invited to write on the following topics in relation to this poem:
1. Picture yourself in your favorite comfortable spot. Write about: "I am happy with myself because . . ."
2. Write about an experience of your own that was similar to the "certain day" of the poem.
3. List the qualities or competencies you are aware of having that make you grateful to be yourself.
4. What have you learned about yourself as a result of this discussion?

3. "when faces called flowers float out of the ground" by e.e. cummings

The poet legally changed his name to e.e. cummings, using small case, and in like fashion, he rejects the conventional punctuation and way of saying things when he writes his poetry. Some regard him as a master of the whimsical, for he is very apt yet unexpected in his use of imagery. If you, the facilitator, are searching for a poem that would point out the contrast between the joyousness of a generous spirit and the binding, blinding qualities of self-absorption and stockpiling, this is a good choice. Or if some remarks in a pre-

155

vious session have opened up the issues of selfishness or egocentrism, use this poem. When the value of generosity comes up, this poem unequivocally states, "giving is living."

The title given is, in fact, the first line of the poem. This is customary for cummings since he numbers the poems in his many volumes of poetry, so to distinguish them, the first line is used.

This is a poem to use with group members who find it challenging to respond to unusual poems which make demands on them, or to wrestle with mental puzzles that may tell them something about themselves. This is also a great poem to bring out the delights of choral reading. The rhythm, the cadence, the choice of words and images, the subtle, but very positive messages, and a certain lightheartedness all contribute to make this three-stanza poem a true delight.

Cummings states the heartwarming qualities of "giving" three times in several lines of the poem. In each stanza, the second line states the positive message—in stanza one, "wishing is having"; in stanza two, "having is giving"; and in the third stanza, "giving is living."

The opposite aspect, that of hoarding, is pointed out in the third line of each stanza: "Keeping is downward and doubting and never" in the first stanza; "keeping is doting and nothing and nonsense" in the second stanza; and "keeping is darkness and winter and cringing" in the third stanza.

In the last three lines of each stanza, cummings whimsically brings in images of "pretty birds," "little fish," and "mountains celebrating life." These are unexpected, contrapuntal observations that lighten his serious message about generosity and hoarding. As facilitator, you decide if they need discussion.

Suggestions for Discussion and Writing Experiences:

To open the exchange about the poem, ask group members to mention and discuss words in the poem that strike them as surprising or meaningful. In the course of the discussion someone may mention "wishing" or "giving," or "living." Carefully facilitate their personal understandings of both these positive attitudes and the contrasting ones conveyed in "keeping is doubting, and doubting and never," "keeping is doting and nothing and nonsense," or "keeping is darkness and winter and cringing." Not every one will agree with the author's evaluation of the value of "giving" and the negativity of "keeping." This disagreement may add to the intensity of involvement in the dialogue. The dialogue can lead to an awareness of the now almost forgotten value of the once universally acknowledged Golden Rule: "Do unto others as you would have them do unto you." That maxim is not stated, but it could be inferred in a good exchange among the group members. What does it mean to those in this group? Or, if someone expresses a different reaction, explore it.

How do each of the group members' contrasting points of view about possessions influence their actions in daily life? If they are "keeping" people, what do they do with the things they own? Is that different from what "giving" people do with "things"? Ask for examples from the members' experiences that might illustrate their points.

Has anyone suggested that "giving" people and "keeping" people have different personalities? What about the conflict in one's own heart between being a "giving" person and a "keeping" one? Does a sense of humor have any place in these differing personalities? What details might someone add to the brief metaphoric contrast between spring and winter?

The therapeutic value of the poem is primarily in the concepts of "giving" and "keeping." Having the members write even briefly about that personal understanding is very important. And the dialogue is often very rich around these ideas, taking up the therapeutic hour. Thus the facilitator might choose to ignore mentioning the "pretty birds," the "little fish," and the "dancing mountains" or might ask about their significance. There are no right or wrong answers as to why cummings uses these phrases except as an author's privilege for a charming diversion, but if it seems important to some members to discuss this, you will make your best facilitating decision.

A totally different way of examining this poem might proceed from an idea suggested by a grief counselor who was a member of a group of adult women years ago. At the meeting following our usual spontaneous reactions to the poem handed out and discussed, this woman said, "Look at this, in going over last week's poem, I discovered that I could rewrite it, only by changing the order of the lines and using the author's words. Listen."

e. e. cummings' poem rewritten

when faces called flowers float out of the ground
when every leaf opens without any sound
when more than was lost has been found has been found
and breathing is wishing and wishing is having—

157

As the above four-line excerpt shows, the grief therapist had simply rearranged the order of cummings' lines, adding nothing of her own. She re-ordered the lines of the poem by using the first line of each stanza consecutively, then the second line of each stanza, and down through poem, resulting in three stanzas of nine lines, six lines, and a concluding six line stanza. In this re-ordering of the lines, the serious message seems to come together and is easier to grasp.

There are many possibilities for ways this rewritten version might be handled: What are the contrasting messages in the first stanza? What are the reactions to these messages? Can someone in the group refer to a personal experience that gives witness to one or the other point of view?

The choice of a cummings poem is a challenge. The facilitator needs to be perceptive about how to encourage reactions to the images and metaphors. He or she needs to explore the many directions the dialogue may take and be ingenious about strategies to direct the exchange. These are materials for eager minds. The explorations they evoke are worth the effort and reward both for the group and the facilitator.

4. "The Pedestrian Woman" by Robin Morgan

The title of the poem itself is a play on words, and the sequence is unusual, as if the poem were saying, "Read Carefully." The poem is about one woman, perhaps middle-aged or thereabouts, and consists of flash-photos of her life. The final two stanzas are also about her but present something like a still life image of her interior world. This poem can well be used with a group of any aged persons to mull over the differences/commonalties between exterior actions and an interior image of the person.

In the beginning of the poem, we see a woman "waiting to stride" across the intersection in her "inimitable" way, with her "shoulderbag banging against one hip," hair "promiscuous in the wind." Then she is sitting at her "typewriter / . . . writing messages" to the world at large that will result in "trouble with the boss." In the fourth stanza of this page-long poem, we see her doing ordinary things like riding the subway, warming "leftovers for her supper," and feeding the dog. We, then, are asked a serious question about whether we can see the "vision" of her dreams; the "passion, irony, and wit" that "are disguised / in all her daily movements"; and the "love" and "courage" within her activities. Next is an enigmatic and provocative one-line stanza: "Ordinary is a word that has no meaning."

The last two stanzas present a metaphoric picture of her life as "a fine piece of Japanese pottery," which the poet presents as raising many issues. The color—a "high-glazed hyacinth blue"—fires the ensuing mental images.

Suggestions for Discussion and Writing Experienes:

The facilitator might begin a group discussion by asking for very brief summaries of the poem, using as an example the phrase: "You can't tell a book by its cover." A preliminary examination of the poem might well emerge in the dialogue about the summaries. After a few minutes, one might ask about the theoretical and actual life distinctions between the "ordinary" and the "special." How do the participants respond to the single line stanza, "Ordinary is a word that has no meaning"? What are the group members' reactions to the last two stanzas?

After this introductory discussion, there is potential for the members to look deeply within. Getting the participants to turn their gaze inward on themselves is a proper objective for a poetry therapy dialogue, so this first part of the session should not be prolonged—just enough to get the group involved in the potency of the poem. Moving the considerations of the members to themselves can be done by offering the participants the choice to share the fruits of the following writing opportunities for this day's session.

Ask the members to write a brief description of themselves, modeled on the first four stanzas of the poem. Give them a time limit and tell them there will be another piece of writing to follow, just as the poem seems to have two distinctive parts. The writing process itself is therapeutic, and if people have written about personally sensitive matters, they may hesitate to share verbally. If sharing aloud has been explained as part of the therapeutic contract at the beginning, the question will not arise. After a few minutes of silence, the following writing opportunities can be presented from which to choose a final writing topic:

1. How do our preconceptions get in the way of truly valuing our own good qualities or those of others?
2. What are the qualities each group member sees within that are valuable or unique? Some members might more readily find a focus if it is suggested that they model their writing about themselves on the last two stanzas.
3. How do our special qualities emerge from our ordinary activities?

The conclusion of the session might be an evaluation by the participants of the poem and the dialogue that emerged as the members shared their writing aloud and responded to others' writings. Or it might be suggested that a poem be written about each one's journey in life described as if it were a piece of pottery, or a painting, a quilt pattern, music, or a basket. Alternatively, either a discussion or a writing experience on what it is that makes a person—man or woman—"pedestrian" might open up some fresh insights that can lead to the next question: What of you?

This poem has been used in a group that is diverse in terms of age, occupation, and gender. Some of the interventions to stimulate discussion were the following: What do you people think about using this poem in a group of both men and women? Does this poem mean anything to the men here? What does the title, "The Pedestrian Woman," mean to you? How do you see the two parts of the poem relating to each other? What does the word "ordinary" mean in the single-line stanza, "Ordinary is a word that has no meaning?" Is it true (or untrue) in a different way for men than it is for women? Are there any common qualities between the reactions of men versus women? The last half-hour or so of the meeting might be used in asking the participants to write their own version of a poem titled either "A Pedestrian Woman" or "A Pedestrian Man," reading the writings aloud and then having a group discussion about each poem.

5. "Finding Her Here" by Jayne Relaford Brown

"Finding Her Here" is a poem that has potential for exploration of several issues that interest adult women members of poetry therapy groups. Brown is very up-front about the thesis of her poem. In this case, the first line sets the keynote: "I am becoming the woman I've wanted." However, one's goal as a biblio/poetry therapist is to stimulate the group members to discover for themselves what this piece leads them to see and feel about themselves. So group members would not be asked to identify the theme of the poem at this point, for it might well tilt the discussion away from themselves to focus on the poet's point of view. The goal of the facilitator might be to help the women find an answer to the question, "What kind of a person have you always wanted to be?" Therefore, the facilitator might ask if the phrases the poet uses are those that anyone in the group would use to describe herself, phrases such as: "Soft body, delighted," "survivor," "a deep weathered basket," "arms strong and tender," "sufficient," "travels with passion," "remembers she's precious," "not scarce," and "plenty to share." Note carefully the specific phrases members choose.

Suggestions for Discussion and Writing Experiences:

Since this poem is written in the first person singular, it easily lends itself to getting a member to choose phrases that she could honestly use about herself. However, if a member thinks none of the poet's words apply to her, regard that as a good thing. Openness encourages genuine responses that are quite different from those in the poem. This may be especially freeing if the members are from culturally diverse groups, or are of different ages. Ask the group members what specific words depict themselves, and encourage them to discuss their versions.

With a group that enjoys writing, the facilitator might decide to make this into a free-write blitz. We suggest that members take a few minutes to write their own dreams of "becoming the woman I've wanted," using the first line of the poem. It could be pointed out that this is a freeing and exploratory experience and that discussing briefly and rewriting different versions almost immediately is a way to open wide the doors of perceptive insights. The second brief writing experience would focus on "becoming the woman I've longed for," using the first line of the second stanza. You may want to point out that there may or may not be a difference between the two questions, but it would be personally helpful to know the difference, if it exists. Take another brief period to write and discuss these new poems, finding the nuances of differences between the two versions, if they differ. Another writing option would involve creating a final version titled, "Finding Myself," and noting the changes each one made—or did not make—in the three writings.

In closing, the last scheduled session dealing with this poem could consist of a discussion of a final re-write of the topic. Propose they take their written versions home and, later, in some quiet time, review, and possibly rewrite, the three renderings to see what then emerges. Pondering the experience helps each person learn something about herself. Each member takes time at the final meeting to present the conclusions about herself.

Another focus for writing might be to take another look at the third stanza. In this stanza, is it possible that the word "becoming" has a different connotation than in the first two verses? The first use of the word, "becoming" in the dictionary seems to be implied in the first two stanzas—"to grow or come to be." But there is another meaning of "becoming" that is a discreet way of describing a woman's beauty, as in "She is very becoming," meaning, pleasing or attractive. It would be good if someone has already made that interpretation, or if you, as facilitator, can guide the members to discern this other possible meaning in the third stanza. The women in the group could then explore the factors that contribute to their assessment of their own beauty.

Depending on the ages of the persons in your group, it might also be appropriate to turn the discussion about the third stanza on to pre- and/or post-menopausal notions of what a "becoming" woman would look like. The tone and nature of the facilitator's interjections might be directed to help the members shed society's view of worshiping youth and to focus on one's face and skin-tone, one's figure and weight, and other emphases members would suggest. As facilitator, you might ask if the consideration of healthy qualities has a place in the picture. Then continuing the positive approach, explore what are the "becoming" specifics each woman now feels free to celebrate about herself. To lead to an in-depth exploration of opinions, it might help to ask participants if this poem would or would not work with males?

Another way to explore this poem is to focus on the lines, "knows she's a survivor— / that whatever comes, / she can outlast it." How each group member views "survivorship" may bring forth a lively discussion. Then members might begin to bring out the circumstances which they felt they have "survived." Questions to address might include: What are the personal strengths of survival? What was involved in the choices the women made? What wisdom did each person gain by doing it her way? Or what unexpected benefits were there for those who accepted life just where it seemed to be leading them? Have there been any advantages? Or, in what way has acceptance been disadvantageous?

Further writing suggestions include the following:

1. Share some of the helpful thoughts that led you to a strong sense of self-esteem. Write a poem describing: "How I have become the woman I've longed for."
2. Write on the topic: "I am a survivor, one who has outlasted what has gone before."
3. Focus your writing on the subject: "As you have grown older, whatever your age, what kind of a person do you want to be in the future?"

4. Write on the theme: "Acquiring self-esteem is significant to our mental health. How might the resultant concept of self-worth differ if one focuses on one's personal appearance or upon the relevance of one's wisdom, temperament, and personality traits?"

6. "Here" by Cheryl Marie Wade

The poem, "Here," is situated in the present but, as in life, draws on the past to illuminate the now. Therefore, it is a compelling poem for use in women's groups, particularly with battered women and those who have survived incest.

In forty-eight lines, Wade presents several contradictions she wants us to know about. She begins by saying she is middle-aged, "with long legs and a short fuse." (This is a good example of her light touch with deep and heart-felt issues.) In the second stanza she moves on to say she "has scars / visible and otherwise" but is one who "believes / in magic," loves "stones" and "can picture Springsteen's thighs / anytime anywhere." The third stanza pictures a woman "here / with a stiff back / and incredible flexibility." Wade also "tells lies for protection / the truth for survival." Proudly she is one "who survives to dream dreams." A transitional one-liner tells us that she braids her hair in her dreams. The next to last stanza is about loving, and the group may want to interpret what "love" means to her. Then she notes her need for "love" and hatred of it, followed immediately by "eyes shadowed by memory." She goes on to say she wants, and yet is "afraid to be loved / I love so easily." Wade concludes her self-description with the words: "full of colors / A survivor / who survives to be / a woman / here."

Suggestions for Discussion and Writing Experiences:

There are so many contrasts packed into this poem that the facilitator's introductory reading needs to be augmented by one or two additional individual and/or group readings, or fresh re-readings during the session if questions about content arise. The many contradictions in "Here" can be examined for their value to the participants. How does Wade's ability to identify the contradictions in her experience seem to help her deal with the stresses she has met? It may be helpful to the participants to draw up a list of the contradictions in their lives to frame their own survival techniques. Members may choose favorite phrases and explain to the group why these appeal to them; or members may choose words or elaborate on phrases that are seen as negative. Also members may be asked if they see a metaphor in the single line: "I braid my hair in my dreams"?

The facilitator could suggest concluding writing exercises to be discussed in the group based on an initial contract made with the participants.

1. I identify with the words or phrases: _____ for the following reasons:
2. Write your own poem: "Here."
3. Write about your personal colors of survival.

ANNOTATED BIBLIOGRAPHY OF POEMS
ON CELEBRATING SELF-WORTH

Brown, Jayne Relaford. "Finding Her Here." *Silver-Tongued Sapphistry.* Silver-Tongued Sapphists Press, 1988. Also in *I Am Becoming the Woman I Wanted.* Ed. Sandra Haldeman Martz. Watsonville, California: Papier-Mache Press, 1994.

A woman who is a graying and maturing survivor tells us in twenty-eight lines, "I am becoming the woman I've wanted." This is her first line. Her singular point of view will provide participants with specifics to agree or disagree with and fantasize about for themselves, as they talk or write about their own future.

Note: See detailed analysis earlier in the chapter.

Clifton, Lucille. "homage to my hips." *The Two-Headed Woman.* Massachusetts: University of Massachusetts Press, 1980. Also in *The Norton Anthology of African American Literature.* Eds. Gates, Henry Louis, Jr., and McKay, Nellie. New York: W.W. Norton and Co., 1997.

This witty fifteen-line poem is a testimony to the powers of this woman's hips. She "owns" her hips with pride and a savviness and knows the potency of them. Clifton says these hips "go where they want to go / they do what they want to do. / these hips are mighty hips. / these hips are magic hips." The poem is a good example of body integrity and the feelings of competency and strength that accompany a positive and integrated self-image.

Clifton, Lucille. "to my friend, jerina." *Quilting Poems 1987-1990.* Brockport, New York: DOA Editions, Ltd., 1991. Also in *Every shut eye ain't asleep: an anthology of poetry by African Americans since 1945.* Eds. Harper, Michael S. and Walton, Anthony. Boston: Little, Brown and Co., 1994. Also in *No More Masks! An anthology of twentieth-century American women poets.* New York: Harper Perennial, 1993.

This poignant poem addresses the subject of incest and sexual abuse with sensitivity and eloquence. Written as a letter to her friend, jerina, the survivor speaks of her vulnerability and sense of shame initially and then describes her readiness for what she "has earned / sweet sighs, safe houses, / hands she can trust."

cummings, e.e. "when faces called flowers float out of the ground." *Appalachian Wilderness: The Great Smokey Mountains.* New York: E.P. Dutton, 1970.

This delightful, complex poem focuses on the themes of keeping and giving. A summary of the message lies in three phrases from the three stanzas of this twenty-one line poem: "wishing is having," "giving," and "living." The relevant converse of giving is keeping. The three phrases in each stanza for this theme are: "keeping is downward," "doting," "darkness and winter." Since these are basic human traits, there is much to unpack. Furthermore, the poem also refers to birds and fish and mountains that do not seem entirely relevant.

Note: See detailed analysis earlier in the chapter.

Gilpin, Laura. "Spring Cleaning." *Hocus Pocus of the Universe.* Garden City, New York: Doubleday, 1997.

"Spring Cleaning" opens with "All morning / I have been pulling / skeletons out of the closet / the old bones that / keep me awake at night." The reader accompanies the poet through her process of emptying the closet and facing the skeletons so she can ultimately let them go. Even if the past remains, it can be "invisible as an angel" once the old bones are buried.

Ginsberg, Allen. "Now and Forever." *Cosmopolitan Greetings: Poems 1986-1992.* New York: Harper Collins, 1994.

The choice of words in this Ginsberg poem shows a master's depth of vocabulary and may initially be overwhelming to the reader, so several readings might be in order to capture the full meaning of this remarkable poem. The essence of the poem relates to the desire for immortality, not in literal terms, but through continuity of beauty in nature

("star-spangled high mountains / waning moon over Aspen peaks"),
through language and words, and through the perpetuation of genera-
tions and human nature ("Now and forever boys can read / girls dream,
old men cry / Old women sigh / youth still come").

Hynes, Timothy. "Quiet." unpublished.
This nine-line poem juxtaposes the words "Quit," "Quietly," and
"Quick" to deal with letting go of the past in order to move forward. It
advises the reader to "leave the past / to its self" and to "quit quietly
but quick."
Note: See copy of this poem at the end of the chapter.

Kinnell, Galway. "Saint Francis and the Sow." *Selected Poems*. Boston:
Houghton and Mifflin Co., 1982. Also in *The Norton Anthology of American
Literature: Vol. 2*. New York: W.W. Norton, 1994.
The first eleven lines of the poem seem theoretical but the significance
of the theme of "self-blessing" carries throughout the work. The last
thirteen lines specifically depict the accurate, earthy details of the
"sow's" beauty. Many participants smile at the reality of the images and
rethink the applicable message in ways that apply to themselves.
Note: See detailed analysis earlier in the chapter.

Levertov, Denise. "Variation on a Theme by Rilke." *The Book of Hours, Book
1, Poem 1, Stanza 1. Breathing the Water*. New York: New Directions, 1987.
The topic of this poem is the occasion of being given a strong sense of
self-assurance. The line, "A certain day became a presence to me" sets
the tone. The conclusion is "it was I, a bell awakened" and "my whole
self" came alive with "what it knew: *I can*."
Note: See detailed analysis earlier in the chapter.

Morgan, Robin. "The Pedestrian Woman." *Cries of the Spirit: A Celebration
of Women's Spirituality*. Ed. Marilyn Sewell. Boston: Beacon Press, 1991.
In thirty-four lines, this poem describes how a friend, the speaker, sees a
woman striding across the street "in that inimitable way of hers." But the
speaker also sees a "vision" of "what love, what courage" this women
shows in facing life. The last two stanzas describe the Japanese pottery
which the speaker uses as a metaphor for her friend's life—dull sienna on
the outside and the beautiful "high-glazed hyacinth blue" inside.
Note: See detailed analysis earlier in the chapter.

Oden, Gloria. "The Way It Is." *I Hear My Sisters Saying: Poems by Twentieth Century Women.* Eds. Konek, Carol and Walters, Dorothy. New York: Thomas Y. Crowell, 1976.

> A woman describes the beauty and essence of her African-American mother through her memories as a child in this forty-six line poem. She says her mother's "willow fall of black hair / . . . billowed in a fine mist / from her proud shoulders / to her waist." The images are fluid and sensual and capture the narrator's sense of her own burgeoning identity and pride in who she has become. The poem ends with, "Dark hair, dark skin / these are the dominant measures of / my sense of beauty."

Wade, Cheryl Marie. "Here." *She Who Was Lost Is Remembered: Healing from Incest through Creativity.* Ed. Louise M. Wisechild. Seattle, Washington: The Seal Press, 1991.

> "Here" is full of movement, back and forth, contradiction after contradiction, i.e. "There is a woman here / with a stiff back / and incredible flexibility / who tells lies for protection / the truth for survival." A middle-aged woman goes through the personal descriptions, events, attitudes, and realities of her life and the truth as she experiences it. And the readers will find themselves in many of the lines, aware of their own complexities, and wiser about themselves as they work through these.
>
> Note: See detailed analysis earlier in the chapter.

Walker, Alice. "The Nature of This Flower Is to Bloom." *Her Blue Body Everything We Know, Earthling Poems, 1965-1990.* San Diego, California: Harcourt Brace Jovanovich, 1993.

> Walker's strong survivor poem uses the metaphor of a rebellious petunia which lives "Against the Elemental Crush" and blooms "Gloriously / For its Self." This concise eight-line poem addresses the inherent strength that can be found from within and then flourishes.

Whitman, Walt. From "Part 1, Song of Myself." *The Norton Anthology of American Literature.* Vol. 1. New York: W.W. Norton & Company, 1994.

> This succinct seven line excerpted poem sings of joyous self-worth as the first person voice shares a tremendous sense of value and ecstasy in who he is and what he has become. He says, "I celebrate myself, and

sing myself / And what I assume, you shall assume." This is a very positive and lyrical poem that validates a strong sense of self.

Note: See copy of this poem at the end of the chapter.

Whitman, Walt. "Song of the Open Road (Part 5)." *Complete Poetry and Collected Prose: Literary Classics of the United States.* New York: Viking Press, 1982.

In this inspiring and positive nineteen-line excerpt from Whitman's poem, the persona describes a new found confidence and sense of mastery. He states, "I am larger, better than I thought, / I did not know I held so much goodness." These lines are filled with images of freedom where he "divests [him]self of the holds that would hold [him]" and "ordain[s] [him]self loos'd of limits and imaginary lines."

Note: See copy of this poem at the end of the chapter.

QUIET

QUIT QUIETLY   BUT QUICK

NOT TOO LOUD   BUT SOFTLY

QUIT NOW   LEAVE THE PAST

TO ITS SELF

QUIT AND DESTROY

DESTROY BAD   LEAVE THE REST

QUIT QUIETLY

QUIT QUICK

QUIETLY AND SOFT   THE WORLD TURNS

Timothy Hynes

Reprinted by permission of Timothy Hynes

Excerpt from SONG OF MYSELF, PART 1

I celebrate myself, and sing myself
And what I assume, you shall assume
For every atom belonging to me as good
                belongs to you.

I loafe and invite my soul,
I learn and loafe at my ease observing a
                spear of summer grass

                            Walt Whitman

Excerpt from SONG OF THE OPEN ROAD, PART 5

From this hour I ordain myself loos'd of limits and imaginary lines,
Going where I list, my own master total and absolute,
Listening to others, considering well what they say,
Pausing, searching, receiving, contemplating,
Gently, but with undeniable will, divesting myself of the holds that
        would hold me.

I inhale great draughts of space,
The east and the west are mine, and the north and the south are
        mine.

I am larger, better than I thought
I did not know I held so much goodness.

All seems beautiful to me,
I can repeat over to men and women You have done such good to me I
        would do the same to you,
I will recruit for myself and you as I go,
I will scatter myself among men and women as I go,
I will toss a new gladness and roughness among them,
Whoever denies me it shall not trouble me,
Whoever accepts me he or she shall be blessed and shall bless me.

                                        Walt Whitman

REFERENCES

Dickinson, Emily. "I'm nobody. Who are you?" Poem XXVII. *The Selected Poems of Emily Dickinson*. New York: The Modern Library, 1996.

DeRosis, Helen. *Working with Patients: Introductory Guidelines for Psychotherapists*. New York: Agathon, 1978. p. 6.

Hartmann, Heinz. *Ego Psychology and the Problems of Adaptation*. New York: International Universities Press, 1958.

Moore, B. and Fine, B. *A Glossary of Psychoanalytic Terms and Concepts*. New York: The American Psychoanalytic Association, 1968.

Wallace, Ronald. "A Hot Property," *Looking for the Place My Words Are*. Ed. Paul B. Janezko. New York: Bradbury Press, 1990.

BEING WITH NATURE

Barbara Kreisberg, MS, CTRS, CPT
and Charles Rossiter, Ph.D., CPT

THEMATIC OVERVIEW

HOW OFTEN HAVE WE NEEDED TIME ALONE or time away from the busy, noisy clamor of our daily lives? How often have we heard the expressions "quiet time," "time out," or "alone time" in order to find the sacred space within ourselves? Finding our own inner peace in our highly populated, pressured environment is not easy. With computers, faxes, and cellular phones, the focus is on cramming as much as we can into the shortest amount of time. How can we find tranquility in such a fast paced world? Most of us are drawn to the quiet and peacefulness of nature. Poetic devices such as metaphor, rhyme, rhythm, and images affecting all of our senses used in poems about nature help us to tap into our imagination. A poem can take us where we need to be, even though we may not leave our physical place at all.

Sometimes when we are depressed, confused, or deeply immersed in an emotionally charged situation, it helps to look outside ourselves in order to gain perspective. Some poetry allows us to do this by using nature as metaphor. Simple metaphors can offer major insights into situations that otherwise may be difficult to understand or talk about. Poems such as "A falling petal," "the temple bell stops," "Birdfoot's Grandpa," "The Cast Off," "Stone," and "Flower in a Crannied Wall" help us look outside ourselves.

Another lesson we can learn from the simplicity of nature is that joy and beauty are transient. Nothing lasts forever, and we must seize magical moments wherever we can. This is demonstrated beautifully in "The Act" and "The Yellow Tulip." Through poems such as these, we learn that our struggles and joys affect our existence and we are constantly changing and evolving. We learn that the rhythms of our lives parallel life cycles found in all living things. Focusing on our connection with nature brings contentment and deepens our understanding of ourselves.

Frequently all we need is to meditate and cleanse our minds and bodies of the clutter of everyday life. Poems such as "The Lake Isle of

Innersfree," "The Grasshopper and the Cricket," and "the temple bell fades" help us to pause and use all of our senses to marvel at the moment. Reading or writing poems about the tranquility of nature helps us to be still. For some, these activities may bring about a spiritual or physical cleansing as breathing, pulse rate, and blood pressure decrease. The result may be a decrease in stress and a replenishing of energy.

Other poems about nature may offer a sense of hope to those who feel depressed. "I Wandered Lonely as a Cloud," "Wild Geese," "The Explorer," "Loveliest of Trees," and "Song of the Flower" also teach us that surviving obstacles and striving toward our full potential gives meaning to life's journey.

IN-DEPTH FOCUS ON POEMS IN A THERAPEUTIC CONTEXT

1. "Song of the Flower" by Kahlil Gibran

"Song of the Flower" is a poignant poem that reflects upon the never-ending cycle of life. This is illustrated in the first stanza, "I am a star fallen from the / Blue tent upon the green carpet. / I am the daughter of the elements / With whom Winter conceived; / to whom Spring gave birth; I was / Reared in the lap of Summer and I / slept in the bed of Autumn." By using personification, the poem endows the flower with human qualities of self-reflection and empowerment. Gibran writes, "My plains are decorated with / my beautiful colors, and the air / is scented with my fragrance." The flower's own journey through life parallels that of human existence. It is also there with us during many of our own life experiences. The poem shows us that like the flower, we are born, we live, we celebrate, we sing, we dance, we endure, we rest, and we die. The poem reminds us that we are never alone in this journey of life, as all living things experience the same pattern of existence. The flower is a symbol of so many different things in our lives. It is a symbol of love, of romance, of celebration, of joy, and of sorrow as well.

We learn, through the flower's song, that like the flower we must accept all that comes our way, as it is part of life's journey as illustrated in the last stanza. Gibran writes, "I am the lover's gift; / I am the wedding wreath; / I am the memory of a moment of happiness; / I am the last gift of the living to the dead: / I look up high to see only the light / and never look down to see my shadow; / This is wisdom which man must learn." The poem provides us with a thought-provoking ending; one designed to lift our spirits and offer us hope.

Since the theme of the poem is a universal one, it could be used with clients who are grieving the loss of a loved one, ending a major relationship, adjusting to the loss of physical functioning due to medical illness, or suffering from depression. It can offer hope during a particularly dark period. By illustrating the flower as a part of nature that has similar qualities and life experiences to those of human beings, the poet helps the reader see his/her similarities to the flower. During a poetry therapy session, participants may find it safe to speak of the perceptions and experiences of a flower. As the group progresses, and members feel more comfortable with one another, the facilitator can introduce the idea of substituting themselves or others for the flower.

Suggestions for Discussion and Writing Experiences

1. What do you see as the theme of this poem?
2. Can the flower be seen as a metaphor for something else?
3. What is your favorite line in the poem? Why? Use this line as the first line of your own poem. Write about something significant in your life that relates to this line.
4. Just as the flower has taken on human qualities, can you think of any animal or part of nature you could imagine yourself wanting to be? Try to imagine yourself as something other than who you are, either an animal or a part of nature. Begin to write, "I am . . ." and describe your experience.
5. Write about where you were born, where you grew up, and where you are right now.
6. What do you think of when you read the line, "But I look up high only to see the light, and never look down to see my shadow"? Do you know anyone who has felt this way? Have you? Describe what their or your experience has been like that may have contributed to this way of thinking.

2. "Haiku" by Moritaki

This traditional three-line Haiku captures one moment in time so that we may reflect upon the word picture presented. Here we see a petal "dropping upward." How can a petal drop upward? We think of something being pulled downward by gravity, Yet this petal is resisting gravity and moves upward instead. "Back to the branch" can be seen as returning to its root, or place of sustenance and strength. Seeing the petal as a butterfly and independent speaks to its ability to miraculously defy gravity and soar on its own.

This poem can be presented to anyone who may be experiencing depression and who may be feeling helpless and disconnected due to the difficulties coping with a life stress. Like the petal, we may see ourselves failing downward, farther into a hopeless void. This poem allows us to see how we can be lifted up and turn ourselves around in order to overcome the depression. As the butterfly in the poem learns to fly on its own, so may we be able to receive nurturance and support in a time of need so that we may be able to move on with our lives. Thus this poem offers hope and comfort to those who may feel like giving up.

Suggestions for Discussion and Writing Experiences:

1. Have you ever read a Haiku before?
2. Does this poem have any meaning for you?
3. Can you see any similarities between the poem and life in general?
4. Have you ever been in a situation where you felt like giving up? Write about what was happening in your life at the time and who or what gave you the strength to move out of your despair and into a more positive place. Describe what helped you to change from a falling petal to a soaring butterfly.

3. "The Yellow Tulip" by George Swede

In "The Yellow Tulip," Swede describes the discomfort, the limited resources, and the tortuous elements of nature that this plant has had to endure in order to survive. The last stanza of the poem describes how this fragile plant was able to overcome all of these obstacles so that finally "Nothing else matters." The last line of the poem encourages us to celebrate who we are now, despite difficulties and hardships of our past. It empowers the reader to place value on one's own ability to survive all odds in order to become whole.

This poem is also one that could be used in a variety of poetry therapy settings. It can be used with substance abuse patients who are in the midst of recovery and dealing with great turmoil, guilt, and hardship. It can also be used with clients who have suffered emotional, physical, and/or sexual abuse. The poem suggests that like beautiful flowers, people who have been through unbearable pain and abuse can overcome these obstacles and develop into strong and beautiful beings.

Suggestions for Discussion and Writing Experiences:

1. What is your reaction to this poem? What does it say to you?
2. Are there any lessons to be learned from this poem?
3. Does this poem remind you of an experience that either you or someone you know has had?
4. Write about an obstacle you have had to overcome in your own life. How has that contributed to the type of person you are today?
5. Write a dialogue between you and your obstacle. What would you like to say to it? What do you think it would say to you?

4. "The Act" by William Carlos Williams

This beautiful and elegant little poem is descriptive rather than prescriptive in what it says and, therefore, can serve as an excellent open-ended stimulant for discussion. The poem begins with roses in the rain. Then the narrator pleads with a woman not to cut them. She replies "they won't last." He counters that they are beautiful where they are. In response she says "Agh, we were all beautiful once," cuts the roses, and hands them to the narrator.

The poem is nine short lines long and a good example of Williams' use of the "American speech" of everyday conversation he strove to perfect. Despite the plainness of the diction, numerous small decisions by Williams add to the poem's poetic quality and its impact. Beginning in the first line, rather than simply writing "There were roses in the rain," Williams inserts a comma after the word "roses," a choice which heightens the impact of the phrase "in the rain" and suggests that the roses were particularly beautiful as they glistened with raindrops. In the last line, Williams uses a line break to emphasize the narrator's statement that the roses were not only cut by the woman but then received by the narrator in his/her hand.

The poem's title, "The Act," is accurate. The poem describes a disagreement over whether an act should be taken as well as the result. In relation to nature, the issue raised is whether to let the roses be in their natural state or to cut them or, more generally, to let nature be or to manipulate it to suit our fancy. But this is not the only issue the poem raises. One might also consider the idea of acting for short-term pleasure versus going for the longer-term, assuming the roses will retain their beauty longer if left in their natural state. Finally, there is the issue of resolving differences. In the poem, two different opinions about what should be done are given and reasons for each are offered. Ultimately, the difference is resolved when the woman dismisses the narrator's objections and cuts the roses.

This poem can be particularly useful with couples as a way to open discussion of similarities and differences in viewpoints, decision making, and ways of resolving conflicts. However, the poem is so straightforward and deals with such basic issues that it can be used with a wide range of clients. In any personal growth group, considerations of how one relates to nature, how one deals with others whose views are different, and how one resolves conflicts, can all lead to insights and personal awareness. The poem can also be used with psychiatric patients, as it is sufficiently short and straightforward and thus does not require high level cognitive functioning in order for it to be understood or to stimulate a response. A geriatric population might be interested in the statement "we were all beautiful once," and a group of adolescents might use their passionate attitudes toward the environment as a way into the poem and the personal issues it opens up.

Suggestions for Discussion and Writing Experiences:

1. Do you think the narrator is a man or woman? Does it matter?
2. Which of the two characters in the poem would you rather be? Why?
3. Continue the dialogue in the poem. You might do this either by writing a little skit in which the narrator and the woman continue talking or by pairing with another group member and each assuming one of the roles and continuing the conversation begun in the poem.
4. What do you think of the fact that cut flowers were placed in the hands of the narrator? Does this say something about their relationship? Elaborate.
5. Be one of the "elements" in the poem—the narrator, the woman, the roses, the rain, the narrator's hands that received the roses—and speak from that perspective. Write down what you would say.

5. "The Explorer" by David Ignatow

This eighteen-line poem describes an encounter with a mountain. In the first lines, it is established that the narrator has a dangerous mountain to climb "and no one to stop me." He decides to climb it "for the sake of the living." Voices call out to him to climb and die." He answers that he will climb "and live." In a two-line second stanza, as the narrator "reaches for possession," the voices change their message and tell him to climb and live. In the concluding stanza, the narrator finds joy in the natural world around him—the trees, the grass, and even the "glacial face of the mountain." Finally, he declares triumphantly that he has discovered the mountain to be his own.

The diction in this poem is quite straightforward and clear; however some things are stated in elusive ways that might evoke productive discussion in poetry therapy as when the narrator says he will climb "for the sake of the living" or that he is "reaching for possession." There is also the issue of who "they" are who tell him first to climb and die, and then tell him to climb and live. It is interesting that the voices shout when they say climb and die and whisper when they say climb and live after the narrator has answered softly "climb . . . and live." We may also consider the mountain a metaphor for life and/or life's struggles. The narrator nearly comes right out and tells us as much when he calls the mountain "my own."

The brief narrative of this poem touches on a number of significant human issues such as bravery, cowardice, determination, and responses to challenges; and on human emotions such as fear, exhaltation, joy, and triumph. These issues and emotions are sufficiently basic and the poem sufficiently accessible that it can be used with a wide range of clients. Because the poem does not address a particular real-life decision or difficulty but rather uses the mountain as a metaphor for any issue that must be dealt with, the poem can be useful for those facing difficult life decisions of any type. However, it may be particularly useful for those situations that involve facing a seemingly dangerous, unknown future, such as divorce. Young people, looking forward to life's challenges and rewards should have no trouble relating to the poem. Those with depression or serious diagnoses could also benefit from the use of this poem to help them explore how they view their difficulties and what they might do about them.

Suggestions for Discussion and Writing Experiences:

1. How is the narrator like you or not like you?
2. What does the phrase in the poem "reach for possession" mean to you?
3. Why do you think the narrator says the mountain is his own?
4. What feelings does the narrator express in this poem?
5. Do you have any mountains to climb? Can you name your mountain?
6. Speak to your mountain and tell it what you think and feel about it.
7. Write the letters M O U N T A I N down the left side of your page. Now write a poem using those letters as the first letters of each line
8. Is "The Explorer" a happy poem? Why or why not?

6. "Stone" by Charles Simic

This three-stanza poem explores the characteristics of stones, asks the reader to go inside and become a stone, and suggests that there may be more to stones than meets the eye. In the opening stanza the narrator talks about going inside a stone and that, he'd be happy being a stone rather than a dove or tiger's tooth. In the second stanza, the characteristics of stone are explored. Outside it's a riddle, but within "it must be cool and quiet." The unperturbable nature of stone is considered as the narrator notes the stone's passivity when a cow steps on it or a child throws it in the river. In the final stanza the idea that there's much more light and life to the quiet stone than meets the eye is expressed. After all, "sparks fly when two stones are rubbed." Perhaps, the narrator ponders, there's "a moon shining," "star charts" or "strange writings," and other magical elements inside the stolid stone.

The ostensible subject and simple diction of this poem make it accessible to just about anyone, so it is potentially useful with a wide range of clients. Even quite young children could enjoy thinking about and discussing stones and the ideas suggested in the poem. The ways in which the stone in the poem might represent people is, of course, the poem's great strength for use in poetry therapy. Although the poem could be useful with just about any group, it can provide a particularly powerful stimulus for those who are reticent, shy, or extremely withdrawn. The magical third stanza is particularly validating in its suggestion that we might find wonderful things within the stone (or person) if only we could get beyond the exterior to the inner realm.

Given the concrete nature of its subject matter, the poem lends itself to a different kind of physical group activity. That is, participants might select an appealing stone from a collection of stones brought by the facilitator or, if possible, participants might look around outside to find stones that appeal to them. Writing and discussion can follow. This kind of activity with tangible objects provides another means of communication and a different avenue for encouraging participant self-exploration and discussion.

Suggestions for Discussion and Writing Experiences:

1. Do you know anyone who is like a stone? How are they like a stone?
2. The narrator would rather be a stone than a dove or tiger's tooth. What, in nature, would you like to be?
3. Inside the stone in the poem there is light and things on the inner wall. Imagine yourself as a stone and look at your inner wall. What do you find? Write about it. (NOTE: These instructions are greatly abbreviated.) This activity should be done as a guided imagery exercise by a facilitator who is familiar and comfortable with using guided imagery.)
4. Select a stone from among those brought by the facilitator, examine it, then write about it. Feel free to write anything—thoughts, feelings, descriptions, or even remote associations that result from selecting and handling the stone.
5. Now select a stone to give to someone in the group. Tell them why you are giving them this particular stone.

ANNOTATED BIBLIOGRAPHY OF POEMS CONNECTING WITH NATURE

Basho. "the temple bell fades." Translation by Lee Gurga and Charles Rossiter.

> In this short, three-line haiku, Basho captures a fleeing moment in time and asks the reader to reflect upon this moment. Like most haiku, the response to its meaning can be very different for all those who read it, and there really is no correct interpretation, only the one that has the most meaning for its reader. This poem about the continuing resonance of a temple bell after its actual clanging has stopped can be looked at in several ways. One may see it as meaning that after someone or something that is loud or bold leaves a place, its effects are still felt by those

left behind and its impact is strongly felt even though it has left. Another way to look at this poem is to realize that things or people do not have to be large or loud in order to be heard or noticed and that beauty and meaning can come from the quietest of things.

Note: See copy of this poem at the end of the chapter.

Bruchac, Joseph. "Birdfoot's Grampa." *Go with the Poem.* Ed. Lillian Moore. New York: McGraw Hill 1979.

In the poem "Birdfoot's Grampa," Bruchac writes about an old man and a younger passenger who are driving on a rainy night. They come upon several small toads on the road. "The Old Man / must have stopped our car / two dozen times to climb out / and gather into his hands / the small toads blinded / by our lights." The old man wants to save these toads, and the younger passenger seems to be getting frustrated that they are not making more progress on their journey. "You can't save them all, / accept it, get in, / we've got places to go." The old man responds by saying, "They have places to go, too." The poem describes two types of people, one who is overly sensitive to the needs of others and one who seems determined to achieve a set goal in the shortest amount of time possible. The poem asks us to look at how we make decisions. It asks us to ponder about when it is important to put our own needs before the needs of others and when it is important to put their needs before our own. Most of all, the poem asks us to look at our own values and how our values influence our decisions.

Gibran, Kahlil. "Song of the Flower." *The Treasured Writings of Kahlil Gibran.* Eds. Martin L. Wolf & Andrew Dib Sherfan. Trans. Anthony Rizcallah Ferris. New York: Barnes & Noble, 1998.

This poem is a poignant reflection on the unending cycle of life. By personifying the flower, the poet helps us see the ways in which our own lives pass through life's natural passages, and acceptance of those passages is encouraged.

Note: See detailed analysis earlier in the chapter.

Housman, A.E. "Loveliest of Trees, the Cherry Now." *Immortal Poems.* Ed. Oscar Williams. New York: Washington Square Press, 1960.

This is another poem that suggests we stop, attend more closely, and appreciate more fully. Essentially the poem tells us that nature is beau-

tiful, time is passing, and we should, therefore, get out there and appreciate nature as the poet does when he stops to focus on a cherry tree "hung with bloom along the bough." Carpe diem as it were.
Note: See copy of this poem at the end of the chapter.

Ignatow, David. "The Explorer." *David Ignatow, New and Collected Poems, 1970-1985*. Ohio: Wesleyan University Press, 1986.
The person in the poem has a mountain to climb and, though fearful, climbs it. In the process, he connects with the world around him and achieves a joy that is "skyward." Parallels to other life experiences can easily be seen, and discussion of how one confronts challenges can be stimulated by this poem.
Note: See detailed analysis earlier in the chapter.

Keats, John. "On the Grasshopper and the Cricket." *Immortal Poems*. Ed. Oscar Williams. New York: Washington Square Press, 1960.
This poem might serve as a poetic antidepressant with its message that even when there appears to be no life in nature, life goes on—the trick is that we must pause and attend to those little sounds of life that abound if we will only take the time to notice. In this poem what is noticed is the grasshopper's voice that runs "from hedge to hedge" and the cricket's song.
Note: See copy of this poem at the end of the chapter.

Moritaki "haiku." *The Soul Is Here for Its Own Joy. Sacred Poems From Many Cultures*. Ed. & trans. Robert Bly. Ecco Press, 1995.
A petal falls. No, it's a butterfly. This poem, as haiku do, deals with the juxtaposition of two perceptions. Discussion of our own perceptions of ourselves and the world might consider whether we see ourselves as falling leaves or butterflies. The extended discussion of this poem above considers its possible use with those experiencing depression.
Note: See detailed analysis earlier in the chapter.

Oliver, Mary. "Wild Geese." *New and Selected Poems*. Boston: Beacon, 1993; Also in *Dream Work*. New York: Grove Atlantic, 1986.
This poem provides another angle on the notion that we are all a part of nature and all have a place in nature. I think the key lines are "Whoever you are, no matter how lonely, / the world offers itself to

your imagination." Elsewhere in the poem we find the idea that regardless of who we are, we have a place "in the family of things." The message from this poem is so broadly applicable that the poem might be used with a wide range of poetry therapy patients.

Simic, Charles. "Stone." *News of the Universe.* Ed. Robert Bly. San Francisco: Sierra Club Books, 1980.

This exploration of the nature of stones suggests that the reader go inside and become a stone to discover that there may be more to stones than meets the eye. The concrete nature of this poem lends itself to different kinds of group activities, discussed above.
Note: See detailed analysis earlier in the chapter.

Swede, George. "The Yellow Tulip." *Time Is Flies.* Toronto: Three Trees Press, 1986 (& second printing, 1987).

A beautiful plant endures great hardship and survives. Connections to the lives of clients who have suffered and wish to struggle to overcome the past can readily be made.
Note: See detailed analysis earlier in the chapter.
Note: See copy of this poem at the end of the chapter.

Tennyson, Alfred Lord. "Flower in the Crannied Wall." *Book of Nature Poems.* Comp. A. William Cole. New York: Viking Press, 1969; Also in *Immortal Poems.* Ed. Oscar Williams. New York: Washington Square Press, 1960.

In this poem, the writer looks very closely at a flower from a distance and without judgment. In the last line, "Little flower—but if I could understand / What you are, root and all, and all in all, I should know what God and man is." Tennyson seems to be implying that if only we could be objective and neutral when looking at the world and all that is in it, we could then gain enormous wisdom about life. He also implies that understanding the simplicity of a flower may be the key to understanding the complexity of mankind.
Note: See copy of this poem at the end of the chapter.

Williams, William Carlos, "The Act." *Collected Later Poems.* New York: W.W. Norton & Company, 1967.

This quiet, yet highly-charged little poem concerns two people considering whether or not to cut some roses and can be used to stimulate discussion of power in relationships and ways in which conflicts are handled.

Note: See detailed analysis earlier in the chapter.

Wordsworth, William. "Daffodils." *Book of Nature Poems*. Comp. A. William Cole. New York: The Viking Press, 1969.

Wordsworth paints a magnificent picture with words as he describes: "A host, of golden daffodils; / Beside the lake, beneath the trees, / Fluttering and dancing in the breeze." The reader is taken to a place where nothing but a vast scene of flowers is seen in the mind's eye: "Ten thousand saw I at a glance, / Tossing their heads in sprightly dance." The poem is seen as a memory that has made such an impact on the writer, that its recall becomes a comfort and a pleasure whenever the writer feels sad or lonely. He writes, "For oft, when on my couch I lie / In vacant or in pensive mood, / They flash upon the inward eye / Which is the bliss of solitude; / And then my heart with pleasure fills, / And dances with the daffodils." One can use memories to help carry us through dark times in order to elevate our mood.

Note: See copy of this poem at the end of the chapter.

Yeats, William Butler. "The Lake Isle of Innisfree." *The Norton Anthology of Modern Poetry*, Second Edition. Eds. Richard Ellman & Robert O'Clair. New York: W.W. Norton, 1988.

This pleasant, quiet poem suggests the benefits of retiring to a natural setting for the peace and solace one might find there. It also mentions an intrinsically strong connection that might be felt between us and nature when the sound of a lake lapping on a shore is heard "in the deep heart's core."

Note: See copy of this poem at the end of the chapter.

THE TEMPLE BELL FADES

the temple bell fades...
but the tolling continues
out of the flowers

Basho

This translation by Lee Gurga and Charles Rossiter appears in print here for the first time by permission of the authors.

LOVELIEST OF TREES

Loveliest of trees, the cherry now
Is hung with bloom along the bough,
And stands about the woodland ride
Wearing white for Eastertide.

Now, my threescore years and ten,
Twenty will not come again,
And take from seventy springs a score,
It only leaves me fifty more.

And since to look at things in bloom
Fifty springs are little room,
About the woodlands I will go
To see the cherry hung with snow.

                                   A.E. Housman

ON THE GRASSHOPPER AND THE CRICKET

The poetry of the earth is never dead:
  When all the birds are faint with the hot sun,
  And hide in cooling trees, a voice will run
From hedge to hedge about the new-mown mead;
That is the Grasshopper's—he takes the lead
  In summer luxury,—he has never done
  With his delights; for when tired out with fun
He rests at ease beneath some pleasant weed.
The poetry of the earth is ceasing never:
  On a lone winter evening, when the frost
    Has wrought a silence, from the stove there shrills
The Cricket's song, in warmth increasing ever,
  And seems to one in drowsiness half lost,
    The Grasshopper's among some grassy hills.

John Keats

THE YELLOW TULIP

For weeks
it struggled
through the hard crust
of the spring earth
and a foot
of air

Just to be
scorched
by the sun
jolted
by raindrops
blasted
by the wind

But on this gentle
May morning
as it opens
yellow petals
to the sky

Nothing else matters

George Swede

FLOWER IN THE CRANNIED WALL

Flower in the crannied wall,
I pluck you out of the crannies,
I hold you here, root and all, in my hand,
Little flower—but if I could understand
What you are, root and all, and all in all,
I should know what God and man is.

Alfred Lord Tennyson

DAFFODILS

I wandered lonely as a cloud
That floats on high o'er vales and hills,
When all at once I saw a crowd,
A host, of golden daffodils;
Beside the lake, beneath the trees,
Fluttering and dancing in the breeze.

Continuous as the stars that shine
And twinkle on the milky way,
They stretched in never-ending line
Along the margin of the bay:
Ten thousand saw I at a glance,
Tossing their heads in sprightly dance.

The waves beside them danced; but they
Out-did the sparkling waves in glee:
A poet could not be but gay,
In such jocund company:
I gazed—and gazed—but little thought
What wealth the show had brought:

For oft, when on my couch I lie
In vacant or in pensive mood,
They flash upon the inward eye
Which is the bliss of solitude;
And then my heart with pleasure fills,
And dances with the daffodils.

William Wordsworth

THE LAKE ISLE OF INNISFREE

I will arise and go now, and go to Innisfree;
And a small cabin build there, of clay and wattles made;
Nine bean-rows will I have there, a hive for the honey-bee,
And live alone in the bee-loud glade.

And I shall have some peace there, for peace comes dropping slow,
Dropping from the veils of the morning to where the cricket sings;
There midnight's all a glimmer, and noon a purple glow,
And evening full of linnet's wings.

I will arise and go now, for always night and day
I hear lake water lapping with low sounds by the shore;
While I stand on the roadway, or on the pavements grey,
I hear it in the deep heart's core.

William Butler Yeats

REFERENCES

Rossman, Martin. *Guided Imagery for Self-Healing*. Tiburon, California: H.J. Kramer Inc., 2000.

V
SHARING THE JOURNEY: TRAVELING TOGETHER IN AND OUT OF STEP

THE PARENT-CHILD CONNECTION

Geri Giebel Chavis, Ph.D., LP, CPT

THEMATIC OVERVIEW

THE PARENT-CHILD CONNECTION IS NOT ONLY obviously essential for the survival and well-being of the human race but exerts a powerful ongoing impact on our view of ourselves, the shape of our lives, and our characteristic style of relating to significant others and casual acquaintances. In our lifetime, we share our journey in an intense way with our parents and our offspring, and, as the title of this section suggests, the voyage can take us through both smooth and turbulent waters. As therapists, whether we focus on the present, the past, the future, or a combination of all three time dimensions, we are always somewhere in the territory of this primary human tie. Even an absent or largely uninvolved parent profoundly influences who we are and how we act. Moreover, in a world where a mother's and a father's roles are in flux and where divorces, remarriages, re-structured stepfamilies, and inter-marriages are so common, the experiences parent and child have with one another are often quite complex and multi-faceted.

From both personal and professional experiences, I have come to believe that despite their diverse individual circumstances, parents and children harbor universal desires. While parents characteristically want to protect their children from harm, pass on their values, and receive respect, children desire guidance and role modeling, yet crave unconditional positive regard and freedom to become their own person. Parents usually want so much for their children—the fulfillment or achievements they never attained—and thus often impose rules designed to "insure" that their children will not make the same mistakes they have made. They frequently experience a sense of disconcerting failure if their children defy their rules or principles in forging a path to become unique individuals. The parents of teenagers that I see in my practice are usually reluctant to relinquish the control they had when their sons and daughters were youngsters and feel the pain of losing their status as wise, all-knowing figures. They often find it difficult or unnatural to respond to their teens as young adults and feel person-ally rejected in the face of their adolescent's anger, rebellion, or criticism. If therapeutic intervention becomes necessary, mothers and fathers often fear being judged as "bad" parents who have made irrevocable mistakes, while their offspring frequently harbor guilt from disappointing or disobeying par-ents and causing pain and disruption within the family. Thus, the parents and children that therapists treat are frequently locked in power struggles, with anger, mutual blaming, depression, somatic symptoms, and anxiety masking deep fears of abandonment and anguish over loss of connection and perceived personal failures.

The thirty-five poems discussed in this section can be useful in work-ing with individuals of all ages who are grappling with their role as child or par-ent, or with families going through a variety of developmental transitions, con-flicts, and life-changing events. Twenty poems focus on the parent's view and most, but not all, of these are directly addressed to a child. Fifteen poems focus on the child's view, but in a majority of these, there is not a direct address to a parent; instead, we hear the voice of an adult male or female recalling a parent and recounting a childhood experience through a long vista of years. The par-ent poems fall roughly into three categories: those evaluating success or failure in parenting or defining the parental role; those expressing parents' expecta-tions for their children and their recognition of the ways their children either resemble or differ from them; and those in which parents voice fear or experi-ence loss due to real or imagined dangers or developmental changes that involve the child's psychological or physical leave-taking. The child poems also fit into three categories. The first are those which assert uniqueness of self, sep-arate from parents, and express the need for independence in the face of parental worry or limit-setting. The second set delineates the effects on the child of a parent's life style, actions, or expectations. The third consists of mem-ory poems through which a child, experiencing an ambivalent mixture of feel-ings, clarifies or revises his/her view of a parent.

IN-DEPTH FOCUS ON POEMS IN A THERAPEUTIC CONTEXT

I. "On Children" by Kahlil Gibran

Gibran's well-known poetic passage on parent-child relations can help parents recognize that their children do not "belong" to them. There are many lines in

198

this work that will challenge parents who are experiencing difficulty giving up control of their children's lives and who have very high expectations regarding their children's academic, athletic or social achievements. While it tends to be more didactic than poems I usually find the most therapeutic, its fresh, accessible imagery and universality make it a desirable choice for a poetry therapist working with parents of teens. Moreover, the didactic tone is muted rather than aggressive, as is seen when Gibran suggests to parents regarding their children: "You may give them your love but not your thoughts." This line can be quite useful for stimulating a discussion of privacy and control issues. Parents of "acting-out" teens often feel threatened by secrets being kept from them. Yet, parents often discover that their most rigid and angry attempts to violate their child's privacy lead to the most extreme forms of rebellion. The chief attitude fostered by Gibran's poem is acceptance of life's natural rhythm or release of control in order to remain the healthy stabilizing force in the background. While there are many lines and powerful images that may provoke resistance or evoke painful emotion in parents, the rhythm created by the parallel structures in the poem is soothing, and the speaker's tone is quietly self-assured. Thus comfort and challenge go hand in hand in this work, as evidenced in the first stanza where Gibran tells parents: "Your children are not your children. / They are the sons and daughters of Life's longing for itself. / They come through you but not from you, / And though they are with you yet they belong not to you." The phrase "Life's longing for itself" is memorable for its alliterative quality and personification of life that fosters a sense of perspective. "Life" comes alive as a vital entity transcending the everyday conflicts or power struggles that parents and children experience.

In the second stanza, parents may be shocked by the metaphorically powerful message that the "souls" of their children "dwell in the house of tomorrow" which parents "cannot visit" even in their "dreams." Also the line "You may strive to be like them, but seek not to make them like you" may irritate parents who fervently wish to mold their child's life into a familiar shape. For this reason, I would be particularly alert and sensitive to parents' reaction to this line. Perhaps it will tap parents' underlying desire to recover their lost youth or encourage parents to focus on the features they admire about even an unruly, disobedient teenager. Through asking parents to think about what features of their child they might want to emulate, the therapist can create the opportunity for re-framing a parent's harshly critical stance. Yet in spite of the above challenging lines and even though Gibran concludes this stanza saying that "life goes not backward," he does not leave parents out in the cold. Mothers and fathers can "give" their "love" to their children even if they cannot give their "thoughts" and can "house" the "bodies" of their children by offering nurturing and protection.

In his last stanza, Gibran couches his advice in a visceral metaphor of a bow and arrow, inviting parent-readers to visualize themselves as the "bows" from which the "living arrows" of children are sent forth. He tells us, "Let your bending in the archer's hand be for gladness; / For even as He loves the arrow that flies, / so He loves also the bow that is stable." This image is a hopeful rather than a hurtful one because it conveys the sense that a divine force honors all generations and also relieves parental guilt by recognizing one's limit of control once the "arrow" is in the air.

Since the "archer" seems to be some form of divine being or force holding the bow or parent in its "hand," some clients may feel as if a religious view is being imposed on them. In order to respect clients' diverse spiritual beliefs, the facilitator can invite reactions to the archer figure or the notion of a grand plan beyond the human, and ask if Gibran's image fits for them.

Suggestions for Discussion and Writing Experiences:

The best question to ask in relation to this poem may be an open-ended one, namely, what lines or images are particularly striking or moving for you? This broad question provides room for a wide range of individual responses. In a somewhat more specific vein, the therapist can encourage parents to personalize their responses to this poem, by soliciting their reaction to the lines, "You may give them your love but not your thoughts, / For they have their own thoughts." I would invite parents to share their "thoughts" aloud and speculate on the "thoughts" of their children, thus providing an opportunity for them to express their grief or frustration over their inability to "transmit" their thoughts to their children, while helping them affirm their offspring's uniqueness. I would invite parents to recall their role as children in relation to their parents as we look at such lines as "You may house their bodies but not their souls, / For their souls dwell in the house of tomorrow, which you cannot visit, not even in your dreams." These are, in my opinion, very poignant lines that are likely to evoke emotion. The word "dreams" suggests another question: What are your dreams for your child? Where do you think these dreams have come from? These questions are designed to help parents explore the expectations they have for themselves and for their children, and the ways in which these expectations sometimes become fused.

Writing activities that can be used in conjunction with this poem include the following:

1. Create an acrostic poem, with each letter of the word, P R I V A C Y placed at the beginning of a separate poetic line, to form a framework for creative expression.
2. Imagining yourself as a "bow" and your children as "arrows," identify where you are positioned, who or what is the "archer," and where the arrows are flying, and free-write on your thoughts with these images in mind.
3. Choose another set of cognate images like bow and arrow that fits more aptly your particular relationship with your child right now, or the relationship you want to have.
4. Write a response to Gibran, telling him what you want him to know about you as a parent or about your child.
5. Choose a line, set of lines, or image that reflects you when you were an adolescent interacting with your parents, and free-write using that line or image as the beginning of your poem.

2. "Circus Song" by Patricia Goedicke

This is a poem I have introduced to clients who are mothers struggling with teenage daughters. It is also a favorite choice of mine in mother-daughter growth groups, where participants explore the dynamics of their relationships with their mothers and/or daughters and work toward increased self-understanding. Comprised of eleven very short (two to three-line) stanzas, the mother-speaker of this poem addresses her daughter directly with a mixture of love, compassion, earnestness, and frustration. While the speaker is a wise parent and effective role model for distressed mothers, she is facing the real messiness of encounters with an angry, ambivalent daughter.

Besides the direct addresses using words like "Dear," "Little yeasty thing," and "Dear clown, dear savage daughter," the vibrancy of this poem resides chiefly in its metaphors, kinesthetic sensory quality, and the universality of its paradoxes. The mother's reference to her daughter's "yeastiness" is part of an image pattern in the poem involving bread baking. The daughter is like "dough" that is "twisting / And turning" in the mother's hands and "Wrapped" in her "warm coverings" until she is ready to "rise." Like the dough, the daughter's "guilt" is "Just sticky enough to keep [her] / Right

201

where [she] want[s] to be, trapped / Trying out [her] weapons but safe." The mention of weapons fits with the more violent images in the poem, which appear mostly couched in the form of wild cat metaphors. The mother tells us she is called "animal trainer" and is accused of keeping her daughter "in the same cage" from which the mother believes she is trying to release her daughter. In a surprising reversal of image, the daughter goes from being the "hungry cat in a circus" to the one who "crack[s] the whip" over the mother's "bones." This reversal raises the question of who is training or controlling whom.

It is paradoxical that the mother who is facilitating the daughter's passage to adulthood is viewed as the obstructing force. Yet this mother accepts her daughter's fighting spirit, as is apparent in the poem's remarkably resonating final stanza: "No matter how much it hurts / Sharpening your claws on me first / Is how you begin to grow." As painful as these lines are, they capture another important underlying paradox within this poem—that the beloved parent is the safest target for the teenaged daughter's anger, and it is natural, perhaps even necessary, for a daughter who admires and trusts her mother to express criticism and rage as she attempts to define her separate self. This insight can provide comfort for the parent who cannot see the light at the end of the tunnel and may feel personally rejected by an individuating daughter. Mothers will realize they are not alone when they hear this poem's speaker voice the paradoxical lines, "For every step forward you take / Three backward and blame me."

Suggestions for Discussion and Writing Experiences:

Since the experience captured in "Circus Song" is so universal for mothers and daughters, it makes sense to ask a question such as, "Is there a line or two here that seems familiar to you or that you can relate to? As an opener for discussion, another question to ask is "what do you think of the mother and the daughter in this poem? In responding to this question, clients may find themselves focusing on the choices made by the mother and daughter in the poem, while expressing how these choices resemble or differ from their own. This question is also likely to stimulate a sharing of diverse personal experiences, involving accounts of mothers' failures and successes with their teen daughters and the dilemmas mothers face as they watch their daughters mature and rebel. Since guilt is so often the "glue" that binds mothers and daughters, I may invite participants to discuss the ways guilt has affected their relationship with their mothers and daughters or how guilt influences their present behavior and view of themselves.

After facilitating a discussion of this poem, I often ask group participants to react to a particular line and use it as a catalyst for their own writing. When they have written for about ten minutes, I often ask them to read their poem to themselves, select one striking phrase they have generated, and make this phrase the beginning of a second poetic expression. I call this activity, "the opportunity to go deeper."

Another writing activity that fits well with Goedicke's poem because of its vivid animal imagery is the invitation to select animals that embody both you and your daughter at the present time and to create a set of lines that develops your chosen animal images. For mother-daughter growth groups, I may ask participants to describe the "animal" they resembled when they were teens growing up with mom. To encourage sensory development, I may add such questions as "How did your animal self move, speak, eat, breathe, or react to mother?"

3. "Going" by Patricia Fargnoli

This poem establishes dramatic immediacy by its unique narrative form and vivid, down-to-earth visual and auditory imagery. Reading like a series of quickly passing camera shots, "Going" begins with an image to which all parents of growing and grown-up children can relate: "The children walk off into crowds of strangers, / their laces are tied, their backs straight. / They wave to you from platforms you cannot reach." Right away, we as readers are drawn in by the persona's use of "you," and when she conveys to us the words, "You want to hang on," she gets right inside our parent-head and heart and stays there throughout the poem.

Fargnoli's poignant single stanza poem is basically all about hanging on and letting go, about facing the loss of your offspring's childlike state of dependency. It is an ideal selection for both middle-aged and aging parents and their adult offspring who may or may not currently have children of their own. It explores some of the ways parents "hang on"—"Running after" their children with gifts or "small packages," care-taking with "vitamins," or bestowing a legacy of "guilt."

Immediately following this list of "gifts" that parents try to give their children, the poem's narrator tells us that children may "keep discarding" their parents' "dreams," a line that mirrors an issue raised by Gibran's poem discussed earlier. The narrator tempers the rejecting behavior of offspring by reminding the reader that children will "carry" the "admonitions" of parents in their "pockets" and "their children will sing" the parents' "lullabies," thus suggesting these are the truths that allow parents to "let go."

After the line, "you let go" which has a peaceful, wistful feel to it, Fargnoli's poem moves into its last thematic section, with aging parents "[settling] back" and receiving the visits of their adult offspring. While the children "serve up slices of their lives" at Sunday dinners, "it's not the same" as it was when parents knew every detail of their children's lives. The poem ends with a powerfully understated set of domestic memory images—"long braids," "a ribbon streaming," "a quilt tucked in," and "small things snapping on a line." These images provide an opportunity for parents and adult children to express grief over a lost time and to affirm the bond that unites them across the stretch of years. Those who have recently lost a parent or child are likely to find this poem very moving and cathartic. They will know they are not alone in a grief process that is fueled by the seemingly insignificant images of everyday life.

Suggestions for Discussion and Writing Experiences:

The broad topic of gift-giving between parents and children provides a richly loaded mine for the poetry therapist who can ask such questions as: What "gifts" did your parents give you? Which ones were welcome and which ones did or do you want to reject? What kind of gift-giver and gift-receiver are you? Clients can be invited to write a journal entry on the best and worst gift their parent ever gave them, or they ever gave their parent. Since gifts passed between parent and child so often take on emotional resonance and symbolic dimensions, the discussion of, reflection on, and writing about gifts can uncover a great deal of therapeutic material. Both parents and children can gain insight into their healthy and dysfunctional interactions by such explorations of the gift-giving issue.

The phrase, "let go," often elicits much feeling-laden discussion involving a set of important questions such as: What does it means to let go? What makes it easier or harder to let go of one's children? Does letting go mean losing? Do we gain anything when we let go?

The loaded word, "admonitions" can also provide ample food for discussion amongst parents and offspring alike. The poetry therapist can ask clients to identify or write a list of parental "admonitions," sayings, or warnings they "carry" or desire to keep or discard. Clients may be asked, "Is it possible to discard these admonitions, and if so, how does this discarding take place?

Fargnoli's mention of lullabies as an intergenerational link provides other fruitful activities. The therapist can invite clients to share the "lullabies" they recall and even create a lullaby or song of comfort they wish they had heard from their parents or perhaps would like to sing to their children.

4. "Those Winter Sundays" by Robert Hayden

An adult speaker recalls his father's generous acts, which he never noticed or acknowledged as a child. With its powerful alliterative thermal images of "blueblack cold" and "banked fires" that "blaze," this poem recreates the ambience of the speaker's childhood household and his father's painful working class life. The poem begins with the words, "Sundays too my father got up early" which immediately tells us that even on his day of rest, this father warmed the house before others awakened, in spite of his "cracked hands that ached / from labor in the weekday weather." The latter lines provide a powerfully concise metaphor for a whole lifetime of backbreaking labor, which this son now realizes he took for granted. He recalls "Speaking indifferently" to his father, a fact he now regrets. The short statement that bluntly and emphatically closes the first stanza amplifies the speaker's regret: "No one ever thanked him." The entire poem also concludes with a straightforward question highlighting the regretful tone with its repetition of key words: "What did I know, what did I know / of love's austere and lonely offices?"

Despite the comfort of a warmed house in the second stanza, the image of the cold "splintering" and "breaking" reflects the persona's memory of awakening with fear caused by "the chronic angers of the house." Given the suggestions of this phrase, Hayden's poem is an appropriate selection for clients who come from abusive backgrounds or dysfunctional families, and can be useful for adult males or females attempting to introduce more balance into their negative view of parents or trying to resolve grief over parents' shortcomings. I can also envision its potential use in family counseling sessions involving adult children or teenagers and their parents.

Suggestions for Discussion and Writing Experiences:

The poem's final, regret-filled question is quite likely to evoke reader response. It invites us to answer the question of what are the "austere" or indirect ways people close to us show their love? It invites us to be more receptive to those "lonely offices of love," those tasks performed for us that escape our notice, those caring gestures that elude us, especially when we are angry. This work also stimulates readers to discuss the question of how anger as well as fear may blind us to the positive side of others.

Hayden's poem invites a variety of writing exercises. Since it reads like a vignette of the past, clients can be asked to write their own short memory poem of "Sunday morning" or more pertinently, their memory poem focusing on a kind act of the particular parent for whom they feel the most resentment. In a family therapy setting, family members can be invited to use the frame, "When I do _____ for you, I am showing I love you," or can be invited to compose a list poem directly addressed to one another, beginning with the words, "I want to thank you for . . ." Even an adult child whose parent is no longer alive can complete this "thank you" list as a tribute or create an "In Memorium" poem.

If adult children are at the stage where their anger or fear is still raw, they can be invited to designate Hayden's line "fearing the chronic angers of that house" as the opener for their own poem. These words are likely to conjure up for some readers a host of sensory memories that can function as a catalyst for sharing the chaos and pain that surrounded them in the past. Asking individuals from abusive backgrounds how they dealt with the "chronic angers" they faced or how they managed to find "safe places" can highlight client's courage and resiliency and increase awareness of current coping strategies that help or hinder clients in their present lives.

As facilitators stimulate discussion and provide activities in conjunction with this poem, it is important not to leave clients in a place of unresolved rage or deep regret. As clients relate and react to the poem's imagery and emotional tone, the facilitator needs to find ways to encourage forward movement and provide opportunities to help heal past wounds.

5. "I Knew This Kid" by James Kavanaugh

In the first stanza of this poem, the first person narrator, using painful visceral imagery, recounts the story of a kid he knew who tried "to prove his courage" and live up to his macho father's expectations. He grew up "Proving he was brave enough to be loved" as he suffered the agony of a hurting tailbone and stumbled in oversized shoes on the tackle football field. Our sympathies are immediately drawn to this vulnerable child craving a parent's love, "holding his breath / And closing his eyes / And throwing a block into a guy twice his size."

The two-stanza format works very well in this poem, since both stanzas begin with the line "I knew this skinny little kid," a repetition that emphasizes the child's fragility. While the first stanza introduces the child performing unnatural feats to please his father, the second stanza develops, in a soothing sensory way, the nature-loving habits of this little boy. After telling us that the child is drawn to "cattails and pussy willows," "muskrats and gawking herons," the kindly narrator raises the most important question of the poem in the closing lines: "And I wonder what he would have been / If someone had loved him for / Just following the fawns and building waterfalls . . . / I wonder what he would have been / If he hadn't played tackle football at all."

Although the images are very specific and the main character in this poem seems to be a particular child the narrator has known, the situation depicted is universal and one that therapists encounter repeatedly in their offices. The narrator's softly reflective tone encourages the reader to respond reflectively as well. The closing wistful question taps into a deep desire for unconditional love and can be the vehicle for a process whereby clients begin to voice this desire, actively grieve and, perhaps, even eventually accept the limitations of their parents.

This poem can also be quite therapeutic for young adult/late adolescent clients who have lost sight of what feels right for them on a personal level, because they have spent so much time and energy trying to mold themselves into what their parents want them to be. Differentiating what we do for ourselves and what we do to please or not disappoint significant others is an essential aspect of development for young adults and continues to be a challenge for many in their more mature years as well. This poem is also particularly useful for parents who are stubbornly promoting their own agenda with their children, forgetting to affirm their children's uniqueness in their desire to ensure their success or happiness.

Suggestions for Discussion and Writing Experiences:

Clients resonating with the "kid's" experience in Kavanaugh's poem can write their own two-part work, the first, naming things they have done to please others and the second, voicing their inherent talents and tastes, their natural bent.

The facilitator may draw attention to the lack of self-nurturing that is evident in the "kid's" behavior. Clients can be asked what they do for themselves that feels really good and caring. They may also be asked to write a letter of advice or encouragement to the "kid" in this poem. What would they want to say? What would they want to do for this "kid"? Through focusing on this fictional character, clients can imagine healthy solutions for themselves.

In discussions of this poem, the poetry therapy facilitator can also invite clients to actually answer the speaker's closing question—to imagine what this boy would have been, if his natural tendencies had been encouraged. Using the speaker's words, "if someone had loved him," the poetry therapist can ask clients if there was "someone" other than a parent who was present to guide them in a way that took their needs into account.

To humanize the very imperfect "daddy" in this poem, the poetry therapist might ask clients to imagine what the father would be thinking and feeling if he knew that his son's tailbone was hurt and that he was stumbling in misery. Clients may also be invited to imagine what their own father's parents were like and what their fathers did to please these parents. Questions like these open the door to acceptance and forgiveness.

6. "I Wanted to Be a Cauliflower" by Gladys Wellington

Like Kavanaugh's "I Knew This Kid," Wellington's poem focuses on a child's molding of self to fit what she thinks her parent wants. In this case, the daughter, now a woman, tells us how she tried to resemble her "bland" mother when she was a child so her mother would "love" her. She denied her personality in becoming like the "cauliflower" without the "hollandaise" that reflected her mother's temperament. Yet, her efforts backfired, since her "sister who led a pastrami life" was the center of the mother's attention.

Continuing with food metaphors in the second stanza, the daughter-speaker tells us that with the passage of years, her sister's "pastrami's turned green" and she has "found a bit / of sauce" for herself. These lines introduce hope and joy into the poem, suggesting to readers that the "good" conforming child can come into her own, that in fact we all have the potential to realize our true selves more fully as we mature. The humor of the poem's last lines also provides relief for many readers, for here we are told that the formerly lifeless "cauliflower" daughter can even "offer" her mother "hot chili peppers" when she "comes to visit." The ambiguity of this last image opens the door for multiple interpretations and reactions. The daughter here could be expressing some anger over past experiences, may be working to open her mother's eyes, may wish to show her zesty personality, or may be trying to add "spice" to her mom's colorless life.

Besides its focus on the speaker's relationship with her mother, Wellington's poem creatively deals with the theme of sibling rivalry. It metaphorically raises the issues of a parent's favoritism and the behaviors of children that capture a parent's attention. Since the poem deals with at least two time frames, it also introduces the notion that parents' relationships with and view of their children can and often does change over time.

"I wanted to be a cauliflower" is a poem I have used repeatedly in a variety of settings—in mother-daughter developmental growth groups for women of varying ages, in therapist growth and training groups, in women's psychotherapy groups, in seminars on parenting, and in courses on the mother-daughter relationship. I have found that everyone relates enthusiastically to the food images here and is easily enticed into creative expressions involving her or his own food choices.

Suggestions for Discussion and Writing Experiences:

The poem's opening set of lines, "I wanted to be a cauliflower / when I was a child / so my mother would love me," provides material for a provocative writing exercise. Clients or group members can be asked to use the structure of these lines, substituting their parent's favorite food for "cauliflower" and then allowing themselves to free-associate on what comes to mind regarding this food and their relationship with their parent. I have found that this exercise always yields important insights for the writer.

Often, I have introduced a more open creative writing possibility in conjunction with the discussion of this poem. It involves choosing a favorite or most distasteful food and working either with the frame, "I wanted [or want] to be a [favorite food]" or "I didn't [or wouldn't] want to be a [least favorite food]." Clients are encouraged to develop their words beyond this initial line, using the sensory features of the particular food choices they make. Not only do respondents have a good time with this activity, but they have the opportunity to voice desires and resistance, to name ways they are unique human beings distinguished from their family members. In working with women's groups focusing on the mother-daughter connection, I have invited participants to write a two-part poem, in which stanza one begins with the words, "I am [my favorite food] and stanza two begins with the words, "But my mother is [her favorite food]." While the structure of this poem encourages the writer to differentiate self from mother, changing the "But" to an "And" at the beginning of stanza two encourages the writer to identify similarities between self and mother. The choice to use one or the other or both frames will depend on the goals and particular issues of the participants.

The two-part shape of Wellington's poem, separating past and present, provides another key to a poetry writing activity. Clients can be asked to write their own two-stanza poem, choosing two foods in order to metaphorically capture the way they used to be and the way they are now with a particular parent or family member.

The multiple possibilities inherent in the speaker's "offer" of "hot chili peppers" at the end of the poem are bound to generate a variety of personal responses that can be juxtaposed for a therapeutic effect. Clients may be asked to write their own short poem using the opening line, "now when my [parent] comes to visit, I offer her [or him] _____." The word "offer" opens up possibilities for an in-depth discussion of what children of all ages offer their parents, and what motivates these offerings.

Addressing the sibling issue, the poetry therapy facilitator can encourage a discussion of who is the "cauliflower" and who is the "pastrami" sibling in your family? Clients can be asked to identify a food that fits the personality or role of each sibling and to discuss the changes that have occurred over the years. Clients may also be asked what specific behaviors received positive and negative parental attention when they were growing up in a household with their siblings. Clients who have no siblings can be encouraged to explore their parents' reactions to cousins or close friends who spent so much time in their home that they may have been almost like a sister or brother.

ANNOTATED BIBLIOGRAPHY OF POEMS
ON THE PARENT-CHILD CONNECTON

Bond, Alec. "Flower Girl." *Poems for an Only Daughter*. Peoria, Illinois: Spoon River Poetry Press. (P.O. Box 1443, Peoria, Illinois 61655.)
   A father, getting ready to photograph his young daughter in the role of flower girl, likens her to "a young Persephone" on this autumn day. His image sets the somber tone for the grief he anticipates when she will

become the bride, "the sad-eyed girl in the basement" and he the anxious parent "waiting" with her "for the groom." He sees his daughter as "part of a ceremony" she does "not understand" but whose "power" she feels. The allusion to the Demeter-Persephone-Hades myth intensifies and universalizes this parent's sense of loss, for the ancient story involves the underworld god's abduction of an innocent daughter of the earth. Since it is a myth embodying both grief and the inevitable cycle of death and rebirth, the father's reference to Persephone suggests a complex blend of despair and hope. This poem is an apt catalyst for a discussion of losses that parents and children face in the course of various developmental phases.

Brooks, Gwendolyn. "Life for My Child Is Simple and Is Good." *Selected Poems*. Perennial Classics. NewYork: Harper & Row, 1999. Also in *The Conscious Reader*. Eds. Caroline Shrodes, Harry Finestone & Michael Shugrue. Third Edition. New York: Collier Macmillan, 1985.

A parent describes her/his son who "knows his wish" and enjoys mischievous, often dangerous, adventures. While the parent shares the son's zest for life, its "joy of undeep and unabiding things," she/he emphasizes the child's belief in his infallibility and his complete lack of fear in reaching for what he wants, perhaps suggesting the difference between this parent and child. The parent's ambivalent mixture of admiration and worry is evoked by the last two lines, "His lesions are legion. / But reaching is his rule." This poem is likely to elicit discussion on how parents can protect children while also encouraging them to be risk-takers.

Brooks, Gwendolyn. "a song in the front yard." *The World of Gwendolyn Brooks*. New York: Harper & Row, 1963 and 1999. Also in *I Am the Darker Brother; An Anthology of Modern Poems by Negro Americans*. Ed. Arnold Adoff. New York: Macmillan, 1968; *The New Oxford Book of American Verse*. Ed. Richard Ellmann. NewYork: Oxford Univ. Press, 1976; *The Norton Anthology of Modern Poetry*. Eds. Richard Ellmann & Robert O'Clair. Second Edition. New York: W.W. Norton, 1988; and *The Poetry of Black America: Anthology of the 20th Century*. Ed. Arnold Adoff. New York: Harper & Row, 1973.

The feisty adolescent daughter-speaker of this poem contrasts the "front yard" world where her mother wishes her to stay safe, proper, and innocent; with the "back yard" world where "wonderful fun," sexual awakening, and mischief abound. She boldly states that she "want[s] to go in the back yard now" and "have a good time today." The daughter's attempt to differentiate herself from her mother is apparent when she voices her desire to imitate a girl whom her mother tells her "Will grow up to be a bad woman." The poem's speaker asserts her desire to "wear the brave stockings of night-black lace" in spite of her mother's "sneers." This poem provides an entertaining stimulus for a serious discussion of issues related to sexuality, sex education, parental authority, and role models.

Bruce, Debra. "Father, Son, Grandson." *Passages North.* Vol. 1, No. 2. Spring/Summer, 1986. (William Bonifas Fine Arts Center, Escanaba, Michigan 49829.)

An adult son addresses himself throughout this poem in a distant sort of way, using an unusual "you" pronoun point of view. Beginning with the line, "Your father tosses your baby toward the sun," the male speaker in the middle generation juxtaposes his present visit to his father's home with his early painful memories of growing up. The mature son watches intently as his once abusive, "red-faced" father gently bonds with his baby grandson and lovingly care-takes his garden. The father's hands that "used to twitch toward his belt" are now "stroking the round rich shapes" growing in his garden. As the adult son looks on, aware he is between aging and youthfulness himself, he feels isolated from his child and his father. Yet, while he bitterly recalls his past angry father, he does ask himself the somewhat hopeful question, "Who is this man who takes the time / to touch inside a flower?" This poem suggests that change is possible, while also raising the question of how one can grapple with painful memories and negotiate a new relationship with once hurtful parents.

Bursk, Christopher. "Don't Worry." *Poetry Magazine.* October, 1994. (Modern Poetry Association, 60 West Walton Street, Chicago, Illinois 60610)

A worried father addresses himself as if he were a third person. He sits awaiting the return of a son who has left in anger and is driving in the night. The hours weigh heavy as the father imagines disaster—"wet roads" and his "son's foot heavy on the pedal." He accepts his human need to agonize over what has happened between him and his son, differentiating himself from the trees, plants, and starlight in his world, which do not share his struggles as a human being. One can assume that father and son have disagreed over an issue related to independence because the parent-speaker asks "Does the tree argue with itself / over whether it is giving its leaves too much / or too little independence?" This is a poem about letting go and staying connected, as evidenced in the final image of the wind "acting as if it could / shake loose / the grip of the old maple" on its leaves and branches.

Dunn, Stephen. "Climbing Ladders Anyway." *Poetry Northwest*. Vol. XXIII, No. 3. Autumn, 1982. (University of Washington, 4045 Brooklyn Ave. N.E., JA-15, Seattle, Washington 98105). Also in Dunn's *Not Dancing*. Pittsburgh: Carnegie-Mellon University Press, 1984.

As the title suggests, the adult child of this poem employs ladder imagery in his recollections of his dad. He remembers holding, with trepidation, a wooden ladder with a missing rung that his father climbed in order to complete a necessary household task. This experience becomes for him the prototype of a lesson about the necessity of going "beyond" where he feels "good about going." From his father, he "learned / to be afraid of ladders and to climb them / anyway." Following his dad's example and acutely aware of the continuity between the generations, this son, now a parent, climbs a ladder of his own, with his children watching and probably learning a lesson about courage and determination that they will carry into their future.

Fainlight, Ruth. "Handbag." *100 Poems on the Underground*. Eds. Gerald Benson, Judith Cherniak & Cicely Herbert. Cassell, 1991.

The sensory exploration of a mother's "old leather handbag," smelling sweetly of mints and make-up and "crowded with letters . . . carried / all through the war," evoke, for the poem's speaker, vivid memories and definitions of womanliness, love, and grief. The handbag, blending everyday feminine "necessities" with a unique set of "worn" letters from a soldier-husband, take on symbolic meaning for the adult child. This poem is ideal for stimulating writing exercises involving one's memory of a parent or a special, meaning-laden object.

Fairchild, B.H., Jr. "Work." *Poets On: Generations*. Vol. 4, No. 2. Summer, 1980. (Department of English, 5500 University Parkway, San Bernardino, California 92407-2397.)

In a striking way, this poem links the very different occupations of father and son with cognate images. The adult son here conjures up early memories of his father cutting iron with a steel bit while his "jaw set tight to metal screams" and he stood "knee-deep in curls of hot blue shavings." Although this son intently watched his dad work, he grew up "wanting words instead." When he saw his father's job eliminated because of changing economic conditions, he responded to an inner voice that told him to "let words be steel . . . cut into an empty page" to "scream against the silences of time." This poem is likely to stimulate discussion on how parents' type of work and work habits affect their children's lives. On a more universal level, Fairchild's words can be very useful in helping parents and their sons and daughters explore the ways in which ostensible differences between them, in fact, often reflect underlying similarities.

Fargnoli, Patricia. "Going." *Necessary Light*. Logan, Utah: Utah State University Press, 1999. Also in *Poet Lore*. Vol. 78. No. 4. Winter, 1984.

Using everyday metaphors very effectively and addressing parents with the word "you," this poem graphically and concisely conveys the process of letting go, as young people mature and leave home. For example, the "children" are described as "walk[ing] off into crowds of strangers" and "wav[ing] to you from platforms you cannot reach." However, while the poem delineates what is lost when sons or daughters reject parents' gifts and dreams, it also shows that much remains— in the form of parental "admonitions" carried in children's "pockets" and in the "lullabies" that live on.

Note: See detailed analysis earlier in the chapter.

Note: See copy of this poem at the end of the chapter.

Freeman, Grace Beacham. "Family Treasure." *No Costumes or Masks*. Rock Hill, South Carolina: Red Clay Books, 1975, 1981. (Box 3405 CRS, Rock Hill, South Carolina 29730).

An adult child reflects on her quiet father, "a generous listener" and a "miser with words." She thinks of the few precious words and "sayings" he chose to voice during the ten years he lived in their household, comparing these to "rare coins" that, "rubbed to a shine / on memory's shirtsleeve," have become increasingly valuable as time has passed. This poem can act as a catalyst for reflections on the legacy of family expressions and for discussions on the advantages and disadvantages of silence in the context of parent-child relationships.

Gibran, Kahlil. "On Children." *The Prophet* (1923). New York: Alfred A. Knopf, 2000.

A voice of wisdom addresses parents telling them to shed their possessiveness in relation to their offspring and accept their children's uniqueness along with the inevitable displacement of the old generation with the new. Parents are reassured that a divine being or spiritual force honors equally the parents' role as stable foundation and the child's role as the harbinger of the future.

Note: See detailed analysis earlier in the chapter.

Goedicke, Patricia. "Circus Song." *Tangled Vines: Poems to Celebrate and Explore the Relationships Between Mother and Daughter.* Ed. Lyn Lifshin. San Diego: Harvest/Harcourt Brace Jovanovich, 1992. Also in *Tangled Vines,* First Edition, Boston: Beacon Press, 1978.

Addressing her daughter directly, the mother-speaker in this poem captures through a dynamic, paradoxical combination of wild animal and domestic bread-baking imagery, the ambivalence of the adolescent who needs to fight her parent to become her own person but also still needs security and feels guilt for her attacks. Through her wise words, the parent suggests a model of positive parenting while still acknowledging the pain and challenge involved in parenting.

Note: See detailed analysis earlier in the chapter.

Hayden, Robert. "Those Winter Sundays." *Angles of Ascent: New and Selected Poems.* New York: Liveright, 1975. Also in *The Rag and Bone Shop of the Heart: A Poetry Anthology.* Eds. Robert Bly, James Hillman & Michael Meade. New York: HarperCollins, 1992/Harper Perennial, 1993; *The Top 500 Poems.* Ed. William Harmon. New York: Columbia University Press, 1992; and *The Vintage Book of African American Poetry.* Eds. Michael Harper & Anthony Walton. New York: Vintage/Random House, 2000.

With its strong sensory images, this poem highlights the indirect ways a seemingly cold father can show love or caring. The adult speaker recalls his father's efforts to warm their home, feeling a gratitude he wasn't able to experience when, as a child, he feared "the chronic angers" of his house and spoke "indifferently" to his hard working, austere parent.

Note: See detailed analysis earlier in the chapter.

215

Hughes, Langston. "Mother to Son." *Selected Poems by Hughes*. New York: Alfred A. Knopf, Inc., 1926, 1954. Also in *The Vintage Book of African American Poetry*. Eds. Michael Harper & Anthony Walton. New York: Vintage/Random House, 2000.

Using an earnest conversational tone established with the opening line, "Well, son, I'll tell you," the mother-speaker of this poem passes along her wisdom. Through a stairway image that permeates the poem, she tells her son that in spite of her life of hardships with its "splinters" and "boards torn up," she never stops "climbin' on, / And reachin' landin's, / And turnin' corners," even when all is "dark." She beseeches her son to follow her model of determination, so that he too will survive in a life that is "no crystal stair." In response to this poem, readers of all ages may find themselves evaluating the tone and nature of this mother's advice. Parent-readers are likely to reflect on how they prepare their children for adversity or communicate the value of perseverance. In conjunction with this poem, parents can be asked to write their own "Parent to Child" advice poem as a way to heighten awareness of their expectations and values in relation to their daughters and sons.

Kavanaugh, James. "I Knew This Kid." 1971. *Will You Be My Friend*. Nevada City, California: Argonaut Publishing, 1984. (P.O. Box 189, Nevada City, California 95959-0189)

A third-person narrator tells of a child who tried to live up to his macho father's expectations and suffered the pain and humiliation of going against the grain of his inherently gentle nature. The sympathetic speaker raises the haunting and universal question of what the child would be like if he had not been pressured and had been encouraged to follow his unique tastes and inclinations.

Note: See detailed analysis earlier in the chapter.

Kerr, Kathryn. "Wolves." *First Frost*. Illinois: Stromline Press, 1985.

Interweaving the wolf image throughout this poem, the daughter-persona focuses on what her mother provided, but more on what her mother did not give her. She says, "That mother of mine / gave just enough milk / to keep me alive / and hungry." Likened to a she-wolf, the mother ensured and taught survival but left her daughter ravenously hungry for nurturing, self-expression, and the assurance of safety. In response to the mother's message, "Don't cry," the daughter's "caged cries, like wolves" are "never tamed" and continue to "leap at [her] throat" and "gnaw at [her] stomach." Individuals who have been taught not to cry are likely to resonate to this poem's powerful depiction of emotional hunger.

Knight, Etheridge. "A Watts Mother Mourns While Boiling Beans." *Born of a Woman*. San Francisco: Harper & Row, 1992.

A mother, never "free from fright" since her child's birth, imagines the dangers awaiting her restless, hot-blooded son out late on the ghetto streets. After expressing the desire that this "blooming flower of [her] life" come home, she forces herself to attend to the everyday chores facing her, for her "husband is coming / and the beans are burning." Relentless internal pain and external drudgery characterize this portrait of a parent sorely in need of nurturing. This poem can help foster awareness of the fear and pain parents endure when they are compelled to raise children in dangerous environments. It also can function as a springboard for discussing how burdened mothers/housewives who focus on others' needs and wellbeing all the time can begin to find sources of much-needed support for themselves.

Kunitz, Stanley. "The Portrait." *The Poems of Stanley Kunitz 1928-1978*. Boston: Little, Brown, 1979. (Originally in *The Testing Tree*. Boston: Little Brown, 1971). Also in *First Light: Mother and Son Poems*. Ed. Jason Shinder. Harcourt Brace Jovanovich, 1992; *In the Midst of Winter: Selections from the Literature of Mourning*. Ed. Mary Jane Moffat. Vintage Books, 1992; *Poetspeak, in Their Work, about Their Work*. Ed. Paul Janeczko. New York: Macmillan, 1991; and *The Rag and Bone Shop of the Heart: A Poetry Anthology*. Eds. Robert Bly, James Hillman & Michael Meade. New York: HarperCollins, 1992/Harper Perennial, 1993.

With its startling first line, "My mother never forgave my father for killing himself," this poem conveys the memory of an adult son who is now sixty-four years old. He vividly recalls how his mother reacted when he found a portrait of the father who had killed himself before his son was even born. While the "pastel portrait" eloquently introduces a father who is a "long-lipped stranger / with a brave mustache / and deep brown level eyes," his mother angrily "rip[s]" the painting "into shreds," utters not a single word, and slaps her son "hard." While the mom "locked" the father's "name / in her deepest cabinet," her son, nevertheless, "could hear him thumping," and the mother's slap echoes through a lifetime, with the aging son feeling his "cheek still burning." This poem powerfully drives home an important truth that family ghosts or secrets as well as non-verbal messages have a profound, long-lasting effect on family members' functioning and can be essential for understanding a family's dynamics. It also shows the power of the mother's anger for the son and the duration of shaming and blaming events in one's life. In addition, this poem is likely to evoke discussion of the ways in which parents and children handle their grief over suicide in the family.

Lee, Li-Young. "A Story." *The City in Which I Love You.* Brockport, New York: BOA Editions Ltd., 1990 (92 Park Avenue, Brockport, New York 14420). Also in *The Rag and Bone Shop of the Heart.* Eds. Robert Bly, James Hillman & Michael Meade. New York: HarperCollins, 1992/Harper Perennial, 1993.

    The speaker recounts the tale of a father who has trouble generating new stories to tell his five-year-old son and anticipates a time when the disappointed boy will "give up on his father" and leave his house. The father's desire to be special to his son renders him mute when the son begs for a new story. "In a room full of books in a world / of stories, he can recall / not one." Parents who want to be perfect and fear falling off the pedestal as their children grow up will resonate to this poem, as will parents who want to be accepted as they are, with their "old" stories, in the face of their children's somewhat unrealistic demands.

Levertov, Denise. "Mid-American Tragedy." *Claiming the Spirit Within. A Sourcebook of Women's Poetry.* Ed. Marilyn Sewell. Boston: Beacon Press, 1996.

    This is a poignant poem told in third person about parents whose gay son is dying, possibly from AIDS. It contrasts the mother and father's image of themselves as the perfect traditional parents of the eight-year-old boy of their memories, with their present lack of real connection to their adult son who struggles for breathe "as Jingle Bells / pervades the air." The parents "chatter" but "won't listen," pride themselves on accepting their son, but "never give him / the healing silence" in which they can learn who he really is. This poem can act as a wake-up call for parents of children who are ill or dying or who have chosen life styles very different from those of their parents. It is a work that shows how parents' idealized expectations of themselves can diminish their openness to what their child truly needs.

Madgett, Naomi Long. "Offspring." *Pink Ladies of the Afternoon* (1972). Also in *Cries of the Spirit: a Celebration of Women's Spiritualities*. Ed. Marilyn Sewell. Boston: Beacon Press, 1991; *The Garden Thrives: Twentieth-Century African-American Poetry*. Ed. Clarence Major. New York: HarperCollins, 1996; *The Forerunners: Black Poets in America*. Ed. Woodie King. Washington, D.C.: Howard University Press, 1975; and *Sound and Sense: an Introduction to Poetry*. Eds. Laurence Perrine & Thomas Arp. Eighth Edition. New York: Harcourt Brace Jovanovich, 1992.

Using primarily a tree image, this poem is divided into two stanzas that highlight the contrast between the advice a parent wanted to give her child and the decisions made by that child. The parent, the "I" of the poem, wanted her offspring to grow in ways that maintained intergenerational continuity, but the child chose her own pattern outside the range of the parent's expectation, outside the "far atmosphere" that "Only my dreams allow." Instead of a "twig" that is "bent" in the "way" the parent advises, born of the parent's "trunk" and "strengthened" by the parent's "roots," this child has become a "very individual" and "unpliable" being who walks down "an unfamiliar street." In spite of the persona's disappointment and fears, she or he does acknowledge the offspring's "feet confident" and "smiling" face. This poem is particularly useful for family and individual therapy as well, for parents and children struggling with a variety of individuation issues related to career and life style choices.

McGinley, Phyllis. "Girl's-Eye View of Relatives (First Lesson)." *Times Three: Selected Verse from Three Decades*. Foreword by W.H. Auden. New York: Viking Press, 1960.

As the title suggests, the speaker of this poem is a daughter. In a wry tone, she speaks in universal terms of the way fathers worry about their female offspring and resist their passage to womanhood. She humorously points out that "fathers" are "dragon-seekers, bent on improbable rescues" and believe "change is a threat." She catalogues the specific fears fathers often have, from physical accidents to "books," "snakes," and "angular boys," but asserts that daughters must take their journey to adulthood in spite of

219

these paternal anxieties. The subtitle, "First Lesson" reflects the speaker's desire to convey a message fathers "must learn" about their daughters— that "you have a journey to take and very likely, / For a while, will not return." This conclusion suggests that growing up does involve independent experiences but not permanent separation.

Meinke, Peter. "This is a poem to my son Peter." *The Night Train and the Golden Bird*. Pittsburg, Pennsylvania: University of Pittsburgh Press, 1977. Also in *The Pittsburgh Book of Contemporary American Poetry*. Eds. Ed Ochester & Peter Oresick. Pittsburgh: University of Pittsburgh Press, 1993.
Through strong kinesthetic and visual images of his ten-year-old son's vulnerability, a father voices deep regrets at hurting his male child and diminishing his self-confidence because of his own "weakness / and impatience." In his memory, he sees his son's "large" eyes "glazed in pain," his "pale freckled back / bent in defeat," and his "thin wrists and fingers hung / boneless in despair." Recognizing he erroneously assumed his son knew his own worth, this father now realizes children need to be affirmed repeatedly in order to flourish.

Pastan, Linda. "Aubade." *Tangled Vines: Poems to Celebrate and Explore the Relationship Between Mothers and Daughters*. Ed. Lyn Lifshin. San Diego: Harvest/Harcourt Brace Jovanovich, 1992. Also in *Tangled Vines*. First Edition. Boston: Beacon, 1978.
As its title suggests, this tranquil poem recounts a morning scene. At the breakfast table, the parent experiences the growing distance between her adolescent daughter and herself, providing a poignant image in the phrase, "a heart drifts out of reach / on the surface / of the milk." Yet the poem concludes on a hopeful note suggesting possibilities for a new kind of connection and the experience of joy, when the daughter, taking "the day into her hand / like fresh baked bread," offers the parent a piece. Thus, she offers a "piece" of her life but not ownership of it. The ending suggests that parents of adolescents and adult children are wise when they remain open to their child's invitations to renewed closeness. This poem reflects the satisfaction that parents can feel if they let their child go, allowing them space to discover their own modes of re-connecting.

"The Right Set of Fears."Author and source unknown
Addressing her mother in a monologue, a daughter recounts the advice she received in order to help insure her safe, successful passage through

life. The fears mother passed along as a legacy are embodied in the words: "don't walk alone at night; / don't quit, or settle for defeat; / don't marry the romantic for his brief delights." While the daughter thanks her mother, she asserts that no one can be saved from "strife" and that she needs to resist her present "vision" which "still is checked by fear." As the poem concludes, the daughter rejects her mother's lack of risk-taking, her practical advice that focuses on "old age, and heat in winter." Also, it is clear that the daughter does not want to repeat the pattern of her mother's lifeless existence epitomized by "the laundry and the kitchen" and "a wandering husband." The phrase, "the right set of fears," invites readers to generate their own list and to speculate on what could be considered "the wrong set of fears."

Pastan, Linda. "To a Daughter Leaving Home." *A Fraction of Darkness*. New York: W.W. Norton & Co., 1985.

In recalling how she taught her daughter to ride a bicycle, the mother in this poem focuses on her "surprise" when her daughter "pulled / ahead down the curved / path of the park" and coasted speedily away without falling. This early experience becomes the prototype for the young adult daughter's present leave-taking, and the memory of the daughter "screaming / with laughter" with her "hair flapping / behind [her] like a / handkerchief waving / goodbye" becomes a necessary step in the mother's grieving process. This poem is an ideal choice for parents entering the "empty nest" phase of their lives and can act as a catalyst for their own memories of their children's early acts of independent assertion. The poignant handkerchief image in the last lines can be used to introduce the topic of how parents say goodbye to children leaving home and how they face and fill the emptiness left behind.

Pickard, Deanna Louise. "Not Letting Go." *Passages North*. Vol 7, No. 2 (Spring/Summer, 1986). (William Bonifas Fine Arts Center, Escanaba, Michigan 49829)

With its dream-like quality and ocean imagery, this poem intimately captures the experience of a mother who perceives her "gypsy" son at a stage between childhood and manhood. While aware of his growth because "His voice sounds stilted" and "His milk mustache has darkened," she still feels her breasts "aching with mother's milk," thus suggesting her difficulty in relinquishing the primacy of her role in his life.

This poem conveys and helps normalize the often unacknowledged presence of pain and grief that parents feel when a child matures. It can help readers recognize that losing a central role in their lives can at times feel almost as painful as the death of a loved one.

Plath, Sylvia. "Child." *The Collected Poems of Sylvia Plath.* Ed. Ted Hughes. New York: Harper & Row, 1960.
A parent perceives the "clear" and "absolutely beautiful" eye of her newborn baby as a pool where only positive images ought to be reflected, images like "color and ducks, / The zoo of the new." She expresses her wish that joy, not the pain she knows, will be her child's portion and believes her baby, perfect in its innocence like a "Stalk without wrinkle," should never have to experience life's "troublous / Wringing of hands" or "dark / Ceiling without a star." This wistful poem vividly captures a universal desire of parents.

Roethke, Theodore. "My Papa's Waltz." *The Collected Poems of Theodore Roethke.* New York: Anchor Books/Random House, Inc., 1991. Also in *The Rag and Bone Shop of the Heart: A Poetry Anthology.* Eds. Robert Bly, James Hillman & Michael Meade. New York: HarperCollins, 1992/Harper Perennial, 1993; and *The Top 500 Poems.* Ed. William Harmon. New York: Columbia University Press, 1992.
In this powerfully ambiguous poem with its carefully constructed four quatrain stanzas, a son directly addresses the father of his memory, recalling the drunk man's attentions to him. The images of a small boy being rapidly waltzed by a whiskey-breathing father are largely violent, yet there is a suggestion of the child's tender attachment to the male parent who frightens him and makes his mother frown. While the son gets "dizzy" from the whirling and finds "Such waltzing was not easy," he, nevertheless, remembers being danced to bed, "Still clinging to [his father's] shirt." Individuals with alcoholic parents will find this poem to be a fruitful source of discussion on parental abuse, neglect, and indirect expressions of affection. Through this poem, alcoholic and/or abusive parents have an opportunity to experience the child's sense of fear, helplessness, and yearning.

Walker, Alice. "Forgiveness." *Good Night, Willie Lee, I'll See You in the Morning.* San Diego: Harcourt Brace Jovanovich, 1984. Also in *Her Blue*

Body Everything We Know: Earthling Poems 1965-1990 Complete. San Diego: Harcourt Brace & Co., 1993; and *Tangled Vines: Poems to Celebrate and Explore the Relationship Between Mothers and Daughters.* Ed. Lyn Lifshin. San Diego: Harvest/Harcourt Brace Jovanovich, 1992.

The "I" in this poem is a parent aware of a three-generation cycle of corporal punishment, yet unlike Meinke in the poem discussed earlier, Walker's persona focuses on forgiveness rather than guilt. When she physically punishes her daughter, she "becomes" her mother, yet when she sees in her daughter's visage, the reflection of her own former "sad / and grieving face," she forgives herself for the offenses she may have committed as a child and wishes she can continue to forgive herself. The parent's awareness of her own innocent child self and her ability to nurture self become vehicles whereby the cycle of abuse can be interrupted.

Walker, Alice. "Poem at Thirty-Nine." *Her Blue Body Everything We Know: Earthling Poems 1965-1990 Complete.* San Diego: Harvest/Harcourt Brace & Co., 1993. (Originally from *Horses Make a Landscape Look More Beautiful*)

At mid-life, the daughter-speaker of this poem grieves the loss of her father, beginning with the poignant, simple line, "How I miss my father," a line repeated in the center of the poem to augment its effect. The daughter thinks of her father whenever she balances her checkbook or cooks meals with a flourish. As she remembers him, she assesses what he taught her and the ways in which she resembles or differs from him. While she tried to "escape / the life he knew" and recognized she caused him some trouble as she was growing up, she clearly affirms what they shared and asserts that "he would have grown / to admire the woman" she has "become." This poem is likely to stimulate discussion of the legacies inherited from parents and explorations of who we are in relation to our parents' values and talents. It also is an excellent resource for exploring the process whereby children grieve the death of their parents.

Wellington, Gladys. "I wanted to be a cauliflower." *Contemporary Women Poets.* Ed. Jennifer McDowell. San Jose, California: Merlin Press, 1977. (P.O. Box 5602, San Jose, California 95150)

This poem focuses on a child's desire to attain love by imitating her mother and conforming to what she thinks her mother wants. Using the first person, the daughter, now an adult, recognizes that she has found her own style and can openly proclaim it in her mother's presence. With its entertaining food images that merge humor and poignancy, this poem also introduces the subject of sibling rivalry and the way in which the presence of a sister affects the mother-daughter relationship.

Note: See detailed analysis earlier in the chapter.

Note: See copy of this poem at the end of the chapter.

White, E.B. "Complicated Thoughts about a Small Son." *The Fox of Peapack and Other Poems*. New York: Harper & Row, 1932.

The parent persona openly projects his desire onto the image of his child and unabashedly admits the full extent of his expectations that the "small son" fulfill the adult's unrealized dreams. The opening of the poem conveys this theme of projection through the words, "In you, in you, I see myself, / Or what I like to think is me." The poem's speaker also celebrates his "little man" as his most miraculous achievement, as the "manuscript" the parent will "leave for death." Providing an interesting counterpoint to Gibran's work discussed earlier, White's poem highlights what is often a subtle yet profound process affecting parent-child interactions throughout a lifetime.

Winters, Ivor. "At the San Francisco Airport (To my daughter, 1954)." *Collected Poems by Winters*. Athens, Ohio: Ohio University Press, 1952; 1960.

A father faces the moment when his daughter leaves "the nest" to begin her work in the world. Using a powerful double entendre, the speaker begins with the words, "This is the terminal." The hard bright lights of the metallic airport world highlight the starkness of their separation. The speaker confronts his loss and stage in life in bald terms saying "I am past, and that is all," but qualifies his pain by reflecting on the traits and attitudes he and his daughter share. He accepts that his daughter is taking "the way" she "must take" and ends staring in white light, "awake." This final word invites us to ask what this parent is "awake" to and where he will or can go from here.

GOING

The children walk off into crowds of strangers,
their laces are tied, their backs straight.
They wave to you from platforms you cannot reach.
You want to hang on.
running after them,
you thrust out small packages:
vitamins,
a new blouse,
guilt.
But they keep discarding
your dreams for their own.
Still,
they carry your admonitions in their pockets
and their children will sing your lullabies,
so that, finally, knowing this,
you let go.
They blur, fade.
You settle back.
The years pass, silent as clouds.
Sundays, they come for dinner,
serve up slices of their lives,
but it's not the same.
Sometimes,
in a crowd,
you will catch a glimpse of long braids,
a ribbon streaming,
and you will remember
a head beneath your hand,
a quilt tucked in,
small things snapping on a line.

Patricia Fargnoli

Reprinted by permission of Patricia Fargnoli

I WANTED TO BE A CAULIFLOWER

I wanted to be a cauliflower
when I was a child
so my mother would love me.
I, too, was bland
like her favorite vegetable,
with no hollandaise
to give me verve,
but she looked past me
to my sister
who led a pastrami life
all over the world.

Years have passed,
the pastrami's turned green,
and I've found a bit
of sauce for myself,
so now when my mother
comes to visit,
I offer her hot chili peppers.

Gladys Wellington

Reprinted by permission of Merlin Press

REFLECTING ON COUPLES CONNECTIONS

Lisa Friedlander, MA, MSW, LICSW

THEMATIC OVERVIEW

NOWHERE BUT IN THE PROXIMITY of a significant relationship do the taut strings of ourselves get so much play—zinged, plucked, strummed, stroked to fine resonance, and sometimes snapped. In the context of salient relationship, people feel driven by two opposing impulses—the urge to tune oneself to another and create harmony, and the deep desire to sing one's own melody whether or not it pleases the other's ear or receives applause.

Living within the context of a couple, opportunities abound for closeness and distance. The dance that each does to regulate the proximity of one soul to another often requires subtle but fancy foot work. We recognize this dance, even as we stand on adult feet, because each of us as a child has done it with our mother, slipping from her lap across the kitchen, and hurling back to her arms a thousand times in our quest for independence and autonomy on one hand, and attachment on the other. Oh, to have and to hold. Oh, to let go, free-falling in what looks limitless and without demand.

The landmark event of individuation in our culture moves us to hear the call and leave home. To stake claim on our own turf, whether down the street or across the planet. Like a tricky Gestalt pattern, physical and psychic space can appear as foreground or background for us, emphasizing to what degree we require our boundaries defined. The imperative for adult couples involves learning new skills: how to grow oneself up, reconfigure the nest as needed, and how to do this without flying off.

Often in life, we find ourselves leaving, or we find ourselves coming home. And if all leavings have as their forebear that ultimate leave-taking, death, then in leaving our lovers we practice dying. In returning home to them, we buttress ourselves against death, we look into the eyes of someone whom we know well, who knows us in all our brilliant particularity, whose hands have taken our exact measure, who can tell our stories, who has put our photographs in his album, whose breathing has been our lullaby. In the

227

"we," an "I" can take refuge against all that it means to stand alone, unfused and unhitched.

In the daily practice of making themselves individuals, couples often jostle and nudge against each other, anger fueling the boundary-making process. Pushing against one another results in separateness coming into higher relief, though at the expense of harmony. One client, who constantly felt angry and hostile towards her husband and experienced a loss of sexual desire, told me she was tired of being "and-Susan." She had experienced her entire adult life "joined at the hip." She defined herself as the "and-Susan" part of "Rob-and-Susan." She saw no other way of experiencing just Susan than to take leave of her husband. And yet she feared leaving: what if Susan couldn't live up to all her promise? Worse, what if Susan failed to materialize after all? She had put so much of her self-creating energy into fighting her husband and withholding her affection from him that it seemed frightening to imagine channeling that energy into the unknown realm of creating, without a guidebook, a life with the kind of purpose and meaning about which she could feel proud.

The central struggle of couples in therapy often has to do with finding room to be an individual in close proximity to the other. Couples engage in this struggle by warring over who has power and control of the relationship, by fighting to have the last word, by punishing each other for being an "other" rather than a mirror of the self. A wife wants more respect and validation from her husband, while he wants more affection or sex or time to pursue his hobbies. She wants him to talk more or to listen better. He wants her to stop trying to change him. In the jostling and bumping and friction between the couple, each defines boundaries and blurs them all over again for the pleasure of merging. There is no stasis. There is only the constant atomic dance of attraction and repulsion, of coming together and moving apart, of communing and distinguishing, of singing a solo and blending voices in duet.

When I sit in a room with a couple, I hear many voices. There is her voice and his, or his and his, hers and hers. There are the voices of the four (or more) of their parents. I have my voice and the voice of my father and mother, of my teachers. The voice of the poet also comes into the room, and the voices of the poet's time and place. Each of us spills or whispers, or halting, pulls the poem from our own mouths and hearts. And where we wander, minstrels in search of a song, will surprise us. At times we find our voices easily and with volume, while at other times a voice may be muffled or even lost. Sometimes laughter fills the room, or silence, or fury. Amazement. Guilt. Forgiveness.

Paradoxically, the more each partner reveals about herself or himself, however controversial or conflicting, the more intimacy the couple experiences. Intimacy has to do with revelation and the toleration of the anxiety that often accompanies raw disclosure. Closeness does not always follow suit. Closeness often demands homogeneity, "be more like me," and maintaining the status quo. Closeness reduces anxiety. Intimacy has to do with the possibility of dancing awkwardly or eloquently next to a partner who may never have seen you dance that way before. By connection or identification with, or response to a poem, these profound revelations of desire, dreams, experiences, weaknesses, may more easily come to light. The power of the vehicles of metaphor, rhythm, and enchantment, the bedrock of poetry, serve to connect unconscious material and processes to conscious expression. By utilizing more aspects of self in the therapeutic encounter, primary process material as well as conscious thought, each member of a couple connects more fluidly to the other, and at a level of greater intimacy.

The poems in this chapter reflect a variety of approaches to connection and to love. Broadly categorized, they address four areas: love as saving grace; the resilience and mystery of connection; the I/we struggle between demands to distinguish the self, and to merge in relationship; and falling apart—whether disconnecting from a self-destructive relationship or dealing with the loss of a treasured one. Below are six poems that illustrate the clinical use of poetry for exploring, gaining insight, and healing in the context of working with couples.

In some of these poems, the reader will pick up, unconsciously if not consciously, the notion that the struggle is often about the self, the self as experienced in the context of relationship. The "other" in a couple often becomes the canvas on which one partner paints the aspects of his or her self that feel untenable. Almost paradoxically, poems also poignantly reveal that the personality or energy of the couple includes dimensions that arise from the space between the couple, the space in which their interactions and chemistry combust, blend, or catalyze. I have chosen at least one poem from each of the four broad categories mentioned above, with two sections having two poems each.

You may find some favorite poems from this group. It is often useful to limit yourself to a handful of poems that you bring to couples' therapy. Introducing these poems to different couples will allow you to assess the different possibilities and the kinds of discussion that ensue. With this kind of process it is easier to generate new exercises and to tweak the ones you have already initiated. You can fully learn a poem's possibilities for generating movement in your couples' relationships.

IN-DEPTH FOCUS ON POEMS IN A THERAPEUTIC CONTEXT

1. "At a Window" by Carl Sandburg

In "At a Window," the poet speaks directly to the gods, giving the piece an immediacy, a voice made almost audible while still on the page. The poem has an elemental, ancient feel, a direct supplication to higher powers to answer this most primal need—the need for "a little love." The poet is willing to strike a bargain with the gods that hover, the gods "that sit and give / The world its order." The poet asks for pain and want, for hunger, even for shame and failure, as long as he can "wait and know the coming / Of a little love." If I must receive the poison, he suggests, at least give me the antidote. The antidote may be just a small portion of love, thus emphasizing love's power to heal.

The poem, in the present tense and first person, speaks of the poet going to the window in the second of the two stanzas. The image of the poet inside a darkening room, and the gods in the larger changing world outside, capture his sense of loneliness and smallness within life's vast possibilities. He sees "One little wandering . . . star" which reinforces the image of a small but intense being as foreground to the darkening backdrop of shadows. Metaphors for love include a voice "to speak to me in the day end," and a hand that will offer touch "in a dark room."

Many times couples come into therapy with one or both partners feeling desperation—a need unfulfilled. Harville Hendricks suggests couples find each other, partly out of an unconscious desire to fulfill a need left over from struggles within their family of origin. Identifying that need and offering it up as something one partner might help the other achieve is one aspect of his approach. Murray Bowen would have suggested, or currently David Schnarch would suggest, that need-identification is helpful, but for the purpose of individuation, a person needs to learn to soothe herself and nurture her own fulfillment, rather than demand this fulfillment from a partner or project onto the partner selfishness or withholding attributes.

Suggestions for Discussion and Writing Experiences:

"At a Window" might be used in several ways to foster life partners in their understanding of what drives them. What does each seek in order to soothe a troubled brow or massage an aching heart?

1. Have each member of the couple read "At a Window" to the other. It is important to give voice to a poem, and for each person to invest his or her own emotional tone and emphasis into the poem. Ask each person to comment on the experience of asking for something so directly. Is that consistent with how they try to get what they need, or do they manipulate, hint at, repress or demand what they need? Ask each partner to tell the other how they experience being loved. Is it through touch? Is it felt when one does the other a favor? Listens well and carefully? Communicates love verbally? Ask each one to describe an experience of "the long loneliness," and relate a fantasy of how they might feel comforted by their partner, and how they might soothe themselves. Ask them if they agree that a "little love" provides their deepest source of life-giving energy during down times or whether they would see something else as more important.

2. Using the supplication format of "At a Window," ask each member of a couple to write his/her own entreaty to either the gods or to the other partner. Include in the supplication both what the person needs and what the person is willing to give (the bargain element of the Sandburg poem). After each person has written a piece, ask them each to read their poem to the other. Ask each partner to comment on how he/she felt in response to the other's poem. What did each learn about the longings of the other? Were there elements common to both or very different? How does each feel the longings of the other and their own longings contribute to their conflicts? Does either partner feel inspired to make some changes that respond to the other's expressed desires?

3. Ask each partner to choose one line in the poem as a starting point for his/her own writing. Perhaps it is "One little wandering, western star," or "Let me go to the window." By leaving the pen or pencil on the paper, just continue to write whatever wants to follow the line in the poem. Ask each person to read the poem aloud to the other and then to comment on the process of writing it and on the surprises or expectations that emerged. Ask the listener to share thoughts and feelings provoked while listening to

the other. Did each learn something new about the other? Did either find implications for him or herself in the work of the other? How does each poem relate to themes and dynamics in the relationship of which they are aware?

2. "For What Binds Us" by Jane Hirshfield

Whenever I ask a couple to tell me about what drew each to the other, they say things like, "He was funny and seemed like he would make a good father," or "She seemed enthusiastic, and she believed in me." Or, "I liked the way he looked, and he was smart and a hard worker," or "she stuck by me when I was going through some really hard times." People meet in college, on a job, at a bar, at the home of a friend. People are introduced or bang into each other in a grocery aisle. People are looking for a relationship or not looking for a relationship. People feel immediately comfortable with each other or grow on each other. One partner initially wants the relationship while the other does not, or they both "know" in an instant that "this is the one." A partner can seem "like all the other partners before," or "like no one ever met previously." They have long or whirlwind courtships. Yet all these descriptions seem, somehow, generic, even nondescript. Inarticulable, even ineffable, seem the adhesives, the attractions, the chemistries that bring people together to share a life or part of a life. And beyond that, a time and place provides context—one of support and encouragement or one of stones in the path. The mystery and resilience of intimate connection finds its best description in poetry.

Poet Jane Hirshfield speaks of the mysterious forces that bind couples in her poem, "For What Binds Us." She says there are names for these forces. In physics, scientists use the terms "strong forces," and "weak forces," which Hirshfield adopts as metaphors for human connections. "Proud flesh," the description of an equine scar, is also used to metaphorically describe the bond or scar tissue between couples who have wounds as well as joys in their lives together. "When two people have loved each other . . ." they become "a single fabric." The human experience of affiliation, attachment, or connection, Hirshfield suggests, has all the tenaciousness of the laws of physics ("skin that forms in a half-empty cup," and "nails rusting into the places they join.") or the biological processes of physical healing (the link between two lovers is "like a scar between their bodies").

Hirshfield's poem speaks directly to the reader. "There are names for what binds us," she declares in the opening stanza. "Look around, you can see them," we are told. The poem invites couples to become alert to the present sense of their connection to focus on what is still there, on what is possible. Focus is shifted from the divisive past to what the past has rendered for now.

Hirshfield's poem emphasizes the resilience of a couple's bond. Something that "nothing can tear or mend." Something strong and resilient but not necessarily without a wounding or painful element to it. The strength of their bond is something that can motivate, captivate or prompt partners to think about what is at stake in their conflict, or what is at stake when each tries to individuate.

Suggestions for Discussion and Writing Experiences:

1. Ask each partner to read Hirshfield's poem to the other. Again, it is important for each member of the couple to give voice to the poem, to inspirit the words with his or her own interpretation, lilt, rhythm, and pacing. It is important that the poem be breathed in and out by each person, taken into the body, warmed, and returned to the room swathed in pitch and volume. In this way, the poem is embodied, becomes a real presence in the therapy room. Ask the couple to take a moment just to breathe, to inhale the poem and the sense of its personal meaning or resonance. Ask one partner to take the hands of the other and to convey through their contact his/her sense of the poem. Ask the other partner to do the same with her/his individual-felt sense of the poem. Now each of the partners holds the poem in hand, grasping it in a physical way.
2. Ask both members of a couple to draw their own images of the bond (or binding force) between them. It could look like moss clinging to a rock, two cords braided or knotted together, vines clinging to the branches of a tree, two links in a chain, or a peanut butter and jelly sandwich!
3. Suggest that each member of the couple do some spontaneous poetic writing on the theme of "what binds us." Encourage them to look for descriptive metaphors for their attachment. This will be particularly useful with couples who say they have grown apart or don't feel close any more. Often these are the couples most fused and bound, who have less air space around them. But the bind may have a negative rather than a positive charge. When they are finished writing, have each person read his/her piece to the other. Have the listener identify and respond to the qualities

of attachment mentioned. Ask the couple to consider both the troubling as well as the satisfying qualities or images of their bond.

4. Invite each member of the couple to write a short piece on his/her vision of a healthy bond between each of them and the significant other. After each person has read his/her poem, contrast these ideal visions with the previous poem's images in activity 3.

3. "June Heat" by Susan Dion

Sex and sexual attraction certainly rank high on the list of bonding agents for many couples. Avid and eager sex typically characterizes the "honeymoon" phase of a long-term relationship, and yet sexual communication often grows more blissful and intimate over time. While sex can wax and wane in importance to any given couple, the loss of sexual contact—through illness or psychological trauma, as a result of hormonal changes or physical incapacity/discomfort—can elicit conflict, depression, self-condemnation, loss, and grief. While an expansive sense of sex and sexuality permits some couples to find ways of creating intimate enjoyment, for others, a single sexual problem can spell doom.

Susan Dion's sparkling poem, "June Heat," captures the joy of sexual connection after extreme medical interventions. The physically descriptive poem brings the reader "up close and personal." The intimacy between the lovers is enhanced by the specificity, the mapping of the lover's body.

Dion's poem speaks to the resilience of love and sex. It inspires and excites. The poem, immediate at first, also steps back to comment on the connection—"There is cause for celebration." The poem is set up as a piece written from one lover to her partner, "You come to me in daylight," and yet the poet's voice also moves outside the immediacy of the lovers' connection to tell us "Hidden for a lover / Are thumb-sized depressions / identifying locations, chest tube traumas." Dion creates a poetic experience in which we hover, in varying degrees of proximity, near the couple in the poem.

Dion's use of a list of active verbs—"guiding, beating, whispering, confiding, pleasing"—provides a sense of immediacy, muscularity, and kinesthetic excitement. The "dense, hot" air brings us in touch with the physical aspects of the atmosphere as well.

"June Heat" would be helpful with couples who have experienced some kind of loss in their relationship, or are experiencing some hurdle to closeness, whether sexual, geographical, emotional, or in terms of interests. It is a poem that speaks to a sense of celebration in spite of injury. The poem also sports a sense of making the most of opportunity. "The children are gone," so the lovers jump at the chance to get together, perhaps at a time, "in daylight," when they might not usually make love. This part of the poem brings up the often-lost spontaneity that generally graces the younger years of a relationship as well as the post-children-at-home era.

Suggestions for Discussion and Writing Experiences:

1. Have each partner read the poem aloud to the other. What does each feel about the poem? Does it feel courageous? Inspiring? Daunting? Does it remind the couple of any particularly erotic, exciting, or playful experience they shared together?

2. Ask the couple to write poetic pieces or poems, describing in sensory detail, the time, place and atmosphere of the context in which they shared a treasured and intense experience. Use plenty of action verbs and set the piece in the present, as if unfolding now. The power of the writing process and reading of the poems will be heightened by using the present tense. The present tense elevates the poems from reminiscence to re-experience. The present unfolding of an exciting couple's experience will also hypnotically suggest to the couple that they can and will create this kind of encounter for themselves—not only on paper!

3. By prior arrangement, ask each partner to bring in a favorite photograph of the two of them. Have each share the photograph with the other and describe the time and place in which it was taken, what they were doing at the time, and what it means to each. What is left from that time together, and what has been lost? Have each partner describe the couple in the favorite photograph as a piece of poetic writing. Pay as much attention to detail as possible. Suggest that the writing include some reference to what moment comes after the snapshot, or what moment has just preceded it.

4. "The Cold," by Wendell Berry

In "The Cold," Wendell Berry utilizes the metaphor of winter's cold as a personal perimeter, separating himself from all else including the partner he addresses in the poem. Melting becomes the metaphor for reunion, a softening of boundaries. Even in his frozen-like state, the poet is poised towards his lover. The poet self-consciously enjoys his pure separateness; he sees it echoed among the "cleanly divided" trees. The poem's basic message, framed in simple, straightforward language, is that separateness has its "goodness," and it is "good also to melt." For some couples, separateness, individuation, distinguishing oneself from the collective may require shoving and pushing, withholding or hiding. For others it may represent something fearful and lonely, a threat to the harmony and closeness of the union. For the latter any sign of separateness may feel like a chasm opening up around them. In this poem, Berry addresses the dance between self and other, the elastic rhythm of joining and disengaging, the necessity of both. Relationships that calcify into a static state differ markedly from those in which flexibility and movement make it possible to experience both a strong sense of self and a close proximity to the other. Berry's poem describes a healthy and joyful I/we dance. In the poem, he makes clear that loving to be with oneself, alone, does not represent a betrayal of the partner or the couple's togetherness. The poet's voice remarks that the other is "perfect too in your solitude."

Suggestions for Discussion and Writing Experiences:

1. Invite the partners to read "The Cold" out loud. The couple in the poem feel comfortable, good, alone as well as together. Ask the partners to share their own experiences of being alone and being together. Does each feel whole, or do they feel like halves of a whole, only achieving a sense of goodness when together? If the couple experiences problems with fusion and lack of differentiation, or if the couple projects a lot of material onto one another, invite each to think about a singular moment of happiness or fulfillment (at any point in their lives) when they were alone. What experience, accomplishment, or event in which they participated yielded a solid and positive sense of self? Perhaps this occurred before they got together, if not during their relationship. Next, ask the couple to think about what each sees as a highlight of their experience as a couple. A journey? A moment of reckoning? How they faced a crisis together? How they overcame an obstacle whether financial, logistical, emotional, or other?
2. Ask the partners to write a poetic piece on how it feels to be together or how it feels to be alone, referencing the other. Suggest that they use imagery which symbolically represents the quality of aloneness or togetherness for each. For Berry the metaphor is cold and melting. Other images

might include a barnacle on a rock, a gestalt of foreground and background, two birds sitting on a telephone wire, two towels drying on a line, the stems of two flowers loosely intertwined, etc. After each has finished, allow time for the partners to read each other their pieces and to respond to the readings by taking a deep breath and then offering some personal feelings that their partner's poem inspired. A more sophisticated next step, appropriate for a couple at a mature developmental level, might be a second poem that describes an image of a relationship towards which the partners can envision themselves striving.

3. Ask each of the partners to make their own collage using cut-outs from magazines, old photographs, scribbles or drawings, quotes from the poem above and/or other poems or literature, fabric, photographs, etc. The collage may contain images that represent things each likes to do/think about/be alone with, as well as images of together times. Invite each person to share something about the process of putting together the collage. And have the partner-viewer comment on what moves them about the other's collage. Each person may give her collage a title.

5. "The Meaningful Exchange" by Marge Piercy

Berry's poem could be used in conjunction with this poem by Marge Piercy, called "The Meaningful Exchange." In sharp contrast to Berry's piece, Piercy's poem describes an unhealthy, fused relationship in which the man and woman have calcified roles, the woman a borrowed rather than true self, the man a person buoyed by his woman's sympathy.

In "The Meaningful Exchange," Piercy utilizes the image of a teapot with "a dark green brew of troubles" for the man. The woman is the receptacle, vessel, "belly" in which the man pours his brew. In this unhealthy, exploitative relationship, both man and woman mistake their fusion, their needy dependence, for love. The poem perfectly describes "enabling," such as found in addictions literature. In this case the woman's life gets co-opted by the man's, and what moves her has to do with putting his life into some kind of shape. In turn, the man siphons off his anxiety by spilling his guts to the woman. Fueled by her sympathy he then "watches women pass. / He whistles."

A deeply disturbing poem, it would not be useful for couples in crisis, for couples with fragile ego structures, or for concrete people who lack the capacity for insight. In addition to using this poem with some couples, it would be useful with a woman "who loves too much," one who is addicted to love and/or sex.

In using this poem with a couple, the facilitator might frame the purpose as examining an unhealthy relationship in which the characters in the poem are having a difficult time living together as strong individuals. In reading the poem and exploring the emotional content, the couple could consider which character seems more dependent, or in what way each depends upon the other. What would happen to each without the other? Would the women feel empty without carrying "his sorrows away / sloshing in her belly"? Would the man, who "swings off lighter" after unloading his misery, feel too depressed or heavy "for business"?

Suggestions for Discussion and Writing Experiences:

1. Ask each person to read the poem aloud and talk about the central exchange between the characters in the poem. Ask each to pick out the metaphors that most impress them. At the end, the woman character says "How heavy I feel . . . this must be love." Do the partners see this exchange as one of love? Does the woman's identification of taking on her lover's burdens as her own make sense as love? How would each member of the couple define a loving relationship? How would they compare the couple in this poem to the couple in the Berry poem? Which relationship seems more fulfilling and why?

2. After reading "The Meaningful Exchange," ask the couple to write their own poems with the same title and substitute their own poetic dialogue. Write it in the third person, as if they are looking at themselves, or another couple, from a distance, and focusing in on some element of the relationship dynamic. Whereas in the Piercy poem, the man pours his bilious brew into the woman, perhaps the image in another poem might be one of cooperation, of adventuring together, of brainstorming on a problem, of coming to an understanding, of playing a game like chess. After they have written the piece, have each read his/her piece to the other. Have them compare perceptions, noting differences and commonalties. Ask each to assess for him/herself where he/she is on a continuum of depending on the other for fulfillment at one end, and feeling self-fulfilled but disconnected at the other extreme. To what degree does each experience both a sense of independence and of intimacy?

3. Ask each partner to think about his or her own parents. They will hold an image or multiple images of their parents in mind. As they sit and breathe with that imagery, ask each to get the "feel" of their parents' relationship. Perhaps one parent died young, perhaps the parents were divorced, perhaps one parent abandoned the family young, perhaps the person has adoptive parents or a stepparent who is the "real" father or mother, perhaps someone has parents who are still together after fifty years. Whatever the family configuration, each one should get a felt sense of what, as a child, he or she knew as a marriage (or equivalent). Was it warm and cozy? Hard and cold? Conflictual? A roller-coaster? A safe haven?

4. Invite each member of the couple to write a short poetic piece describing a "moment" in the relationship between whomever he considers his parents. This moment may be real or invented, as the purpose is to establish consciously what has always been felt as the paradigm of adult relationship. Whether the couple considers themselves different or similar to their own parents, their parents' relationships constitute important reference points for them. To what extent does each partner consider her parents similar or different from the couple in the Piercy poem?

5. Have each member of the couple read his poem to the other. Then ask each to share the way they see themselves as similar or dissimilar to their parents in relationship. What kinds of emotions does each experience? Is there a modeling or inverse relationship between the couple's modus operandi and that of their parents?

6. "Report of Health," by John Updike

Whereas the previous two poems address, in both healthy and unhealthy ways, the I/we tension at the core of relationships, this last poem addresses coming apart. Since roughly half of marriages end in divorce, one has a high probability of dealing with couples or individuals whose relationships have come apart at the seams. Emotions often run high at such a time. Jealousy, resentment, feelings of betrayal, rage, loss and grief, feelings of abandonment and rejection, fear, guilt, a sense one is defective or the partner is evil, even traumatic shock, are all possibilities. The termination of a relationship may feel a lot like a death at times. In other circumstances perhaps, it feels like freedom, such as when a woman emerges from a domestically violent relationship.

John Updike's "Report of Health" can be a particularly helpful poem to use with couples or an individual untangling from a significant relationship. In the poem, the speaker, writing in the first person, declares himself "alone" and "unwell." He says, "The wrong I have done you / sits like a sore beneath my thumb. . . ." These lines model taking responsibility for one's own contribution to the degradation, damage, or destruction of a relationship. Many couples come in blaming each other for the problems encountered, deflecting energy away from where it needs to go—towards meeting the personal challenges provoked by the break-up.

Updike's poem has three parts. The first focuses on the speaker's sense of aloneness, his lover's "bright love leaving," the "sunlight passing from a pattern of streets." Part two brings the reader to "Another night." In this part, he has heard that his lover seems "happy and well." The poet speaks to the difficulty of imagining his lover, the lover "shaped so precisely for me," as eloquently happy without him. "As for me," he says, "you are still the eyes of the air." The poet expresses a searing and compelling longing for his wronged lover.

The third part begins, "I may not write again. My voice goes nowhere." It reads as a despairing lament, a living hell, in which he wants what he cannot have, and "the lilac bush is a devil / inviting me into your hair." The poet declares a paradox, that he is "well" to the extent of being happy to "dwell in a world whose Hell I will. . . ."

To take the poet's words into one's own mouth, to utter the "I" belonging to the poet at the same moment one experiences one's own "I" coming up for air, provides a potent experience of coming to grips with one's own behavior, thoughts and feelings. It models speaking for oneself, addresses what one manifests in one's own life. Like lancing a boil, it both hurts and relieves to open and acknowledge what one has done out of smallness or desperation, out of malice or strategy, out of ignorance or lack of caring, from fear or greed or need.

Suggestions for Discussion and Writing Experiences:

1. Ask your client or clients to read aloud Updike's poem and to comment, first, on the feelings aroused by the poem. Whether longing or anger or sadness, ask the person to follow that feeling deep down into the body, to find the place where the feeling lodges or lives right now. What does that part of the body, rumbling with such emotion, want to say? If it could speak, what would it say (in the first person singular)? There is one image

in Updike's poem where he says, "My viscera, long clenched in love of you, / have undergone a detested relaxation." While this poet's description takes place at one remove from speaking as if from the voice of the viscera, it gives an example of the kind of awareness which will benefit your client.

2. Ask the couple or individual to write a eulogy for the "dead" relationship. Even couples who sometimes reunite must rise from the ashes of the unworkable relationship, creating new dimensions of interaction for themselves as a couple as well as new goals for their continuing development as individuals. A eulogy generally focuses on the most meaningful aspects of the late relationship and offers a chance for heartfelt empathy or even apology. These eulogies should be read with a sense of ritual, and perhaps read again out of the therapist's office with a candle lit, or in a place where one would see the old relationship buried—perhaps a place in nature that has meaning.

3. A very challenging therapeutic assignment involves writing that difficult thank-you letter to the ex-partner. In this letter, which involves the use of positive reframing and expanding perceptions, one person writes about the ways in which he or she has grown, has had to cope with new challenges and develop new skills as a result of the upheaval and loss. What strengths have been fostered, what hidden inner resources have emerged, what kindnesses have come forward from strangers or friends? To where has heartache led? What did one learn from the other? Appreciate? What kinds of challenges had to be overcome? How was self-esteem affected? How was being alone negotiated? How did a sense of trust in oneself and others hold up? The letter may not ever be sent, but it will be written and read out loud, finding its niche in the world, and documenting a moment of rare vulnerability and nakedness, of the elaborate workings of pain to promote healing even as it hurts.

In Alcoholics Anonymous, one of the twelve steps involves making amends to those whom one has hurt in the past, which is a similar kind of process that may involve writing letters or speaking with people directly. It often has a profound effect on one's perception of getting closure, of feeling able to move on, of remembering but letting go.

ANNOTATED BIBLIOGRAPHY OF POEMS
ON COUPLE CONNECTIONS

Anderson, Teresa. "Where the False Word Ends." *Speaking in Sign*. Minneapolis: West End Press, 1979.

Words can be hollow or full, full of sweetness of destructive potential—"honey" or "liquid lead." The poet speaks of wives dying "of hunger for words," and of men using words to cover up, and hide their true selves from their wives. There is the weight of the "unsaid," a "molten" place where there is as yet no form. The word creates a reality, Anderson seems to tell us, and if the unsaid (actions, feelings, experiences) does not get deployed into words, then words lose their validity as conveyors of what feels real. What we say to each other must have emotional verisimilitude.

Angelou, Maya. "Just for a Time." *And Still I Rise*. New York: Random House, 1978. Also in *Maya Angelou: Poems*. New York: Bantam Books, 1993; and *The Complete Collected Poems of Maya Angelou*. New York: Random House, 1994.

Angelou's poem is a reminiscence, idealizing first love, the perfection of the young girl whose image was of "Everything / That caused me to sing." Time moves. Love is transient. We can hold onto the past in a poem, or let it go in a poem, make it present by giving our memories a page, a voice. Young love, full of hope, represents all that is possible in love.

Atwood, Margaret. "Habitation." *Procedures for Underground*. Toronto: Oxford University Press, 1970. Also in *Selected Poems, 1965-1975*. Boston: Houghton Mifflin, 1976.

For Atwood, marriage is a matter of having survived something very primitive, "cold," and "unpainted." The "habitat" of marriage produces both pain and wonder and recapitulates the striving of the ancients to make fire. It is often the case with young couples, that they do not anticipate the amount of work involved in creating a sustainable relationship and in creating processes that will hold them together while allowing each breathing room. The metaphor of ancients' making fire, like "reinventing the wheel," may accurately describe the anticipated striving of a couple co-creating a life together.

Berry, Wendell. "The Cold." *Openings*. San Diego: Harvest/Harcourt Brace Jovanovich, 1968,1980.

Berry takes us to the woods in winter, to the solitude of the warm body divided from all else by the cold, to the solitude of "self-suspension," so necessary as counterpoint to coming together.

Note: See detailed analysis earlier in the chapter.

Berry, Wendell. "Marriage." *Openings*. San Diego: Harvest/Harcourt Brace Jovanovich, 1968, 1980.

In this poem Berry emphasizes the brinkmanship required to maintain oneself through thick and thin. Berry writes in "Marriage" of turning against, and turning towards, his wife, hurting and getting hurt, as well as turning to his wife for healing. Always in flux, "it is never whole," he comments at the end.

Bible, King James Version. "The Song of Solomon."

One of the most luscious and erotic paeans to love, "The Song of Solomon" (the King James version here), dwells on all of the sensuous aspects of love and the lover's body. Even the lover's "name is as ointment poured forth." "The Song of Solomon" also extols the attachment of one soul to another, merging the sexual and the spiritual and resoundingly endorsing the power of love as having "a most vehement flame. Many waters cannot quench love, neither can the floods drown it. . . ." These poems speak of human love as the light, the balm, the succor amid suffering and confusion, the connection to joy, even bliss, in a beleaguered world.

Note: See copy of excerpt (Chapter 1, Verses 7-17) from this poem at the end of the chapter.

Clifton, Lucille. "a woman who loves impossible men." *Quilting: Poems, 1987-1990*. Brockport, New York: BOA Editions, Ltd., 1991.

Clifton's powerful poem, like Curran's "A Family Matter," laments the addictions of women who love unavailable, abusive, or dehumanizing men. A woman who loves impossible men "walks by kin / forgets their birthmarks / their birthdays / remembers only the names / the stains of impossible men." This poem, like the previous one, should be used with discretion and with clients who have developed a trusting relationship with their therapist. It may not be appropriate to use with couples. In any abusive relationship, each member of the couple should pursue individual counseling before working together so as to avoid any confusion that perpetrators of violence have cause based on provocation by their partners (victims).

Curran, Judith M. "A Family Matter." *Journal of Poetry Therapy*. Vol. 2. No. 4 (1989).

In this poem, a woman leaves home because of an abusive husband. Her make-up and turtlenecks hardly manifest the most dangerous levels of concealment she has used to make herself stay with him. Denial, confusion, making excuses, and loving him still, have been far more potent. The poem poignantly illustrates the cycle of abuse and apology experienced by many women and kept secret. Sharing the poem with a client in this situation can have the effect of bringing light into a dark and dismal region.

Davy, Claudia. "Resignation." *Hiding Place*. Acme, Pennsylvania: Glendel Press, 1984.

Sometimes a partner must let go of a lover who leaves, either in person or in spirit. Resignation to lovelessness is captured in "frozen tears" and silence, a concave acceptance. "One afternoon," the poem says, "You buttoned up your coat of ritual, / and fastened your cap of rules / — never to take them off again." The tone of the poem captures the silent acceptance that love has no "passage" any more.

Dion, Susan. "June Heat." in *Poetic Medicine* by John Fox. New York: Jeremy Tarcher, 1997.

In "June Heat," Susan Dion writes an erotic poem celebrating a post-surgical sexual encounter. Each healed puncture wound, "thumb-sized depression" and "thin scar" maps pleasure as well as past trauma. The couple in the poem find what is possible and move to its music. It is a poignant poem because the sexual aspect of many couples' relationships is very important. I have seen couples who, for medical reasons, or as a result of medical treatment, have experienced losses in libido, in the ability to become aroused, or to function as they once did sexually. The couple must be willing to embrace the unknown, to create new ways of relating erotically and intimately. There are also many ways to touch and to talk and to bridge a silence with poems.

Note: See detailed analysis earlier in the chapter.
Note: See copy of this poem at the end of the chapter.

Giovanni, Nikki. "A Certain Peace." *My House*. New York: William Morrow & Company, 1972.

This poem takes as its frame of reference a bubble bath, the lover enjoying the leisure of catering only to herself, enjoying a day determined only by her own pleasures. Devoting energy to herself makes it possible to feel renewed excitement when her lover comes home later that same night. She writes, "it was very pleasant / not having you around / this afternoon / not that I don't love you. . . ." The poem emphasizes the way in which the experiences of solitude and togetherness complement and enhance each other.

Giovanni, Nikki. "A Poem of Friendship." *Cotton Candy on a Rainy Day.* New York: Quill/William Morrow & Company, 1978.
This poem extols the connection of "what we are together," rather than what lovers or friends do or say or give to each other. "The words we never have to speak" are just as important. The poem revels in appreciation of the union of two people below the surface definitions of their relationship.

Hirshfield, Jane. "For What Binds Us." *Of Gravity and Angels.* Ohio: Wesleyan University Press, 1988.
In this poem, Hirshfield explores the mystery and resilience of a couple's connection. Whether or not partners have common interests or spend lots of quality time together, they are often bound, not only by history or progeny, but by a chemistry that defies elegant explanation. Jane Hirschfield's "For What Binds Us" takes physics as a central metaphor. She speaks of forces between partners that "nothing can tear or mend."
Note: See detailed analysis earlier in the chapter.

Kavanaugh, James. "I Laugh and Cry with the Same Eyes." *Sunshine Days and Foggy Nights.* New York : E.P. Dutton & Co., Inc., 1975.
This straightforward poem addresses the importance of expressing all of oneself in order that one's partner do the same. Many couples share a myth that each is only half of a whole. Kavanaugh's poem appreciates that togetherness works only if each of the partners is whole.

Machan, Katharyn Howd. "Divorce." *Journal of Poetry Therapy.* Vol. 8. No. 2 (1994).
Machan writes in the third person about uncoupling, about the empty places kept alive by each in his/her separate domain. She tells us about

the unclaimed halves of the beds, the empty places at their respective breakfast tables, and the over-determination of each to assert that it is so "much better this way." This is a poem that makes us keenly feel the "presence" of absence, the fullness of loss.

Pastan, Linda. "love poem." *The Norton Introduction to Poetry*, Sixth Edition. Ed. J. Paul Hunter. New York: W.W. Norton & Co., 1995.
Diametrically opposed to Piercy's "To have without holding," Linda Pastan's piece says of love that it is like standing on the edge of a thawing, swollen creek. One false step and the lovers will get soaked. So they must grab each other—grab each other and step back. The creek, like love, plummets headlong towards its destination, carrying everything in its path, absorbing, rushing. The image sets our minds to abundance and danger at the same time. Whereas Piercy's poem offers love as not holding onto, Pastan's canvas paints love as something one must hold onto with everything one has.

Piercy, Marge. "The Meaningful Exchange." *The Twelve-Spoked Wheel Flashing*. New York: Knopf, 1978.
In contrast to the other poems, Marge Piercy writes, in "The Meaningful Exchange," of a connection in which a woman and man relate in calcified roles. The bearer of troubles, the man, pours his "dark green brew" into the listening woman, and she takes this on at the "center of her life," shifting around it so that she loses herself. Unfortunately, she identifies this feeling of heaviness as love. An excellent example of enmeshment, or blurred boundaries, this poem exemplifies the experience of losing oneself in another.
Note: See detailed analysis earlier in the chapter.

Piercy, Marge. "To have without holding." *Cries of the Spirit: A Celebration of Women's Spiritualities*. Ed. Marilyn Sewell. Boston: Beacon Press, 1991. Also available on line via www.google.com/search.
In this poem Piercy compares loving "wide open" to stretching muscles, opening the hand, to "thwarting" the reflexes of grabbing and clutching. This is a way to love differently, she says, and, therefore, a difficult, but ultimately gratifying challenge. She addresses the paradox of letting go in order to truly have something real and authentic. If a couple falls into a negative pattern in which one partner pursues while the other

distances, they may have to reckon with surrendering the fantasy that each can control the other. Letting go of this supposed control, and the manipulations, cajoling, begging and homogenizing that go along with it, may result in a more authentic and emotionally closer relationship.

Sandburg, Carl. "At a Window." *The Complete Poems of Carl Sandburg.* New York: Harcourt Brace Jovanovich, 1970. Also in *Chicago Poems* (1916). Intro. John E. Hallwas. Urbana, Illinois: University of Illinois Press, 1992.

World weary and vacant-eyed from stress and fatigue, many couples need reminding of the banner of their love that, in the slightest wind, flaps and shimmies, catches the light. Carl Sandburg's "At a Window" asks the gods to "leave me a little love," the soft voice at the dark end of the day or the touch of a hand.

Note: See detailed analysis earlier in the chapter.

Note: See copy of this poem at the end of the chapter.

Shakespeare, William "Sonnet 29." *Shakespeare's Sonnets (The Arden Shakespeare).* Ed. Katherine Duncan-Jones. London: Thomson Learning, 1997. Also in *The Norton Anthology of English Literature,* Volume I, Third Edition. Ed. M.H. Abrams. New York: W.W. Norton & Company, 1974.

Shakespeare, in "Sonnet 29," speaks about arising from an outcast state by merely remembering his lover, of shifting, in an instant, from an earthly state of woe to heavenly bliss. When couples fall into a pattern of unremitting complaint against each other, Shakespeare's sonnet models the possibility of making a shift from the closed chamber of conflict, and its attendant stresses, to the alternate perspective of gratitude. Invited to reflect upon what each partner brings to the other, they may find their lark's voices rising from the "sullen earth" of their disenchantments.

Note: See copy of this poem at the end of the chapter.

Updike, John. "Report of Health." *Midpoint and Other Poems.* New York: Random House, 1969. Also in *Collected Poems 1953-1993.* Reprint Edition. New York: Knopf, 1995.

Updike's poem looks at guilt, resentment, and love, the complex emotional strata that gets revealed when partners come apart. Here the narrator looks towards a living Hell as a way to keep the poignancy of his love alive, to keep "the wrong I have done you" at his fingertips. He needs this as a reference point, does not want to heal if it means accepting what has happened. The poem invites readers to delve into their own regrets, guilt, passions, and attachments.

Yeats, William Butler. "When You Are Old." *The Collected Poems of W.B. Yeats.* Revised Second Edition. Ed. Richard J. Finneran. New York: Scribner /Simon & Schuster, 1996.

Yeats' poem looks ahead rather than back, to a time anticipated, when the consummate lover reveals the images that capture his love. He distinguishes himself as the "one man" who "loved" the "pilgrim soul in you" and who could appreciate "the sorrows of your changing face. . . ." As in writing experiences in which one composes an epitaph for oneself or one's lover, this poem offers a model for appreciating, in the present, what the future will encompass.

Note: See copy of this poem at the end of the chapter.

THE SONG OF SOLOMON (excerpt)
(Chapter 1, Verses 7-17)

Tell me, Oh thou whom my soul loveth, where thou feedest,
Where thou makest they flock to rest at noon:
For why should I be as one that turneth aside
By the flocks of thy companions?
If thou know not, O thou fairest among women,
Go thy way forth by the footsteps of the flock,
And feed thy kids beside the shepherds' tents.
I have compared thee, O my love,
To a company of horses in Pharoah's chariots.
Thy cheeks are comely with rows of jewels,
Thy neck with chains of gold.
We will make thee borders of gold with studs of silver.
While the king sitteth at his table,
My spikenard sendeth forth the smell thereof.
A bundle of myrrh is my well-beloved unto me;
He shall lie all night betwixt my breasts.
My beloved is unto me as a cluster of camphire
In the vineyards of Engedi.
Behold, thou are fair, my love;
Behold, thou art fair;
Thou has doves' eyes.
Behold, thou art fair, my beloved, yea, pleasant:
Also our bed is green.
The beams of our house are cedar, and our rafters of fir.

The Bible, King James version

249

JUNE HEAT

You come to me in daylight
The children are gone
The air is dense, hot

Dark hairs flecked with silver
Cover your strong, large chest
Solid

Residual markings in sculpted hollow
Between straight lines of collar bones, base of throat
Old punctures, tracheotomy, worn intrusions

Hidden for a lover
Are thumb-sized depressions
identifying locations, chest tube traumas

Tracing thin scars, center
Surgical site, open heart
Guiding, beating, whispering, confiding, pleasing

Brown red skin entangled with
Pale thin legs,
Arms, fingers, blonde hair

There is cause for celebration
The children are gone
The air is dense, hot.

Susan Dion

AT A WINDOW

Give me hunger,
O you gods that sit and give
The world its orders.
Give me hunger, pain and want,
Shut me out with shame and failure
From your doors of gold and fame,
Give me your shabbiest, weariest hunger!

But leave me a little love,
A voice to speak to me in the day end,
A hand to touch me in the dark room
Breaking the long loneliness.
In the dusk of day-shapes
Blurring the sunset,
One little wandering, western star
Thrust out from the changing shores of shadow.
Let me go to the window,
Watch there the day-shapes of dusk
And wait and know the coming
Of a little love.

Carl Sandburg

SONNET 29

When, in disgrace with Fortune and men's eyes,
I all alone bemoan my outcast state,
And trouble deaf heaven with my bootless cries,
And look upon myself and curse my fate,
Wishing me like to one more rich in hope,
Featured like him, like him with friends possessed,
Desiring this man's art, and that man's scope,
With that I most enjoy contented least;
Yet in these thoughts myself despising,
Haply I think on thee, and then my state,
Like to the lark, at break of day arising
From sullen earth, sings hymns at heaven's gate;
   For thy sweet love rememb'red such wealth brings
   That then I scorn to change my state with kings.

William Shakespeare

WHEN YOU ARE OLD

When you are old and grey and full of sleep,
And nodding by the fire, take down this book,
And slowly read, and dream of the soft look
Your eyes had once, and of their shadows deep;

How many loved your moments of glad grace,
And loved your beauty with love false or true,
But one man loved the pilgrim soul in you,
And loved the sorrows of your changing face;

And bending down beside the glowing bars,
Murmur, a little sadly, how Love fled
And paced upon the mountains overhead
And hid his face amid a crowd of stars.

William Butler Yeats

REFERENCES

Bowen, Murray. *Family Therapy in Clinical Practice.* New York: Jason Aronson, Inc., 1978.

Hendricks, Harville. *Getting the Love You Want: A Guide for Couples.* New York: Henry Holt & Company, 1988.

Schnarch, David M. *Passionate Marriage: Love, Sex, and Intimacy in Emotionally Committed Relationships.* New York: W.W. Norton & Company, 1997.

VI
FINDING A MAP TO
TRAVEL BY

FINDING A MAP TO TRAVEL BY

Kenneth Gorelick, M.D., RPT
and Peggy Osna Heller, Ph.D., LCSW-C, RPT

We shall not cease from exploration
And the end of all our exploring
Will be to arrive where we started
And know the place for the first time.
T.S. Eliot "Little Gidding," *The Four Quartets*

THEMATIC OVERVIEW

IF THE READER IS ORDERLY, THIS IS THE LAST CHAPTER—until launching into new ones elsewhere. If the reader is a browser or wanderer, he/she will loop back to other chapters. A contrarian cannot stand suspense and so begins at "the end." By whatever method one navigates the way, we welcome the view to our perspective on the uses of poetry to help map the journeys through life.

Words, whether from scripture or from Rap, pave paths we travel, providing guideposts of exhortation, route markers to set us on course, demarcations of direction, and detours that take us along the "blue highways" less traveled (Moon).

The journey is an archetypal metaphor for the individual life. Journey is in our deepest nature. We have come out of Africa to populate the whole planet. We even find it in the lowly shaggy-dog story. A man seeking the meaning of life goes through incredible hardships and finally arrives at the cave of an old monk high in the Himalayas. He asks the guru, "What is the meaning of life?" The old man replies, "Life is a fountain." Incredulous, the seeker cries: "What! Have I suffered all this just to be told 'Life is a fountain'?" The sage replies, "You mean, it isn't . . . ?" A Hasidic parable, quoted in Hynes, tells of a seeker who journeys to a distant castle, only to be told by the gatekeeper to return home where his treasure lies buried beneath his hearth. By contrast, Kafka tells of a man who waits his whole life before the castle entry for the gatekeeper to open it, only to be told at his dying breath,

"... this gate was made only for you. I am now going to shut it." The poetry therapy process is a tool to help us find our way into our inner world, and to make our way in the world around us. We will encounter countless doors, some marked, some unmarked, some open, some closed. Which ones will we open, and how?

Metaphor

"Life is like ..." could be a stem sentence opening to many intriguing images. We can say "life is like a journey," but it is a pale image with limited impact. It keeps us at a distance. When we say "life is a journey to an unexplored sea bottom," it begins to move us somewhere. This is the power of metaphor: to move us.

Life can be likened to anything—a web, an ocean, a play. The journey metaphor is rich. It has connotations of stages, of encounters—both friendly and hostile—of obstacles, of plans and surprises, of activity and respite. A journey, like us, has a preparatory phase, a beginning, middle, end, and aftermath. Phases and stages are important dimensions to consider when choosing and using literature as a tool. Above all the metaphor suggests movement: movement through time and space. Through metaphor we can transcend limits.

Metaphor as Bridge Between Inner and Outer Worlds

"I never saw a Moor, / I never saw the Sea [...] / Yet certain am I of the spot / As if the Checks were given," writes Emily Dickinson. What gives sufficient scope to our lives? Is the journey to be measured in miles? What is a suitable degree of worldly ambition? What scope for the inner life and imagination? We are here given another scale to ponder—the point where microcosm and macrocosm converge and where time and immortality intersect. Sometimes who authored a piece is irrelevant to our enterprise, possibly distracting. Here it seems useful to picture Emily self-confined in a space that is small and without clocks. It is easy to imagine that there were no clocks in the small space to which she confined herself. Her time is not linear time but the Great Round. Her map used other-worldly coordinates to measure the life of this world. She found joy in "spreading wide [her] narrow hands / To gather Paradise" ("I dwell in Possibility"). How many delights are there in this world? How many must we sample to have a fulfilled life? Reading, writing, and interchange help us to know our inner landscape better and to right-size our connections with the world beyond our skin. All poetry-making is about the attempt to connect these two domains. Amongst the poems in this chapter, Piercy's "To Be of Use" in the "real world" takes a pole opposite from Dickinson's inner reality.

The relationship between surface and depth is curiously paradoxical. Nearly two hundred years ago William Smith began his solo odyssey across the face of England. In detailing the topographical features of localities, he perceived the deep structure, with its larger movements of time and space. His map made it easier for others to grasp the flow of geologic and biologic evolution and to help break the confines of a static worldview (Winchester). The writer—and that includes participants who write as part of the poetry therapy process—in attending to the quotidian details of his/her life, attends to its larger meaning. See Whitman, to look at grass and perceive the mortal world revealed.

Metaphor as Smokescreen

Emily offers, in her explorations of her inner space, her roadmap for surviving pain and thriving through adversity. Emily speaks a credo of poetry therapists: "Tell all the truth but tell it slant— / The truth must dazzle gradually / Or every man be blind." This is a powerful way to say that it is difficult to look on the truths of our existence. To approach these, we need time to adapt, a protective cloak. This is what imagery and metaphor are exquisitely able to do for us. They are the protective goggles in our explorer's tool-kit. This approach—using image and metaphor as a protective shield—is fundamental to poetry therapy. Metaphor reveals and conceals simultaneously. Our right-brain image-maker can make us aware of things that the left-brain censor would otherwise keep from us. Metaphor is a smokescreen with a hole in it, a lie that leads to the truth.

Poetry as Tool Kit

Journey implies goals, means, and tools. Tool kits include many things—first aid kit, utility knife, compass, and, yes, map. Reading and writing are tools for us that aid in all these functions: survival, safety, comfort, pleasure. ee cummings said "poetry is news that stays news." Accordingly, the poetic tool kit has the latest: GPS—global positioning system—capability that invites us to see ourselves in a social and political context, to think of what imprint we wish to leave on the planet. The political is the macro space-time viewpoint expressed by the novelist Gunter Grass: ". . . I cannot freely choose my subjects. For the most part, my subjects were assigned by German history, by the war that was criminally started and conducted, and by the never-ending consequences of that era. Thus my books are fatally linked to these subjects" (quoted in Gordimer).

Attitude

Also in the tool kit it is handy to have a prism that reveals the many shades of light that can be cast by experience. We are meaning-making animals. Two people can interpret the "same" event completely differently. The compelling story of "Rashomon," a Japanese folktale in which a murder scene is described in entirely different ways by several eye-witnesses, reminds us of this. Meanings can be more harmful or more helpful. Meanings can be altered. For example, we know events can be viewed through optimistic or pessimistic glasses. Borrowing from Shakespeare, we call these the "Jake-ian and Duke-ian" attitudes (*As You Like It*). In his "All the world's a stage" soliloquy, Jaques views life development in a rather sour way, from the stage of "the mewling, puking infant," to the "whining schoolboy," to the "lover sighing like a furnace," to the soldier "seeking the bubble reputation," the judge "in fair round belly," the elderly with "childish treble," to the "last scene" played "sans teeth, sans eyes, sans taste, sans everything." Contrast this with the attitude of Duke Senior, whose life is full of adversity, yet "finds tongues in trees, books in the running brooks, sermons in stones, and good in everything." It is our job as poetry therapists to enlarge awareness of viewpoints and to assist in finding the hope that makes going on through adversity worthwhile. In this chapter's poetry kit, Aeschylus holds us to the harsh realities, while Keats' "Endymion" could be Duke Senior speaking two hundred years after Shakespeare.

On Maps and Map-Making

Maps have their place. The explorer will have no map, or a very limited one, for he/she is entering new terrain. The pioneer has a goal or destination and will seek out maps, will listen to stories, realistic and fantastic ones, and will set out. The settler will need a very different kind of map, a much more local and specific one that fits lifestyle needs. The farmer wants a weather and soil map. The fisherman wants currents and rocks. The poetry therapist has expertise in choosing maps.

The wrong map can wreak havoc. If a map shows the earth coming to an end and falling into the great void, travelers may never set out in a certain direction. A wrong map can doom travelers if the trail is longer than anticipated or if location of food or water supplies is incorrectly marked. Therefore, finding the map—choosing the correct ones and rejecting unsuitable ones—is one of the most important tasks of the voyager. All of us carry inner maps that tell us "go here, that direction is impossible." Poetry therapy can make us more aware of self-limitations and can help us open to new possibilities. With our senses, our hearts, minds, and bodies, using our pens and pencils we can all be William Smiths creating evolutionary, and perhaps revolutionary, maps. William Stafford encourages us with the reminder that writers are not special people with special experiences. A writer is a person who uses paper and pen to discover what he/she doesn't know he/she knows. This notion has been expanded and explicated by poetry therapist John Fox. With pen in hand writing journals, poems, stories, fables, memoirs, letters, we can all be mapmakers for ourselves. Blumenthal may give us some ideas to write "The New Story of Your Life."

Humans have had the advantage of word-maps for about 5,000 years. Story has been a natural form that such maps have taken, and the stories of Gilgamesh as he sought the meaning of mortality and of Ulysses as he struggled to come home from his wars are widely known in our culture. Cavafy's "Ithaka" here represents this same type of story: "Have Ithaka always in your mind / Your arrival there is what you are destined for." At the same time "Ithaka gave you the splendid journey / Without her you would not have set out."

Let us take as permanent and indelible—at least for this moment— the metaphor of imaginal literature as maps for our life's journey. Let us set out on the task of finding maps, using the tool kit provided by the poetry therapy process. Literature, that great psycho-educational master, can teach the rules with the heavy hand of an Aesop's fable whose prescriptive answer is clear and obvious—a Ten Commandments didacticism. Examples in this chapter of such poems include Green's "Don't Make Your Life Too Beautiful," Meinke's "Advice to My Son," Madgett's "Woman with Flower," Sandburg's "What He Shall Tell That Son," and the excerpt from the Tao.

Some people crave and need prescription—at least until they have confidence in their own powers. As facilitators, we need to soften rigidity and instill trust to take the risk of change. Risk, not recklessness. Iconoclasts present the ideas by which we are inspired to test the rules. Our preferred choice of literature for poetry therapy is that which leads to wisdom from examining our lives, motives, dreams, and values. Literature chosen in keeping with the needs, problems, and developmental stages of the participants can, through the subtlety of metaphor, mentor by challenging heart and mind to discover personal meaning that is organic and authentic. See Machado's "Wayfarer," Oliver's "The Journey," and Kinnell's "The Still Time."

Safe Containers

"Things fall apart; the center cannot hold; / Mere anarchy is loosed upon the world." So Yeats reminds us. Metaphorically it may do us good to have our neatly structured world disintegrate from time to time so we can test assumptions, prune, expand, renew. However, some individuals are so vulnerable that the destruction can be literal—suicide, substance abuse, a host of other self-destructive behaviors, or violence to others. Or psychological anarchy in the form of psychosis might appear. Therefore, we need to be aware of safety and containment when using the power tool of poetry therapy with self or others. Yes, we must be aware of the power of the process even for self-application. Kay Adams, at the Wordsworth Center Poetry Therapy Summer Intensive 2001, stated that women with severe psychological trauma told her that by free-writing in their journals without guidance, they fell deeper into the black hole of despair and pain. Therefore, Kay offers a paced and structured approach to journaling. Book discussion groups and writing workshops that touch on personal levels are generally safe because they do not probe too deeply. Facilitators have the responsibility to recognize and protect fragile participants and to monitor the levels of pain intensity. When in doubt, consult with professionals.

In the map box offered here, Boye's "Yes It Hurts" and Oliver's "In Blackwater Woods" call to the deepest levels of grief. Hewitt's "The Enticing Lane," Levertov's "The Fountain," Rumi's "The Guest House," and Sarton's "Myself to Me" speak of pain but offer more protection. We find stronger containment where the pain is more allusive, as in Eliot's "Shall I Say It Again," Hugo's "Be Like the Bird," and Wordsworth's "And O Ye Fountains."

Map Box

Maps don't tell us how long it takes to get there. Time has its own maps. It runs in one direction but can fold back on itself. We live not only in time-present, but simultaneously in past and in future. We grow, make mistakes, learn, change in time. The moon is one constant reminder that everything and everyone goes through phases: beginning, middle, end. We ask in what phase is the person, process, or project before us. In this poem packet, Cavafy, Eliot, Hewitt, Kinnell, Meinke, Sandburg, Whitman, and Wordsworth make explicit the passage of time or the unfolding of developmental stages.

We have referred to the twenty-five poems offered in this chapter. These are a pack full of maps—literary references to take the poetry therapy pilgrim on some hypothetical journeys. Perhaps that pilgrim is the sort of life-tourist who prefers precise, detailed instructions, promising that if he/she goes, let us say west for so many miles, he/she will reach a particular, defined destination. Or maybe the pilgrim is more the vagabond who can puzzle out the meaning of a chart that looks more like a rebus than a map. Wanderlust allows or requires one to infer meaning from the symbols and images in a poetic puzzle map. Our packet contains both denotative and connotative maps as well as some strategies for using them along the way, but we advise, as Adrienne Rich advised the readers of her famously titled tour guide of a poem, "Prospective Immigrants Take Note." We propose to share some packing and unpacking tips, some hints about danger zones, some advisories on highlights. Far more important, however, we share our strategies as a call to adventure, an inspiration for sightseeing.

We invite the reader to travel with us as creative explorers, eschewing for this tour the notion of a poetic Baedeker, a reference made up of "good" poems with effective applications. That is here, of course; moreover, one will find the invitation to use even a random note in a bottle as suitable literature and a challenge to the imagination to bring that word map to life, literally and figuratively.

The poetry therapist's artistry comes from *not* using a "tried and true" bibliography. Rather it is from exhaustive reading, choosing material that is specific for the participants of a particular group as well as being consistent with the general goals of humanistic psychology, so clearly presented in Hynes and Hynes-Berry's *Biblio/Poetry Therapy*, and devising creative methods to present the literature. It also comes from the therapist's creative listening, hearing, and reflecting participants' metaphors and aiding in the application of that symbolic language to the person's self-understanding and growth.

Final Preparations

That said, let us begin this travelogue. We start with the assumption that we ourselves, or our patients, clients, students, or participants come to poetry therapy having lost their way, seeking relief and direction. We ask at the beginning of such a journey: What do you call yourself? What interests you? What are you seeking? Where have you gone before? How did you get there? What worked or did not? What obstacles did you face? Or avoid? What sustained you under adversity? Where do you want to go from here? Then we proceed to the poetry therapy experience. We read, discuss, and usually write, then discuss some more. We do not do writing exercises. These we relegate to the classroom, creative writing workshop, or gymnasium. We conduct writing experiences, explorations, adventures, and the discussion that follows their sharing.

The authors of this chapter work together, and independently. Here is a composite of how we might approach a poem. We like to think of each poem as a potential treasure map, replete with story, music, and pictures. In preparation for using a piece, we ask what images, feelings, thoughts are evoked in me? What is it about this language, style, structure, that speak to me? How does it apply in my life? How do I intuit it will affect others? Which others? With what issues? How do I become a sacred steward evoking valuable personal responses even if affectively or cognitively off-base, and not just a tour guide? When the map is directive, how can I tease out the contrasts or conflicts that are part of responsible life travel? How can I use the words, melodies, images of the piece to elicit polarities and summon forth the thesis, antithesis, synthesis dialectic that leads to dialogue with literature, self, facilitator, group?

As poetry therapists, we are responsible for knowing everything we can about reading and writing poetry and about the particular piece we plan to use, and for applying that knowledge as we plan a session. The challenge then, is to put aside our facts and provide the widest space possible for the participants to form and express their own impressions. And there lies so much of poetry's magic. No doubt, many people have built their successful lives upon a misreading of Robert Frost's familiar poem, "The Road Not Taken." Frost, here a wily cartographer, tells us straight out he "took the other as just as fair . . . ," that "the passing there / Had worn them really about the same . . ." and that "both that morning equally lay. . . ." How he must be winking when later he says he . . . "shall be telling this with a sigh . . ." as if there really had been an essential disparity in the divergent roads that "made all the difference." For the reader whose life challenge it became to take the less-traveled road and who thrived by following this directive, the personal message was far more valuable than the poet's actual instructions on the map. The poetry therapist, unlike the teacher of literature, must step back and let this happen.

As we unfold the maps and share our interpretations, we encourage readers to entertain their own perspectives. We have ordered these poems on the basis of what we see as their emotional depth and confrontation with painful life experience, just as we would structure a progressive process of therapeutic work.

IN-DEPTH DISCUSSION OF POEMS IN
A THERAPEUTIC CONTEXT

1. "Wayfarer" by Antonio Machado

Solvitur ambulando, a phrase attributed to St. Jerome, says "to find a solution, take a walk." In his Poem #47, "Sonnets," Antonio Machado addresses his reader, "Pilgrim, a wonder awaits you on the road." That perspective speaks eloquently again in "Wayfarer." This poem is a pirate's puzzle, filled with subtle clues that seem as much to direct as misdirect, and can, therefore, guide the determined explorer to the buried treasure that resides within the self. It vibrates with possibility, precisely because it appears so simple on the surface but contains links to that secret self that has the energy to create and recreate, take risks and learn from them regardless of outcome. The story is as simple as Machado's language. It says, the only way to live is to make decisions and proceed according to those choices. There is no blueprint or diagram to show the right way. Once one has set his/her own course, he/she can look back to determine what has been accomplished but is now over and complete. The music of the poem is like a chant, reminiscent of the *Hasidic Nigun*, that (in one translation of the Hebrew) repeats and repeats, "All the world's a bridge, a very narrow bridge, and the most important thing, the only thing, is not to be afraid. Keep walking. All the world's a bridge . . . walking."

Machado's chant addresses the reader as "wayfarer" three times in this poem of only ten lines, perhaps playfully, perhaps provocatively, inducing that traveler to go "the only way, no way, the way, no way." The pictures are few: footsteps, path, foam trails to the sea.

When we look at a poem, we try to imagine its range of possible applications. This would be a fine piece for a variety of populations such as people who are over-programmed and needing more spontaneity, teenagers struggling to find their way, special-education students beginning to be mainstreamed, adolescents or adults with depressive disorders, or patients leaving the confines of an institution. Let us consider it here for use with a developmental group of people about to engage in some new endeavor.

After the poem is read once by the facilitator, participants would be invited to chant the short lines, using their combined voices to create the immediate connection that comes from shared experience. Initial discussion might focus on an easy-to-address theme introduced by the question, "where do you enjoy walking?" Each participant would then say his or her first name, followed by a response to the question. Such a simple entrance activity allows each person to risk the often difficult task of putting one's solitary voice out into the public arena. We start with an amplification of a literal quality of the selection, first providing safety in its familiarity, then allowing its more personal and metaphorical aspects to emerge like a developing Polaroid snapshot.

After brief discussion, the facilitator might say, "This poem could be an invitation to walk. Let's experiment." Participants would be asked to choose a "walking partner," with whom they would stroll about the room and, each in turn, tell the other—who simply listens—about a life path he/she has traveled with its positive or negative ramifications. The shift from one speaker to the other can be facilitated with the use of music that stops after about two minutes of playing then resumes. Returning to their seats, participants would write for about five minutes about the proximate previous experience that influenced their choice of that path.

All group members would then be invited to read and to relate the walking/writing/sharing experience to a current life decision issue with the goal of self-awareness and exploration of options rather than solutions. Careful facilitation would elicit from each person, with help from the group, the resilience factors extractable from each narrative, making empowerment an essential therapeutic purpose in the use of this poem.

2. "The Fountain" by Denise Levertov

"Don't say," and again, "don't say there is no water," Levertov begins and repeats her invocation. She speaks directly to us in this, her map for lost travelers, too tired and thirsty to go on, too hopeless of finding their way, and she promises with certainty that help lies ahead. She pledges that no matter how parched our hearts, the spring that will refresh us is there, as it has always been. She knows, because she has been drained, depleted, and has drunk there. She reminds us that we, too, have quenched our thirst there. She bids us find our footholds, climb, and drink.

As if echoing the lines from W.H. Auden's eulogy to Yeats, "In the deserts of the heart / Let the healing fountain start," Levertov inspires with her fervent assurance. The healing fountain is there, right there springing from the rocks. Work with this poem might center on discussion of the times in participants' lives when it seemed that nothing would ever relieve their pain, whether physical or emotional. The question "Has your heart ever felt dry?" can elicit specific examples of such times, expressed perhaps in the idiom of metaphor with its protective shield. The questions, "Who is that woman?" and "What might her scowling expression imply?" can evoke lively discussion. Finally, hope can be restored by participants' writing of their heart's aridity and of the steps they have taken in the past to sustain themselves during such hardship. Discussion and sharing of both actual and metaphorical fountains would allow group members to provide inspiration for each other as they confront difficult travel and desiccation on their journeys.

What if, however, the discussion elicits inappropriately inhibiting commands group members recall as they respond to the poet's, "Don't say." A creative alternative would be to invite participants to write some of the restrictive statements that others or they themselves have used to proscribe their appropriate words or behaviors. This strategy can summon participants' determination to say what they wish or need to say in these quite different circumstances. They might practice saying aloud the forbidden words as the group intones, "Don't say." Such injunctions as, "Don't say to your spouse that you're angry," or "Don't say to your boss that you have been treated unfairly," or "Don't say to your parent that you disagree," or any of the "Don't tell" warnings that have threatened abuse survivors can be addressed with this process and discussed further.

A coda activity, designed to summarize as well as inspire further creative application, could be a return to the hopeful metaphorical message of the poem, that there is a fountain within us, always there and ready to spring forth no matter how hard our hearts have grown. For a final word, participants could be asked, "What might that be for you?"

3. "The Guest House" by Jelaluddin Rumi

Just as a territorial map can expand our perception of exterior space, so can a poetic map enlarge our perception of self, our inner space. In his poem, "On the Threshold," Rumi says, "With each passing moment / a soul sets out to find itself." Yet, Rumi's translated poems often convey an authoritarian tone that may offend some seekers. Translators John Moyne and Coleman Barks disagree. In their introduction to *Open Secret: Versions of Rumi*, they state, "Rumi's odes are not roadmaps for the spiritual path, not directional as perhaps are Han-Shan's poems, for instance. Rumi's odes and quatrains rather are the personal, human records of a man's being given a sharp, clear consciousness of the divine, and enduring it."

Although Rumi's "The Guest House" ends with just such a mystical allusion, it is a piece with enough universal attributes to recommend it even for an agnostic reader or group. How difficult it is for most people to make room within the house of self for unbidden emotions or seemingly uncharacteristic responses to life challenges. We call certain of our emotions "negative" and try to hide them from others and ourselves. We welcome joy with ease, but depression? meanness? shame? malice? a crowd of sorrows? Hardly! How often is self-compassion derided as "feeling sorry for oneself," or self-respect demeaned as selfishness? Rumi entreats us to invite them in, all of them, honoring and entertaining each with hospitality, even with laughter. "This being human," he says, affords us new opportunities to grow in awareness and acceptance each morning. Such a wholesome viewpoint would be accepted by most people, particularly those who have been participating in either a developmental or a clinical poetry therapy group for some time and are working towards termination.

Suppose that, in the initial discussion of the poem, everybody in the group agrees. The mental healthiness of the opinion is acknowledged and can be further explored and affirmed with a writing activity designed to apply Rumi's advice to a specific "unwelcome guest" in each participant's life. Subsequent discussion can expand on personal meanings and applications. Suppose, on the other hand, that the discussion takes a quite different turn. The unwelcome guests of some group members have been and continue to be more than they can endure. The facilitator may have seen the paraplegic member of the group, paralyzed because of an automobile accident at the height of her dancing career, shake her fist at the firmament after each new assault to her well-being and shout, "Enough character-building!"

The challenge for the poetry therapist is to allow room for dissent, making of this piece something more welcoming of a variety of responses than it is on its surface. As it stands, it might be read like a floor plan that shows the precise dimensions of a living room and indicates that the sofa must go here and the TV there, and though one doesn't appreciate the idea of overnight guests, they will come, so get a sleeper couch. That doesn't leave much space for imaginative decorating.

An evocative, creative process that invites a broader range of reaction is a brief write that can introduce not only surprise, but also spontaneity and, often, a freeing of emotional response. Participants can be asked to become the host at the Guest House as seen in their mind's eye, ready for visitors. They would be told that they have the power to admit or reject any potential guest, but just need to be aware of who (or what) is there. When they hear the doorbell, chimed by the facilitator, they may peek unseen or open the door and write immediately who is there, whether literally or metaphorically. They then continue to write, as quickly as possible, a description of the "guest." The facilitator chimes again, after about three minutes, then again after another two minutes, so that participants will have greeted three guests. Sharing can be in dyads, to give everyone a chance to read all three descriptions. Returning to large group process, participants can be invited to share their encountering whomever they considered special guests. They might discuss what it was like for them if they did not want to admit a particular guest and how they handled that situation. Finally, the discussion would focus on what meaning that activity might have in their current life experience. As a termination phase session, the discussion might also focus on how the poetry therapy experience in general has equipped them for their future confrontations with previously "unwelcome guests," who might be their next unexpected visitors, and on what further delights might be in store for them.

4. "The Still Time" by Galway Kinnell

Writers write, and readers read, as a way of dealing with the emotions of intense living. A poem is a container for what is overwhelming, a smokescreen that provides privacy and protection, and a bridge communicating amongst our disparate internal parts and between us and the outside world. This is a "bridge" poem, for it is about "singing" "for one able to groan / to sing, for whatever can sing / to heal itself almost into happiness, by singing." Put it out there, sing your song. There lies beauty and salvation. The recent motion picture "Songcatcher" shows how song adds an immeasurable dimension to the lives of ordinary folk living in daily adversity. They sing of love, betrayal, death, sometimes in voices that croak, yet are beautiful for the truth they sing.

Kinnell's song is a bridge over time, between time then and time now, "so much of it gone / it returns." The "I" who was "young and empty" revisits an "I" who has walked far along the paths of life wondering, "What now?" in the too-few days left. It is in midlife that we revisit the continuous construction of our character. Jung speaks of this time of life as the enantio-dromia, the reversal. Having dealt with basic survival, relationships, career, procreation, we become aware again of our station and re-pose the questions, "Who am I; where am I going; why?" Now we can begin to nurture aspects of our personality and development that we had neglected, to revisit "the road not taken," to consider other options. Money-makers can become char-ity-endowers. Task-driven people can become relationship-oriented. Facts-and-figures people can develop their intuitive and artistic side. The cautious can dare risk. All of these are possible, "now that the fear has been rum-maged down to the husk." And so we have the opportunity to reconsider, "What do I want . . . now."

This poem is also a meditation on emptiness and fullness. Can there be fullness without emptiness? This poem gives honor to the "failed harvests of want," to the "days of not having," to the times "when I was young and empty . . . knowing I would have nothing of anything I wanted." And near the center of the poem, the heart "hollowed out irreversibly" by unfulfilled craving.

And yet there is hope in that empty condition. It waits to be filled. But it does not wait passively. It goes out seeking, and each failed search brings more pain. But now is a time to bless "the misery of each step it took me into the world." And now is a time to harvest, to find the prayerful hands holding something, "the changed air between my palms" which "become[s] the glitter / on ordinary things that inexplicably shine." If we are alive, there is "still time" to harvest.

The speaker in this poem is rich with desire. How has this spark been kept alive? Why has there not been withdrawal from the pain into a more limited world of passive acceptance without the rich luxury of continuing unquenched desire? This is a good poem for those seeking, and for those who have given up in despair. In a group, the facilitator can ask for volunteers to read. Already this is a question about desire, and unfulfillment. We might stop right there, a still time, and process the experience of the reading. Participants could write for just two minutes on "Did you get what you wanted, and how did it feel?" Issues of selfishness and of sharing arise, along with the transcendence of self-imposed limits. For example, the poem is abundant: it can be read twice, or as many times as people want. Participants are invited to repeat lines that have special meaning. They are invited to all speak at once, in a cacophony that is not tuneful but which has a beautiful power.

Inviting discussion about what in the poem speaks to the participants, the facilitator is mindful of especially loaded images in this piece, such as "failed harvests of want." What is a failed harvest? Participants are invited to think about a frustrated desire and what impact it had on them. Did it hollow the heart irreversibly? What sustains you now?

Or, the discussion might reveal that the focus for this session is fear that blocks access to desire. We could write about an old fear, now tamed or less fearsome. How has that happened? Or the focal point of this group might be mortality itself. What is it like as "the wind blows the flesh away" and the "flesh streams itself in its reveries on the wind"? What stories do the dreams of the flesh have to tell? A focal point for writing might be a story about the body. However, facilitators need to be alert: this is very touchy if it goes to deep wounds in the body from illness or abuse.

It is amazing, this poetry, how such a brief poem can be so rich, can contain so many opposites. What are we looking for, praying for? Maybe it is here right between our hands. Can we cast glitter on the ordinary moments of our lives and feel that? Maybe there has been such a highlight in the writing, in the group discussion. We offer that opportunity for participants to capture and honor that moment of contact.

Finally, there is still time. Time to voice something of the heart's desire. Can we find that child's voice, with its "incoherences" and its parrot utterances, and hear what it has to say to us? What utterances have been choked off? Name the fear that chokes. How can it be winnowed down to a husk? Does anyone want to use the group to take a risk: how about singing what you have written?

People in midlife, in any transition, the disenfranchised and unheard, the meek and shy, the cautious, the suppressed, those in grief—there is something for everyone in this poem, which in the beauty of its language and heart, creates communion and bestows blessing. If our Library of Alexandria burned and we could salvage only a few poems to use in poetry therapy, this would be one of them.

5. "In Blackwater Woods" by Mary Oliver

In an exquisite life map that provides no map, Mary Oliver recalls Viktor Frankl, who believed that our essential motivation for survival is to make meaning of the suffering in our lives, regardless of the horrors of our circumstances. A survivor of the Auschwitz concentration camp, Frankl developed the theory and psychotherapeutic practice he called logotherapy. He states in his book, *Man's Search for Meaning*, ". . . we can discover [this] meaning in life in three different ways": (1) achievement: by creating a work or doing a deed; (2) value: by experiencing something in nature or culture or by experiencing someone with love; and (3) attitude: by coping with unavoidable suffering. He encourages us to see the world as it really is and to be responsible. Oliver's "Blackwater Woods" is such a vision. While she depicts vividly the lay of the land, we will have to make our own way.

"Look," she begins. What a way to start a poem, an adventure, a journey! What a way to live a life, with its existential transitoriness, its often dismal circumstances, its seemingly insuperable odds and fleeting joys. "Look." Pay attention. The story in "Blackwater Woods" is of loss, of transfiguration. Nothing remains in its familiar form; the trees transform into light energy, their work fulfilled, their bark emitting its sweet scent as they leave. The cattails burst and float into air; even the ponds have lost their names. They will no longer exist on the map. As each year passes, it takes with it what has been meaningful and known, and we are left to find our way despite the fire that burns substance to ashes and the black river that carries them away. But if we listen to this poem as if it were musical composition, it might be heard to start with a clash of cymbals: "Look." It then sings its dirge of loss in a minor key ending with the sweet resolution of acceptance in a major chord. In only three sentences, Oliver takes us on a philosophical life journey with no magical safety net, no soothing balm. Our eyes are open. This is what is. It is also how we can continue to live. To live, she says, we "must be able to do three things":

> to love what is mortal; to hold it
> against your bones knowing
> your own life depends on it;
> and, when the time comes to let it go,
> to let it go.

The poet does not tell us we must do the three things; she says we must be able to do them, perhaps sharing her own arduous struggle.

Here is how Michael Ondaatje speaks of this confrontation with mortality. "We die, containing a richness of lovers and tribes. . . . I wish for all this to be marked on my body when I am dead. I believe in such cartography—to be marked by nature. . . . All I desired was to walk upon such an earth that had no maps."

How can we travel without a map, when senseless disasters rob us of meaning, when we lose what we love most, when we face the inevitable endings of what we depend upon to last? These are questions people bring into our practices daily: the couple who have lost a child or are unable to conceive, the child or adult whose beloved animal companion has died, the abandoned or widowed spouse or lover, all dealing with having to release what is mortal and cope with continuing the journey without the known, loved other.

In individual therapy, "Blackwater Woods" can be offered as an empathic resonance with the sufferer whose story of unbearable ending has just been disclosed. The poetry therapist can say, "There is a poem I know that seems to echo what you have just told me. May I read it to you (or would you care to read it)?" An always effective opening question after reading is, "What do you think about this?" (Most people seem to get to feelings more readily when asked for their thoughts rather than for their feelings.) Then, "What word or words speak to you?" "What images draw your attention?" The interactive dialogue would serve to expand the patient's view of self in the situation of loss and current inability to move forward with life. The patient would be invited to find, speak, and write the words that describe his or her loss and its current effects, with the encouragement to "get into it" rather than "get over it," at least for the moment. For a person who is not accustomed to writing, an acrostic poem using the name of the lost love will be effective and revealing, as would be the sentence stem or a prompt like, "Look. . . ." Often, the most organic and natural introduction to writing is to repeat a phrase or sentence the patient has just uttered, particularly one that is deeply thoughtful or emotion-laden, and offer a handily kept pen and pad with the gentle imperative, "Write that, and then just continue writing whatever comes for about five minutes. I'll just sit here and be with you silently." (That empathic witnessing helps the patient to contain and cope with the words and emotions that are evoked in the writing process.) The therapist can then offer to hear or to read back the patient's words and discuss them further.

So often, the fear of being completely overcome with grief or hopelessness prevents even the most minimal self-compassion. Instead it is usually the opening of one's heart to oneself through the poetry therapy process that permits the "letting go" and moving on. Such a session would be part of a broader process, but it would be a powerful step in the direction of creating one's own new map, the only chart that will work, on unfamiliar territory.

6. "Yes It Hurts" by Karin Boye

Like Ann Sexton and Sylvia Plath, Swedish poet Karin Boye might not have lasted so long without "the discipline and solace of poetry" as Joyce Carol Oates eulogized Sexton in a *Washington Post* book review some years ago. Boye, according to a direct translation of her biography in Swedish, died a "voluntary, or free-will death" at age forty-one in 1941. She was an artist of astounding productivity and tormented psyche whose poetry, as evidenced in May Swenson's translation of her poem, "Yes It Hurts," is startlingly intense and beautiful. Its tearing polarities might hint at the psychological anguish of a bipolar condition. The trained poetry therapist would be alert to allusions of suicidality or violence in the symbolic language of a participant's writing and would explore this language further by means of sensitive questioning and discussion. Sometimes referral to another mental health professional will be recommended.

Boye's suffering is portrayed metaphorically as unbearable pain that accompanies nature's transition from winter to spring. Buds hurt as they burst, but are fevered to open; ice shivers in its uncertainty, fluctuating between cowardice and determination to melt. Finally, when things are at their worst, "blinking away their fears of the new, / shutting out their doubts about the journey," buds open and water droplets fall, "as if in ecstasy." The poem ends describing an instant of "trust in that daring / that shapes the world."

The English translation is rich and moving in its use of sound, inspiring curiosity about its original music. As a map, it is like a child's blindfold game, leading with subliminal cues to a prized end point heralded with shouts of "Yay, Hooray."

Poetry therapy intern, Ingrid Tegner, who is fluent in Swedish, provided much fascinating information about Boye, as well as another poet's translation of this poem. This exciting research is part of the creative process that can inform and inspire the poetry therapist's preparation, and is one of the many delights of our work that we treasure.

Swenson's translation is not only faithful to the Swedish text, it also interprets Boye's poetic story by means of a subtle subtext of sound that drives deeply the ideas and emotions of the poem independent of its surface language. Listen, as the poem seems to weep, whimper, even mourn, or maybe it stutters tentatively, unable to say a word without struggle. Listen to its repeated sound of "er" in hurts, burst, covered, fever, downward, uncertain, cowardly, shiver, firm, worst, journey, world. Listen to its other insistent sound, a beat like that made by the wire comb on a taut drum skin : hurts, burst, melts, its, resists, ecstasy, first, itself, doubts, instant, greatest, trust: ts st ts ts ts st ts ts st st. Coincidence? Perhaps. There is also a seemingly purposeful manipulation of meaning expressed in the use of the long vowel sound, "ay." Listen to the paucity of "ay" sounds in two of the poem's three verses. In the first verse: "hesitate," "pale," and "pain" tell the poem's story in condensed form; in the center of the second verse, the poet conveys the pull of opposing forces with the word, "weight"; in the center of the third verse it is, "veil," that diaphanous membrane between her competing realities; and finally, four of the last eleven words of the poem are "ay" words: "greatest," "safety," "daring," and "shapes." The voice in the reader's mind opens like the mouth in freedom and fulfillment.

What is happening here? To the poetry therapist's trained ear, these intricate nuances of sound convey meaning and feeling as powerfully as does an operatic aria in a totally unfamiliar language. We hear its anxious ambivalence, its terror of leaving the known no matter how horrible that may be, juxtaposed with its willingness to suffer any agonies in its passion for change, and at last, the open, airy, ecstatic freedom that comes of breaking through, making the new journey that life demands. Sensitively attuned facilitators will now relate the poem to circumstances of their own life that have caused such emotional upheaval, write their own response, then put it and other musings aside, and make a detailed plan for using the literature.

We recommend using the following five-stage structural template developed by Peggy Heller to plan a session that interconnects the therapeutic objective, creative process, and special language of the poetry.

Population: high school juniors, making their initial college choices; hospitalized patients getting ready for a day-treatment program; a young adult contemplating a move, marriage, a job change; a man or woman in midlife thinking about retirement.

Goal(s): to explore the doubts that impede and the desires that impel life change; to acknowledge vulnerabilities, enhance strengths, confront realities inherent in the process of change.

Realia: a flower in the bud for each participant.

275

Process Questions/Experiments:

1. Entry—Allowing an easy response that gets the voice going and the person participating: What do you think about that bud you're holding?
2. Engagement—Making an initial connection with the literature: What speaks to you in this poem? What images do you see? What, if anything, turns you away? Do you notice anything interesting about the sounds in this poem? Here, depending on the type of group and its stage, we might introduce the sounds we have heard, simply voicing the repeated "er" sound and asking for responses, but offering none of our own.
3. Involvement—Introducing the turning point towards more personal interaction with literature and others: What are some of the difficulties or hurts about the life change you are contemplating? Must something in your life close for the new adventure to grow? What are some of the uncertainties? What calls you to do it anyway?
4. Incorporation—Putting thoughts and feelings into the body: Write as yourself one year from now, having made or not made the change.
5. Initiative—Applying the poetry therapy experience: Read aloud in the voice and posture of that year from now self and ask for feedback from the group. Make a statement of hope for that intended future.

ANNOTATED BIBLIOGRAPHY OF POEMS
ON FINDING A MAP TO TRAVEL BY

Aeschylus. "He who learns must suffer." "The Agamemnon." (First Stasimon, Strophe 3). *Familiar Quotations John Bartlett.* Ed. Emily Morrison Beck. Boston: Little, Brown & Company, (1855) 1982. Also in *The Orestes Plays of Aeschylus.* Trans. Paul Roche. New York: New American Library, 1962.

Aeschylus, the first recorded "modern" playwright of our Western civilization, in spare words that beat like hammer strokes, distills an existential truth: from pain comes wisdom. This message is sometimes distorted as a polyannish justification for suffering: "suffering is good for you," a message especially unwelcome coming from someone who is not suffering to someone who is. The deeper truth is that deep pain comes from the collapse of what we have come to count on, what has given meaning to our lives. Pain may pile upon pain. When that happens, we can choose to live or die. Through mistake and adversity we have the opportunity to learn and to grow. We might ask those recovering from suffering: What have you learned? Certainly the phrase in this selection, "against our will," leaves room to curse the people, circumstances, fates, and gods that seem responsible for our suffering. This excerpt represents the tragic viewpoint, which, in contrast to the viewpoint of "Endymion," would have us look at life clear-eyed, accept that it is full of pain, and meet this resolutely, stoically, and persevere no matter what.

Note: See copy of this excerpt at the end of the chapter.

Blumenthal, Michael. "The New Story of Your Life." *Against Romance: Poems by Michael Blumenthal*. New York: Viking Penguin, 1987.

Blumenthal's "New Story" is a prose poem that reads like a conversation with the author, who asks us to consider a "what-if" change of attitude toward adversity and suffering. What if it "is not the story of your defeat / or of your impotence and powerlessness"? What if it is "a story that requires of you a large thrust / into the difficult life"? Those who have in their background Homer's *Odyssey* will appreciate the reference to Calypso as a metaphor for all those forces we allow to seduce us from pursuing our own purposes. The attitude of this poem is quite the opposite of the mother who so coddles or swaddles her child that the child loses contact with his/her own power. This is a kick in the shins to co-dependency. However, if one who has suffered much at the hands of others comes to this poem cold, it might seem like a rebuff, an insult. But once the old story has been told, received, witnessed, accepted and honored, once the sufferer has been reminded of strengths and possibilities, this piece could be the measured slap that helps the reluctant newborn utter the first cry of aliveness.

Boye, Karin. "Yes It Hurts." *Iconographs: Translations of Six Contemporary Swedish Poets by May Swenson*. New York: Scribner, 1970.

In her exquisite translation of Boye's poem, American poet May Swenson invites us to hear its anxious ambivalence, its terror of leaving the known no matter how awful that may be, juxtaposed with its willingness to suffer any agonies in its passion for change, and at last, the open, airy, ecstatic freedom that comes of breaking through, making the new journey that life demands. Vivid nature images enhance the moving effects and appeal of the poem for a broad range of applications.

Note: See detailed analysis earlier in the chapter.

Cavafy. "Ithaka." *Greece in Poetry*. Ed. Simini Zafiropoulos. Harry Abrams, 1993.
"Ithaka" is an intimate conversation with a soothing tone. If we know
the Odyssey, the Laistragonians, the Cyclops, and angry Poseidon, then
the destination Ithaka will conjure vivid images of obstacles and adver-
sities. But perhaps it is even better to play the game of "dictionary" and
make up descriptions for these forces of the dark side, for who knows
them better than we do? (Well, perhaps others do, since they see our
blind side, or see further where we have only one eye). The speaker of
the poem says we will not meet these dark forces, unless we carry them
in our soul. Which, of course, we do. Antithetically, certain words echo
in the poem—"full," "long," "sensuous"—so that we may bathe in these
blessings. Our senses are not neglected: "mother of pearl, and coral,
amber and ebony / and sensuous perfumes of every kind." Since there
is nothing new under the sun, every poem retells an old story. This
poem illustrates our view that every poem is a story—this one certain-
ly is. And in poetry therapy we welcome, in addition to poems—stories,
journal, fairy tales, fables, parables, and all manifestations of imaginal
literature, written and oral. We could summarize this poem, saying "the
journey is more important than the destination." But to do so and skip
this marvelous poem would be to deprive ourselves of a real treat.

Dickinson, Emily. "I Never Saw a Moor." *The Complete Poems of Emily
Dickinson*, Thomas H. Johnson, Ed. Boston: Little, Brown and Company, 1960.
Dickinson's poem #1052 in its brevity juxtaposes our smallness with
the immensity of the universe, the unknown. How do we transcend
finiteness: through imagination, through what Emily calls God, or
heaven? Others have other names: spirit, cosmos, infinity, mystery.
There are five "I's" in this eight-line piece, and three "never's." The
repetition reinforces our being "just human," and knowing so little. Yet
in the ocean of this poem, the white sail of Emily's small bark can be
seen. Her faith sustains her. For the seeker who comes to poetry ther-
apy after loss, important questions about values are evoked: How do I
make manifest my finite self in this immensity? When in life do we pare
things down to just two: myself and the All?

Dickinson, Emily. "Tell all the Truth but tell it slant." *The Complete Poems
of Emily Dickinson*, Thomas H. Johnson, Ed. Boston: Little, Brown and
Company, 1960.

Poem #1129 presents the essence of the poetry therapy process. Metaphor and imagery give us an indirect approach to the harsh realities that few of us can bear. Even Aeschylus represented the unbearable in poetry. And yes, the naked truth can pack all the awesome—sometimes destructive—wallop of the lightning bolt, that toy of Zeus. And, yes, when struck that hard by intolerable reality, we might be dazzled blind and, like Oedipus and Jocasta, feel overwhelmed and act impulsively and destructively in an effort to escape. Here Emily effectively conveys the use of the lighter step. She places trauma terror in the comforting context of maternal idiom. She speaks to the power of metaphor, that smokescreen with a hole in it, that lie which leads to the truth. The poetry therapist would note that to continue too long aslant hobbles the relationship with truth, as seen in avoidant and passive-aggressive orientations to life. The therapeutic task for the poetry therapy participant is to discover at the right time the "superb surprise" of truth.

Eliot, T.S. "East Coker." *Four Quartets*. New York: Harcourt Brace Jovanovich, 1943, 1971.

The second of Eliot's *Four Quartets* is a riff on the passage of time. The language is highly intellectual and at first sight will appeal to those whose intellectual function, as Jung describes the function in *Psychological Types*, is primary. Those who lead with feeling function may feel put off by slightly pompous-sounding proclamations like "To arrive where you are, to get from where you are not / You must go by a way wherein there is no ecstasy." With both types present in the room we may have a good discussion going where thesis and antithesis can find a larger integration. Or we might just get conflict, depending in part on the skills of a facilitator. If we stick with it, we progress through a series of existential questions: where am I, where am I going, how do I get there? Conundrums like "what you do not know is the only thing you know" generate puzzlement which mimics the confusions we encounter in life. The underlying rhythm rocks us in a steady beating pattern as though to say, "It's alright, beneath the turbulence of the waves is a steady solid holding current." This is a great midlife crisis poem for those who can enjoy the stilted poetic diction prevailing at the time of its writing.

Green, Kate. "Don't Make Your Life Too Beautiful." *If the World is Running Out*. Duluth, Minnesota: Holy Cow Press, 1983.

This poem is an odd ambiguous piece that can be taken as serious or ironic. Here is an antithesis to "pretty," and at the antipode of Hallmark. It offers a mess of decay and disorder images we usually sweep under the rug, and which wouldn't be caught dead in a Romantic poem—images like "Leave the hole under the fence / the dog dug in the marigolds / that never flowered," like the neighbor's fallen roof shingles that are just right for mold, beetles, and worms, like "the rotten mattresses in the flagstone basement." The genteel reader might feel slightly queasy here, but the unsettled feeling might be a good goad for complacency. On the other hand, at the right moment, it might be an invitation to kick back and watch those weeds grow. Those who have messy attics and unbalanced checkbooks can take heart that others are worse offenders. Therapeutically there are a lot of useful work images here, as we invite participants to consider the unfixed holes in their lives, peer into what is moldering away under there. The depressed will be familiar with letting go and letting things go as "we bend over our hands / in search of something we held and lost." Subtly the poem urges the despairing to change direction, since there are "heartaches enough to live for." But it is okay not to change. She exhorts: "Live out your ecstasy on earth."

Hewitt, Christopher. "The Enticing Lane." *Poets for Life: Seventy-six Poets Respond to AIDS.* Ed. Michael Klein. New York: Persea Books, Inc., 1989.

Here is a man's voicing of the popular, "If I Had My Life to Live Over" essay, that sighs in regret for a life half-lived, and in determination to seize what is left of the too short day. But it is not merely a directive for growing more daisies and eating more ice cream. The poet, a man who has loved a man, speaks of the "Disease," and "Death Unknown," making probable reference to the ravages of the AIDS epidemic. He says that if he, too, were afflicted, he would reexamine his life from a more benign perspective; he would have lived it with more pleasure, more integrity, more adventure. His poem piles sentence upon long sentence of remorseful "should have[s]" separated by one brief fulcrum statement: "But I let myself be dissuaded / by the sensible people." He laments not having allowed himself to walk "the enticing lane" that is there in his "heart's eye." Though the poet is evidently a middle-aged or older man, his poem could evoke open communication, self-awareness, and self-acceptance among youth at risk because of gender-identity anxieties. Evocative work with this poem could include exploring the divergent meanings of "sensible" and establishing the groundwork for developing participants' own life values. This piece is in the middle ages memento mori tradition which contemplates a skull or other signs of mortality in order to have that consciousness affect our life today. The poetry therapist might elicit discussion about the affliction of AIDS as a mortality symbol that can help survivors deal with such shattering phenomena as other life-threatening illnesses, wars, and natural disasters as well as the many facets of post-traumatic stress disorder. Exploration of "the enticing lane" can evoke stories of roads both taken and not, with their life-changing consequences.

Hugo, Victor, "Be Like the Bird." *Splinters: A Book of Very Short Poems.* New York: Oxford Univ. Press, 1989.

This brief piece invites us to try on one image from nature: a small bird feeling the branch give way, but aware he/she has wings, therefore can sing. We have all experienced something giving way under us, less supportive than we had thought. Most find we can fly, though we may forget it in the anxious moment. Often people come to poetry therapy having fallen to the ground and suffered physical or emotional injury. They can learn to fly and to sing for the first time with their authentic voices.

Keats, John. "A Thing of Beauty." (*Endymion*, Book I, lines 1-33). *The Poetical Works of John Keats.* Ed. H. Buxton Forman. London: Oxford University Press, 1931.

In *Endymion* the modern reader first notes the archaic language, some of which has been appropriated by Madison Avenue: "a thing of beauty is a joy forever." Older people, however, might appreciate language that has been depreciated by time. Here is the speech of Duke Senior, expressed by the youthful Keats. Despite "despondence . . . gloomy days . . . unhealthy ways," an "endless fountain" pours onto us from "heaven's brink." The trees, the moon, clear rills "Haunt us until they become a cheering light." This poem pours itself out in wordy exuberance. The young can find cause here to mock the superannuated; at the same time there is opportunity to find an appreciation of what has gone before, either in language now dead, or in our elders still living. We can envision a discussion of poems like this as part of an intergenerational appreciation project. This poem mouths the archetypal truth that finding a way to our puny self with transcendent connection to the large scheme of things—natural, traditional, cosmic, religious—might help lift our existential angst or lighten our clinical depressions.

Note: See copy of this excerpt at the end of the chapter.

Kinnell, Galway. "The Still Time." *Galway Kinnell, Selected Poems.* Boston: Houghton Mifflin Co. 1982. Also in *Contemporary American Poetry* Third Edition. Ed. A. Poulin, Jr. Boston: Houghton Mifflin.

Here is a wonderful passage poem. Its language is more accessible to today's reader than T.S. Eliot's, but it too describes the passage of time as a developmental spiral that returns us to an old place having the ability to take a new direction. There are a lot of feeling words here: "failed harvests of want," "fear . . . rummaged down to its husk," "young and empty," "hollows the heart out irreversibly." Like all good poems it is strong because of its language, its images, and the importance of its questions: how can I go on, how can I hope yet to thrive, despite the adversities, the losses, the passage of time?

Note: See detailed analysis earlier in the chapter.

Levertov, Denise. "The Fountain." *Poems 1960–1967.* New York: New Directions Publishing Corporation, 1983. Also in *Cries of the Spirit: A Celebration of Women's Spirituality.* Ed. Marilyn Sewell. Boston: Beacon Press, 1991 and New York: Houghton Mifflin Company, 2000.

"Don't say there is no water," Levertov begins and repeats her invocation. She speaks directly to us in this, her map for lost travelers, too tired and thirsty to go on, too hopeless of finding our way, and she promises with certainty that help lies ahead. She pledges that no matter how parched our hearts, the spring that will refresh us is there, as it has always been. She knows, because she has been drained, depleted, and has drunk there. She reminds us that we, too, have quenched our thirst there. She bids us find our footholds, climb and drink. Discussion and sharing of both actual and metaphorical fountains would allow group members to provide inspiration for each other as they confront difficult travel and desiccation on their journeys.

Note: See detailed analysis earlier in the chapter.

Machado, Antonio. "Wayfarer, the only way. . . ." *Antonio Machado: Selected Poems.* Trans. A. Trueblood. Cambridge, Massachusetts: Harvard University Press, 1982.

The story of this poem is as simple as Machado's language. It says, the only way to live is to make your own decisions and proceed according to those choices. There is no blueprint or diagram to show you the right way. Once you have set your own course, you can look back to determine what you have accomplished, but it is now over and complete. The music of the poem is like a chant, and the images are few: footsteps, path, foam trails to the sea. This would be a fine piece to bring to a developmental group of people about to engage in some new endeavor, a sea change.

Note: See detailed analysis earlier in the chapter.

Madgett, Naomi Long. "Woman With Flower." *The Garden Times: Twentieth-Century African-American Poetry.* Ed. Clarence Major. Boston: Harper Collins, 1996. Also in *The Forerunners: Black Poets in America.* Ed. Woodie King, Jr. Washington, D.C.: Howard University Press, 1975.

Madgett's poem does not have some of the strong images of "Advice to My Son," which could evoke the street experience. Like "Advice to My Son," the language and structure are uncomplicated. The images, though a bit clichéd, like "the leaf's inclined to find its own direction," can invite interpretation, agreement/disagreement, and exploration. This poem's message might be directed at too-protective parents or too-directive teachers and counselors who coax, watch, or prod too much. Its injunctions to "let the soil rest from so much digging," or "the things we love we have to learn to leave alone" might stimulate discussion amongst parents or teachers regarding the optimal ways to help youth, help patients or clients, to grow. It might invite the over-timid to wriggle from the grasp of the over-controlling.

Meinke, Peter. "Advice to My Son." *Liquid Paper: New and Selected Poems.* Pittsburgh: University of Pittsburgh Press, 1991.

At first look, "Advice to My Son" seems to offer a laundry list. It begins "The trick is, to live your days / as if each one may be your last." This seems like stuffed-shirt advice in the spirit of Polonius' advice to Laertes in Hamlet: "neither a borrower nor a lender be." In this sense it offers an invitation for offspring to gently mock their over-protective progenitors. But the poem can stand in loco parentis for the poorly-parented. The words "men lose their lives in strange and unimaginable ways" and "if you survive" might, in the right setting, offer an entry into the everyday life of young people in our inner cities: their anger, despair, defiance. The poem conveys the idea of beauty as a saving nectar, not alone, but in conjunction with what feeds the belly as well. The poem helps create a space for the future, for the idea of foresight and planning: "marry a pretty girl / after seeing her mother." These specific recipes can open the door to examination of life issues, such as the criteria for choosing a partner. The poem is pretty spare poetically, not too charged with meaning or dense with poetic qualities. It will not hook with its beauty, but its homely quality will not intimidate those just beginning to explore reading and writing, and themselves.

Oliver, Mary. "In Blackwater Woods." *American Primitive*. Boston: Little, Brown, and Company, 1983. Also in *New and Selected Poems*. Boston: Beacon Press 1992 and *Cries of the Spirit: A Celebration of Women's Spirituality*. Boston: Beacon Press, 1991 and New York: Houghton Mifflin Company, 2000.

The story in "Blackwater Woods" is of loss, of transfiguration. Nothing remains in its familiar form; the trees transform into light energy, their work fulfilled, their bark emitting its sweet scent as they leave. The cattails burst and float into air; even the ponds have lost their names. They will no longer exist on the map. As each year passes, it takes with it what has been meaningful and known, and we are left to find our way. How can we travel without a map, when senseless disasters rob us of meaning, when we lose what we love most, when we face the inevitable endings of what we depend upon to last? To live, Oliver says, we "must be able to do three things": love what we know we will lose, hold it for dear life, then let it go.

Note: See detailed analysis earlier in the chapter.

Oliver, Mary. "The Journey." *Dream Work*. New York: The Atlantic Monthly Press, 1986. Also in *New and Selected Poems*. Boston: Beacon Press, 1992 and *Cries of the Spirit: A Celebration of Women's Spirituality*. Ed. Marilyn Sewell. Boston: Beacon Press, 1991 and New York: Houghton Mifflin Company, 2000.

Mary Oliver gives us the map that Greek myth gave to Psyche to guide her quest towards spiritual fulfillment. It is an evocation, a call to adventure for all of us who must learn to hear and heed our own authentic voice, dare to begin our travel in a new way, and risk the hazards of the unknown in order to become our true selves. Whether we do precisely as our parents, teachers, friends have taught us or exactly the opposite, we are still obeying the old rules rather than creating our own based on our own experiences and conclusions. Like Psyche in her little boat, we must ignore any blandishments or warnings from voices not our own, lest we be pulled under and drown. Roger Housden, in his book, *Ten Poems to Change Your Life*, writes: ". . . the new identity is self-born, an immaculate conception of the spirit in you that is on an altogether different frequency and level to the life you have lived so far. . . . [It] does not walk away from the world, but into it." By following this map, we invite the participants in poetry therapy to travel in genuineness, courage, responsibility, and beauty.

Piercy, Marge. "To Be of Use." *Circles on the Water: Selected Poems of Marge Piercy*. New York: Alfred A. Knopf, 1982. Also in *Cries of the Spirit: A Celebration of Women's Spirituality*. Ed. Marilyn Sewell. Boston: Beacon Press, 1991 and New York: Houghton Mifflin Company, 2000.

Here, of course, is the map of work and also of spirit, drawn by Marge Piercy's uncompromising and deft hand. Her metaphor is water, in which we spend our days swimming confidently and joyfully like seals in their element, pulling and plodding ponderously in muck like water buffalo, or swimming synchronously like a water ballet corps, doing what is most ordinary and vital for life. In her first three of the five verses, she speaks of her loving, respectful attitude towards people who work in these ways. In the fourth verse, she steps back and invites us to look at work together, judging the product and its manner of execution rather than its creator. When the work is done carelessly, the water evaporates and mud becomes dust; when work worth doing is done well, it provides satisfaction. In her final verse, she shifts gracefully into a spiritual dimension. First, we see the well-done work of hands that turn clay, which is mud, into things of beauty: amphoras, vases, pitchers; then we see that it is we who are the clay, worked by the unseen hand, longing to be useful, crying to hold work/water/meaning within us. Which character or object speaks for you?

Rumi, Jelaluddin. "The Guest House." *The Essential Rumi*. Trans. Coleman Barks with John Moyne. San Francisco: Harper, 1995.

How difficult it is for most people to make room within the house of self for unbidden emotions or seemingly uncharacteristic responses to life challenges. We call certain of our emotions "negative" and try to hide them from others and ourselves. We welcome joy with ease, but depression? meanness? shame? malice? a crowd of sorrows? Hardly! Rumi entreats us to invite them in, all of them, honoring and entertaining each with hospitality, even with laughter. "This being human," he says, affords us new opportunities to grow in awareness and acceptance each morning. Such a wholesome viewpoint would be accepted by most people, particularly those who have been participating in either a developmental or a clinical poetry therapy group for some time and are working towards termination.

Note: See detailed analysis earlier in the chapter.

Sandburg, Carl. "What Shall He Tell That Son?" (Verse #9 of "The People, Yes" copyright 1936, 1964). *The Complete Poems of Carl Sandburg*, Revised and Expanded Edition. New York: Harcourt Brace Jovanovich, Publishers, 1970.

"Be easy with yourself, so you can do the hardest thing: be yourself" says delightfully this "advice" poem. In the form and tone of an intimate chat, it transcends the pretentiousness inherent in this genre. The device is a chain of transmission: speaker to listener, coaching him on speaking to the son nearing manhood. The speaker does not come off sounding like Jacques' judge in Shakespeare's *As You Like It*: "In fair round belly with good capon lined / With eyes severe and beard of formal cut / Full of wise saws and modern instances." Instead he comes across as the good uncle or granddad, unpretentious and folksy, and the advice is welcoming: "Without rich wanting, nothing arrives." We get some instruction: "money has killed men and left them dead years before burial," and "tell himself no lies about himself." But we get even more imagery, like "rich soft wanting" and paradox, like "Life is hard; be steel; be a rock" and "Life is soft loam; go gentle; go easy." This piece opens us to consider what advice we have received, from whom, how we felt and reacted, what we have rejected and kept, and what wisdom we have for ourselves now.

Sarton, May. "Myself to Me." *Selected Poems of May Sarton*. Eds. S. Hilsinger & Lois Byrnes. New York: W.W. Norton & Co., 1978.

"Myself to Me" is one of the few pieces in our collection constructed in rhyming couplets. Rhyme is one of the constants people associate with poetry, yet it strikes the American reader growing up since the 1950s

286

as a bit quaint. Yet paired lines effectively carry this meditation on love. Rhyme here is part of the containment and lightens the mood. The poet is coping with pain, and shows us herself doing so: "Out of the passion comes the form / And only passion keeps it warm." We need a structured container for painful emotions to keep pain from becoming unbearable. But if the structure is too rigid or impenetrable, we will freeze within. This is an old story, a central story: how to continue making new loves in the face of the pain we hold from old loves. Is it better to have loved and lost than never to have loved at all? This poem begins "Set the table and sweep the floor— / Love will not come back to this door," tells us that "Love all unasked broke down the door / To bring me pain as it did before," and concludes: "Set the table, sweep the floor— / Forget the lies you told before." The form of this poem is an "I-Thou" conversation with self and is confessional, yet contained. In exploring this piece, we can go in the direction of past and current relationships, hurts, gratifications, how we protect ourselves, what kind of door we have, what lies we tell ourselves, and what it is like to be alone.

Tzu, Lao. "I have just three things to teach:" (excerpt) *Lao-Tzu, The Sacred Books of China: The Texts of Taoism.* Trans. Gia-fu Feng and Jane English. Oxford: The Clarendon Press, 1891. Also in *Tao Te Ching.* Trans. Stephen Mitchell. New York: HarperCollins, 1988.

Mitchell's improvisation on Chapters 67 and 22 of the pre-Confucian Tao, is a good example of didactic literature. It imparts traditional wisdom: be modest, don't let ego get in the way. The speaker in the poem talks to the reader of the basics: "simplicity, patience, compassion." To those impatient with being instructed by the elders, this piece is a good launch pad for expressing their feelings about authority. Such persons might be more receptive to the ambiguous lines "Because he doesn't know who he is / people recognize themselves in him," and "Because [the wise person] has no goal in mind / everything he does succeeds." Younger people wrestle with what success is and compare themselves mercilessly to others. To those more experienced in life, this piece is an invitation to share what they have discovered about "simplicity," "patience," and "compassion." Participants of all ages can use this piece as a starting place to write about and discuss "wisdom you have received," "false wisdom you have been given," and "wisdom you have discovered." The poetry therapist can use the structure of cause-and-

effect lines to invite participants to explore, in writing and in discus-
sion, their varying degrees of blindness about the consequences of their
actions. This didactic poem offers opportunity for those who have been
over- or under-parented to confront their attitudes towards authority.

Whitman, Walt. "A child said, What is the grass?" ("Song of Myself" Verse
6). *Selected Poems 1855-1892*. A New Edition. Ed. Gary Schmidgall. New
York: St. Martin's Press, 1999. Also in *Leaves of Grass and Selected Prose*. Ed.
John Kouwenhoven. New York: Random House, 1950; *Leaves of Grass*. New
York: Barnes & Noble Books, 1993; and *The Norton Anthology of Poetry*
Fourth Edition. Eds. Margaret Fergusen, Mary Jo Salter & Jon Stallworthy
New York: W.W. Norton & Co., 1996.

> *Leaves of Grass* resumes, an ocean away and a half-century later, where
> Wordsworth, in his "Intimations Ode," leaves off. Again the eternal
> human struggle against mortality and finiteness begins with the child
> It is a pleasure to follow the poet's tour de force, via a child's question
> "What is the grass?" It is a litany of the one and the many: "the flag of
> my disposition," "the handkerchief of the Lord," a "uniform hiero-
> glyphic," and, famously, "the uncut hair of graves." Whitman does with
> the word "grass" what Mozart does with the simple tune, "Twinkle,
> Twinkle Little Star." All lovers of language will love the dance of
> images. It is a brilliant move to use homely grass as a metaphor that
> links the generations, genders, the living and the dead. This is another
> effort to take the sting from death: "if ever [death] was, it led forward
> life, and does not wait at the end to arrest it. . . ." This poem may invite
> us as reader to unpack the meanings that inhere in common objects.
> What stories inhabit the tree in our yard, the photo on our desk, the
> pen in the drawer, that piece of bric-a-brac, the dishes that we grumpi-
> ly wash? Here is a celebration of the most ordinary.
> Note: See copy of this excerpt at the end of the chapter.

Wordsworth, William, "And O, Ye Fountains. . . ." (Verse XI in "Ode:
Intimations of Immortality From Recollections of Early Childhood." *William
Wordsworth: Selected Poems*. New York: Gramercy Books, 1993. Also in *The
Norton Anthology of Poetry* Third Edition. Ed. Alexander Allerin. New York:
W.W. Norton & Company, 1983.

> This is the final stanza of a poem that looks back from an unhappy
> threshold that marks the end of life, or the end of joy. The grand sweep

of the poem moves from birth "trailing clouds of glory." Life is a decline from original bliss into a "prison house" that snuffs all but the embers of the original flame of delight, liberty, and hope. This poem tries to find antidotes to the necessary relinquishments that life and time bring. The two antidotes are memories of past loves and joys in this world, and a connection to a transcendent mother nature. This is a comforting view that tries to wipe away pain, so different from the standpoint of an Aeschylus, who achieves transcendence by embracing pain. Freud, who embraced the view of Aeschylus, disparagingly called the Romantic merger with nature the "oceanic" feeling. Readers of this poem who are not privileged to have memories of past loves and joys may strongly reject this poem's transcendent viewpoint but can identify more strongly with life as "prison house." Although some readers will be put off by the ornate Romantic language and sentiment, others will enjoy the sweeping flight of syllables and be able to release suppressed tears—especially if this poem is recited aloud with Beethoven or Brahms in the background. If the nineteenth century language is not a barrier, participants can use this map of passage through life to consider whether they have had, or can have, a golden age.

Note: See copy of this excerpt at the end of the chapter.

THE AGAMEMNON (first stasimon, strophe 3)

He who learns must suffer. And in our
sleep pain, that cannot forget falls drop by
drop upon the heart, and in our own despair,
against our will, comes wisdom by the
awful grace of God.

Aeschylus

Excerpt from ENDYMION

A thing of beauty is a joy for ever:
Its loveliness increases; it will never
Pass into nothingness; but still will keep
A bower quiet for us, and a sleep
Full of sweet dreams, and health, and quiet breathing.
Therefore, on every morrow, are we wreathing
A flowery band to bind us to the earth,
Spite of despondence, of the inhuman dearth
Of noble natures, of the gloomy days,
Of all the unhealthy and o'er-darkened ways
Made for our searching: yes, in spite of all,
Some shape of beauty moves away the pall
From our dark spirits. Such the sun, the moon,
Trees old and young, sprouting a shady boon
For simple sheep; and such are daffodils
With the green world they live in; and clear rills
That for themselves a cooling covert make
'Gainst the hot season; the mid forest brake,
Rich with a sprinkling of fair musk-rose blooms:
And such too is the grandeur of the dooms
We have imagined for the mighty dead;
All lovely tales that we have heard or read:
An endless fountain of immortal drink,
Pouring unto us from the heaven's brink.
Nor do we merely feel these essences
For one short hour; no, even as the trees
That whisper round a temple become soon
Dear as the temple's self, so does the moon,
The passion poesy, glories infinite,
Haunt us till they become a cheering light
Unto our souls, and bound to us so fast,
That, whether there be shine, or gloom o'ercast,
They always must be with us, or we die.

John Keats

SONG OF MYSELF, Part 6

A child said What is the grass? fetching it to me with full hands;
How could I answer the child? . . . I do not know what it is
   any more than he.

I guess it must be the flag of my disposition,
   out of hopeful green stuff woven.

Or I guess it is the handkerchief of the Lord,
A scented gift and remembrancer designedly dropped,
Bearing the owner's name someway in the corners,
   that we may see and remark, and say Whose?

Or I guess is itself a child . . . the produced babe of the vegetation.

Or I guess it is a uniform hieroglyphic,
And it means, Sprouting alike in broad zones and narrow zones,
Growing among black folks as among white,
Kanuck, Tuckahoe, Congressman, Cuff, I give them the same,
   I receive them the same.

And now it seems to me the beautiful uncut hair of graves.

Tenderly will I use you curling grass,
It may be you transpire from the breasts of young men,
It may be if I had known them I would have loved them;
It may be you are from old people or from women, and from offspring
   taken soon out of their mothers' laps,
And here you are the mothers' laps.

This grass is very dark to be from the white heads of old mothers,
Darker than the colorless beards of old men,
Dark to come from under the faint red roofs of mouths.

O I perceive after all so many uttering tongues!
And I perceive they do not come from the roofs of mouths for nothing.
I wish I could translate the hints about the dead young men and women,

292

And the hints about old men and mothers, and the offspring taken soon
    out of their laps.

What do you think has become of the young and old men?
And what do you think has become of the women and children?

They are alive and well somewhere;
The smallest sprout shows there is really no death,
And if ever there was it led forward life, and does not wait at the end
    to arrest it,
And ceas'd the moment life appear'd.

All goes onward and outward . . . and nothing collapses,
And to die is different from what any one supposed, and luckier.

                                 Walt Whitman

Excerpt from ODE: INTIMATIONS OF IMMORTALITY FROM RECOLLECTIONS OF EARLY CHILDHOOD

And O, ye Fountains, Meadows, Hills, and Groves,
Forebode not any severing of our loves!
Yet in my heart of hearts I feel your might;
I only have relinquished one delight
To live beneath your more habitual sway.
I love the Brooks which down their channels fret,
Even more than when I tripped lightly as they;
The innocent brightness of a new-born Day
Is lovely yet;
The Clouds that gather round the setting sun
Do take a sober colouring from an eye
That hath kept watch o'er man's mortality;
Another race hath been, and other palms are won.
Thanks to the human heart by which we live,
Thanks to its tenderness, its joys, and fears,
To me the meanest flower that blows can give
Thoughts that do often lie too deep for tears.

William Wordsworth

REFERENCES

Adams, Kathleen. *The Write Way to Wellness: A Workbook for Healing and Change.* Lakewood, Colorado: The Center for Journal Therapy, 2000.

Eliot, T.S. "Little Gidding," *The Four Quartets.* London: Faber and Faber, 1974.

Fox, John. *Finding What You Didn't Lose.* New York: Jeremy Tarcher, 1995.

Frankl, Viktor. *Man's Search for Meaning: An Introduction to Logotherapy.* Trans. Ilse Lasch. New York: Simon & Schuster, 1962, pp. 111-113.

Gordimer, Nadine. "The Writing Life." *Washington Post Book World,* August 5, 2001.

Gorelick, Kenneth. "Rapprochement Between the Arts and Psychotherapies: Metaphor the Mediator." *The Arts in Psychotherapy,* Vol. 16, (1989): 149-155.

Grass, Gunter quoted in "The Writing Life," Nadine Gordimer. *Washington Post Book World,* August 5, 2001.

Heller, Peggy O. "Poetry Therapy Training Manual for Mental Health Professionals." Doctoral Dissertation. Pacific Western University, 1995.

Housden, Roger. *Ten Poems to Change Your Life.* Harmony Books 2001. Excerpted in O Magazine. July 2001.

Hynes, Arleen M. and Mary Hynes-Berry. *Bibliotherapy—The Interactive Process: A Handbook.* Boulder, Colorado: Westview Press, 1986; St. Cloud, Minnesota: North Star Press of St. Cloud, Inc., 1992, p. 1.

Jung, C.G. *Psychological Types.* Princeton, New Jersey: Princeton Univ. Press, 1974.

Kafka, Franz. "Before the Law," *The Complete Stories of Franz Kafka.* Ed. Nahum Glatzer. New York: Schocken Books, 1972, p. 165.

Machado, Antonio. "Sonnet 47" (Verse II). *Antonio Machado: Selected Poems*. Trans. Alan S. Trueblood. Cambridge: Harvard University Press, 1982.

Moon, William. "Least Heat." *Blue Highways*. Boston: Back Bay Press, 1999.

Ondaatje. Michael. *The English Patient*. New York: Knopf, 1992, p. 261.

Rumi, Jellaludin. "On the Threshold." *In the Arms of the Beloved*. Trans. Jonathan Star. New York: Tarcher/Putnam, 1997, p. 61.

Rumi, Jellaludin. *Open Secret: Versions of Rumi*. Trans. John Moyne and Coleman Barks. Putney, Vermont: Threshold Books, 1984, p. xxi.

Winchester, Simon. *The Map That Changed the World*. New York: Harper-Collins, 2001.

Yeats, W.B. "The Second Coming." *The Norton Anthology of Poetry*. New York: W.W. Norton, 1970.

AUTHOR BIOGRAPHIES

Kathleen Adams, L.P.C., R.P.T., is a Licensed Professional Counselor and Registered Poetry/Jouranl Therapist in private practice in Denver, CO. She is the author of five books on the power of writing to heal, including the best-selling *Journal to the Self*, and is the founder/directorof the Center for Journal Therapy. In 1998 she received the NAPT Distinguished Service Award for her groundbreaking work in bringing journal and poetry therapy to populations as diverse as survivors of catastrophic trauma, people living with HIV/AIDS, cancer patients, addicts, and the homeless. She was the president of the National Association for Poetry Therapy from 2001 to 2003.

Rosalie Brown, B.A., R.P.T. (1929 to 2001) was employed at St. Elizabeth's Hospital in Washington, D.C., as the first federally designated bibiotherapist for eighteen years before retiring in 1991. She was instrumental in developing and directing St. Elizabeth's bibliotherapy training program. Ms. Brown was a founding member of NAPT and a long-standing board member. She was chair of the Education Committee until 1989 and, thereafter, was an active member of the Certification Committee of NAPT. In 1991, she was designated as a mentor/supervisor. Ms. Brown was presented with the NAPT Arthur Lerner Pioneer Award in 1999 for "her pioneering dedication to professionalism in poetry therapy." She wrote seven published articles on bibliotherapy.

Geri Chavis, Ph.D., C.P.T., L.P., is an English professor and recent past Endowed Professor of Humanities at the College of St. Catherine, where she teaches courses in poetry/bibliotherapy, literature, writing, women's studies, and family studies. She has been a Vice President of the National Association for Poetry Therapy, has served on the NAPT Board for fifteen years, is an Associate Editor of the *Journal of Poetry Therapy*, and coordinates the Minnesota Poetry Therapy Network. In 1990, she received NAPT's Outstanding Achievement Award. She is a licensed psychologist, certified poetry therapist, and NAPT-approved mentor-supervisor who works with individuals, couples, families, and groups. Over the past twenty-five years, Geri has presented a wide variety of workshops in the area of creative arts therapy. She has edited a short story anthology, *Family: Stories from the Interior*, and authored numerous book chapters and articles in the area of poetry/ bibliotherapy.

Lisa Friedlander, M.A., M.S.W., L.I.C.S.W., currently works as a psychotherapist in private practice with individuals, couples, and families. Within a general practice, specialties include sexuality, mood disorders, adolescent issues, and life transitions. She utilizes poetry bibliotherapy frequently as well as other creative arts such as drawing and movement. She has completed the Ericksonian hypnotherapy course and was a fellow at McLean Hospital in the human sexuality clinic. For thirteen years she taught full time at Russell Sage College and then at Tufts University, developing and implementing programs in movement therapy, psychology of the body, and seminars in creative arts therapies. She was dance critic for Boston Phoenix for five years and has published essays and poetry in a number of venues. She was Vice President of Membership for NAPT, co-editor of the *Museletter*, and conference chair for the 2002 annual NAPT conference.

Kenneth P. Gorelick, MD, R.P.T., was Director of Continuing Medical Education at a major teaching hospital for twenty-eight years and has conducted a private practice of psychotherapy and poetry therapy. He is a clinical professor of psychiatry at George Washington University. He has taught poetry therapy in the graduate programs of The Catholic University of America and Lesley College in Cambridge, MA. A president of NAPT from 1987 to 1991 and the NAPT Foundation, he has presented workshops nationally and internationally. He serves on the editorial boards of *The Journal of Poetry Therapy*. He is a board-certified psychiatrist and a fellow of the American Psychiatric Association.

Deborah Eve Grayson, M.S., L.M.H.C., R.P.T., is a Licensed Mental Health Counselor with areas of specialty in hypnosis, the healing arts, eating disorders, and sex therapy. For twenty years, she served as an active member of the board for NAPT, with six of those years dedicated to serving as the Certification Chairperson. A Registered Poetry Therapist since 1991, and an NAPT Mentor/Supervisor, Deborah was the 1997 recipient of NAPT's Distinguished Service Award. She is the author of three books and is also an award-winning photographer. She maintains a private practice in Fort Lauderdale, Florida, and continues to facilitate workshops and out-reach programs on poetry therapy and the related expressive art therapies. She received the Art Lerner Educational Grant in 2001 for her "Poets for Peace Project."

Peggy Osna Heller, Ph.D., L.I.C.S.W., R.P.T., is a diplomate in clinical social work. She has taught courses in poetry therapy at The Catholic University School of Social Service in Washington, D.C., George Mason University in Fairfax, VA, and the University of Maryland School of Social Work. She serves as adjunct faculty for The Union Institute Graduate School. A lecturer and workshop leader nationally, she is a past president of NAPT and the NAPT Foundation. She has held poetry therapy positions at hospitals and treatment centers and founded the Poetry Therapy Training Institute in 1993. She maintains a private practice in psychotherapy and poetry therapy. Since 1995, she and Dr. Gorelick have co-directed the Wordsworth Center for Growth and Healing.

Arleen McCarty Hynes, R.P.T., is a retired biblio/poetry therapist and a member of a religious community, the Order of St. Benedict, in St. Joseph, Minnesota. She began her career in biblio/poetry therapy in 1970, working with patients at St. Elizabeths Hospital, Washington, D.C. She initiated the Biblio/Poetry Therapy Training Program there in 1974. With Dr. Kenneth Gorelick as mentor, it became the first curriculum-based, 440-hour, two-year program in a training hospital, where didactic work, experiential group work with mental patients, and individual and group supervision were part of the program that continued after she left in 1980, for a total of twenty-five years under the directorship of Dr. Gorelick. Hynes received her C.P.T. in 1974 and R.P.T. in 1989. She served on the board of NAPT until 1986. She has taught short-term academic bibliotherapy courses at universities and numerous workshops since 1974. Over the years, she has worked with groups of mental patients, battered women, persons in chemical dependency units, aging persons, and adult growth groups, and has led Poetry as Prayer groups since 1984. Designed as the first academic textbook to train biblio/poetry therapists in 1986, *Bibliotherapy—the Interactive Process: A Handbook* was published by Westview Press and reprinted in 1992 by North Star Press of St. Cloud, Inc. Mary Hynes-Berry, Ph.D., served as co-author of the work. Hynes helped establish the National Federation for Biblio/Poetry therapy in

1984, serving on that Board to the present. She has received NAPT and other national awards for her pioneering work in this field, as well as contributing chapters to books and many articles to professional journals.

Barbara Kreisberg, M.S., C.T.R.S., C.P.T., is a certified recreational therapist and certified poetry therapist. She has had over twenty years experience working in the area of mental health as an expressive therapist in various hospital settings and presently works as a poetry therapist at South Miami Hospital. She has facilitated a number of writing for personal growth workshops and courses in the community at the Baptist Hospital Women's Resource Center, the David and Mary Alper Jewish Community Center, Florida International University, Gilda's Club and Miami Dade Community College to name a few. Her groups emphasize the use of writing for personal growth, self reflection, and healing. She has also served on the Board of the NAPT and was the Conference Chair for the annual conference in Albuquerque, New Mexico, in May, 2000.

Deborah Langosch, A.C.S.W, C.P.T., is a clinical social worker and psychotherapist in private practice. She specializes in working with children, adolescents, and bereavement issues. Ms. Langosch is a certified poetry therapist and a mentor/supervisor. She has served as the Executive Director of the NAPT and for the Federation for Biblio/Poetry Therapy. Ms. Langosch has been an active board and committee member for NAPT. She was the recipient of the Distinguished Service Award from NAPT in 2001. Ms. Langosch has lectured extensively on poetry therapy and has written a number of articles on poetry therapy and on children and loss. She is currently completing her doctoral work at New York University.

Perie Longo, Ph.D., is a Registered Poetry Therapist and Marriage and Family Therapist. She directs the poetry therapy program at Sanctuary Psychiatric Centers of Santa Barbara, is a consultant for poetry therapy at Antioch University, and is in private practice. She has been on the board of NAPT as vice-president and secretary, served on the certification committee for six years, and is a mentor/supervisor for those seeking certification as poetry therapists. In 1998 she received the Outstanding Achievement Award from NAPT and in 2000 was the keynote speaker for the national conference in Albuquerque. Her speech, "Gathered around the Heart of the Fire," appeared in the *Journal of Poetry Therapy*, Spring 2001 issue. She has authored two books of poetry, *Milking the Earth* and *The Privacy of Wind*.

Nicholas Mazza, Ph.D., is a Professor of Social Work at Florida State University. Dr. Mazza holds Florida licenses in clinical social work, psychology, and marriage and family therapy. He has been involved in the practice, research, and teaching of poetry therapy for thirty years. Dr. Mazza is the founding (1987) and current editor of the *Journal of Poetry Therapy* and the author of *Poetry Therapy: Interface of the Arts and Psychology* (1999, CRC Press). He is past Vice President and current board member of NAPT. In 1997, Dr. Mazza received the Pioneer Award from NAPT. In addition to poetry therapy, Dr. Mazza has practiced, taught, and published in the areas of crisis intervention, death and trauma, family therapy, group work, clinical theories and models, and the arts in community practice.

Sherry Reiter, Ph.D., C.S.W., is a Registered Poetry Therapist/Mentor-Supervisor and Registered Drama Therapist/Board Certified Trainer. She is the Director of the Creative "Righting" Center where she trains professionals in poetry therapy and is a therapist in private practice. Sherry is a past President of NAPT and the current President of the National Federation for Biblio/Poetry Therapy. Her belief in the healing power of creativity is central to her work.

Stephen Rojcewicz is a psychiatrist, with a subspecialization in Forensic Psychiatry. He is committed to the integration of psychiatry and the humanities, and has written numerous professional articles on the interplay between psychiatry and literature. He is also the co-author of a textbook on *Supportive Psychotherapy*, published by the American Psychiatric Association. Steve was the President of NAPT from 1997 to 1999, and remains active on the NAPT Board, and in liaison with other creative arts therapies organizations. He is currently involved in translating poems on the role of the poet.

Charles Rossiter, Ph.D., C.P.T., is a board member and past vice-president of NAPT. He has received an NEA fellowship for his poetry and is the Book Review Editor for *The Journal of Poetry Therapy*, to which he is a frequent contributor. His most recent publications are *Back Beat, Cold Mountain 2000: Han Shan in the City*, and *What Men Talk About*, which won the first Red Wheel Barrow Prize from Pudding Press. He also co-produces and hosty the audio poetry website poetrypoetry.com.

Alma Maria Rolfs, L.I.C.S.W., R.P.T., is a licensed independent clinical social worker, registered poetry therapist, educator, and NAPT mentor/supervisor. She has had a private psychotherapy practice with adults, adolescents, and couples for over twenty years and has practiced and supervised poetry therapy in a wide range of mental health settings. She was director of a multidisciplinary Expressive Therapies Department in a private psychiatric hospital in Chicago, where she also directed a Latino Counseling Services program, making use of her bilingual/bicultural background. She has served as NAPT Newsletter Editor, as member of the NAPT Credential Committee, as Recording Secretary, and as an active member of the NAPT Board for many years, and received the NAPT Distinguished Service Award in 1994. She has taught in the Graduate Art Therapy Program at the School of the Art Institute in Chicago, and presently teaches in the Psychology Department at Antioch University Seattle. She is currently a full-time clinician affiliated with PBHN, a group private practice in Seattle, where she also runs the Northwest Poetry Therapy Training Program and is a Board member of the Northwest Poetry Therapy Group. Her clinical specialties both as psychotherapist and poetry therapist include working with multicultural and identity issues, women's issues, and grief and loss.

Lila Weisberger, M.S., R.P.T., C.A.S.A.C., was President of NAPT from 1999 to 2001, served for four
years as the Chair of the Certification Committee and remains active on the NAPT Board. She received the NAPT Outstanding Achievement Award in 1995. Lila is a Registered Poetry Therapist and a NAPT-approved mentor-supervisor. She is the Director of bridgeXngs Poetry Center and facilitates poetry circles/groups in Manhattan. She has a private psychotherapy practice as a poetry therapist as well as providing training to students of poetry therapy. She was a psychologist in a school district for twenty-eight years and began her professional career as a New York State Licensed teacher. She was recruited by the New York State Medical Association to teach the educators in her school district how to protect children by recognizing and reporting child abuse and neglect. She is the recipient of the 1989 Jenkins Memorial Award for her outstanding work as a School Psychologist, and in 1991 she was selected as the "Suffolk County Chase Mental Health School Professional of the Year."

INDEX TO POETS AND POEMS